Principles of Law
Relating to Overseas Trade

Principles of Export Guidebooks

Series Editor: Michael Z. Brooke

Principles of Law Relating to Overseas Trade

Nicholas Kouladis

PhD, LL M, CPE, DPSA, MC IT, MI EX

First published 1994

Blackwell Publishers
108 Cowley Road
Oxford OX4 1JF
UK

238 Main Street
Cambridge, Massachusetts 02142
USA

British Library Cataloguing in Publication Data

A CIP catalogue record for this book is available from the British Library.

Library of Congress Cataloging-in-Publication Data

A CIP catalog record for this book is available from the Library of Congress.

ISBN 0-631-19356-1

Typeset in 11½pt on 13½pt Garamond Light by Aitch Em Wordservice, Aylesbury, Buckinghamshire, Great Britain.

Printed in Great Britain by Hartnolls Limited, Bodmin, Cornwall.

This book is printed on acid-free paper.

Contents

List of Figures and Specimens

xi

Foreword

This Foreword is written to welcome a book on law for exporters. There are not many authors capable of writing a book which explains legal issues to those who are not legally trained. The fact that Dr Kouladis has succeeded must surely provide a rather special cachet for this book.

The Earl of Limerick, President,
The Institute of Export

Series Editor's Introduction

In launching the second book in this series of guidebooks to the profession of exporting, the series editor – along with others associated with the project – is pleased to welcome Dr Nicholas Kouladis as its author.

This book on legal issues – *Principles of Law Relating to Overseas Trade* – is necessarily more technical than some in the series. The author's contribution to the development of you, the reader, rests on his experience and I present this book with great pride to the exporting public. The author has managed to present complex legal matters in a way that the non-lawyer can readily understand.

All the books in this series are preoccupied with bringing products to foreign markets (what else is export about?) and this – which reviews the subject of law – sets the scene which all our authors are following as they colour in their parts of the plan.

May I welcome you, the reader, and hope to meet you again as the other books in the series appear on all aspects of export which you need to know – transport and distribution, international marketing, market research and export management in addition to the first book in the series which is a review of the whole subject.

I am sure you will appreciate this book with its clearly presented insights.

Nicholas's book is not intended to make a lawyer of you,

but to enable you to discuss these matters with your lawyers confidently.

Michael Z. Brooke

About The Institute of Export Examinations

The Institute is grateful for the initiative of Michael Z. Brooke, the series editor, and Blackwell Publishers in publishing this unique series of books specially written for the Professional Examinations.

The authors for the series have been carefully selected and have specialized knowledge of their subjects, all being established lecturers or examiners for the Professional Examinations.

The books have been written in a style that is of benefit not only to students of The Institute but also to commercial organizations seeking further information about specific aspects of international trade.

Professionalism in export is vital for every company if they are to compete successfully in world markets and this new series of books provides a sound basis of knowledge for all those seeking a professional qualification in export through The Institute of Export's Professional Examinations.

The book covers the following parts of The Institute's syllabus.

Principles of Law Relating to Overseas Trade

Objectives of the Syllabus

1 To describe those aspect of United Kingdom, European

Community and foreign law which bear directly on overseas trade;
2 To describe legal aspects of export payment;
3 To describe basic principles of cargo insurance;
4 To describe the legal aspects of carriage by air, sea and road.

Principles of the law of contract

1 Types of contract – by deed, simple, executory, etc.
2 Essential features of a valid simple contract
3 Conditions, warranties and other terms
4 Misrepresentation and mistake
5 Discharge of contract by breach, repudiation or frustration
6 Remedies for breach

Introduction to private international law

1 The proper law of the contract
2 Circumstances in which English courts will assume jurisdiction over an international contract
3 Unification of international sales law

Introduction to sale of goods

1 Sale of Goods Act 1979
Historical background – conditions and warranties – price – passing of property and risk – delivery – acceptance and rejection of goods – examination – Unfair Contract Terms Act 1977
2 Distinction between international sales, consumer sales and other sales
3 Rights of the unpaid seller – lien – stoppage in transit – resale – Romalpa clauses
4 Remedies of buyer and seller
5 Incoterms 1990
6 Introduction to CIF, FOB and other commonly used types of export terms, as defined and interpreted by the English Courts

Agency

1 Formation of agency
2 Rights and duties of principal and agent
3 Authority and ratification
4 Kinds of agency

Competition law

1 UK
Legislation – duty to notify restrictive agreements – export agreements – monopoly situations in exports – horizontal and vertical price maintenance and market division
2 EC
Articles 85 and 86 Treaty of Rome – Procedure notifications, complaints, fines, interim and final measures, negative clearance, exemption – Block exemptions to Article 85 – Abuse of a dominant position.

Free movement of goods in the EC

1 Article 30 EC
2 Article 36 EC
3 Article 222 EC

Legal aspects of the finance of exports

1 Bills of exchange
  (a) Definition
  (b) Acceptance, endorsement
  (c) Holder in due course
  (d) Payment and dishonour
  (e) Foreign bills
  (f) Claused bills
  (g) Documentary bills

(a) Legislation
(b) Application of regimes
(c) Liability under the applicable regimes

3 Carriage by road
(a) CMR

R.T. Ebers FIEx,
Director of Education & Training,
The Institute of Export

Preface

For some years now, while a part-time lecturer of international trade law at Southampton Technical College and University of Southampton, I have felt the need to recommend to my students a comprehensive text dealing with most of the subjects that embrace the commercial and international trade law papers set by these institutions and by the Institute of Export, the Institute of Freight Forwarders, the Society of Shipping Executives and similar bodies. The absence of such a text has prompted me to write this book which, I hope, will be read in conjunction with the several excellent works already available on international trade and commercial law. It will also, I hope, be helpful to those in commercial organisations who wish to know more about the legal aspects of exporting.

The reader will appreciate that the continuous changes which occur in the law present an insoluble problem to the author of any law text; but within the limits of the possible, every effort has been made to present the most up-to-date information available.

I should like to thank Professor Robert Grime of the Institute of Maritime Law – University of Southampton, and Mr John Bridge of Southampton Technical College, who gave me much useful advice and were a source of inspiration and enthusiasm. My thanks are also due to Mr Robin Ebers of the Institute of Export, and Dr Michael Brooke of Brooke Associates, for their encouragement and support in the preparation of this work.

London, December 1993   **Nicholas Kouladis**

To Anastasia

Part 1

Principles of the Law of Contract

1

Elements of Contract

Definition

A contract can be defined as an agreement enforceable by the law between two or more persons to do or abstain from doing some act or acts, their intention being to create legal relations and not merely to exchange mutual promises. Therefore, in order to have an enforceable contract we need two elements:

1 agreement; and
2 intention to form or create legal relations.

Types of Contract

Contracts may be divided into two broad classes:

1 Specialty contracts. These are known as contracts in a deed. Such contracts must be made in writing, signed by the person making it and delivered by him. Certain contracts, such as conveyances of land, must be made in a deed.
2 Simple contracts are contracts which are not made under seal. They are informal contracts and may be made in any way; orally, in writing, or they may be implied from conduct.

Contracts may also be classified as follows:

(a) Executed; an executed contract is one that is wholly performed on one side.
(b) Executory, a contract which is either wholly unperformed, or in which there remains something still to be done on both sides. For example, an agreement whereby one party promises to give £20 to the other if he performs a given task, is an executory contract.

Furthermore, contracts may also be classified as: express, one which, whether made orally or in writing, has had its terms definitely arranged between the parties; and the contract implied, a contract which arises from the conduct of the parties.

Before going any further into the law of contract, one should be acquainted with some terms used to indicate the legal status of a contract.

The term 'void contract' is a contradiction in terms since the whole transaction is regarded a nullity. It means that at no time has there been a contract between the parties. Any goods or money obtained under the agreement must be returned. Where items have been resold to a third party, they may be recovered by the original owner. A contract may be rendered void, for example, by some forms of mistake.

'Voidable' contracts are founded on a misrepresentation. Also, some agreements made by minors fall into this category. The contract is in every respect a valid contract unless and until one of the parties takes steps to avoid it. Anything obtained under the contract must be returned, in so far as this is possible. If goods have been resold before the contract was avoided, the original owner will not be able to reclaim them.

An 'unenforceable' contract is a valid contract but it cannot be enforced in the courts if one of the parties refuses to carry out its terms. Items received under the contract cannot be reclaimed. Examples of unenforceable contracts are agreements for the sale of land, unless evidenced in writing, and statute-barred debts.

Agreement

Effectively, we are concerned with the process by which the

parties to a contract reach agreement. Generally speaking this process can be said to consist of (a) an offer made by one person, the **offeror**, and (b) an acceptance by the person to whom the offer was made, the **offeree**.

Offer

An offer is a statement to the effect that the person making it is willing to contract on the terms stated, as soon as these (terms) are accepted by the person to whom the statement is addressed; for example X may offer to sell Y 10 tons of coal for £500. When Y says 'I accept' or words to that effect, a contract is concluded. However, it must be noted that this is a simplistic example and in negotiations between parties as to price, delivery dates, terms of credit and so forth, it is difficult usually to say just when an offer has been accepted.

One must remember that an essential feature of an offer is that the offeror must intend to be bound without further negotiation, by a simple acceptance of his terms.

Thus, there is no offer where the owner of a house, in response to an enquiry from a person who wishes to buy it, states the price at which he might be prepared to sell; *Gibson* v. *Manchester City Council* (1979).

This is so even where the owner wishes to sell and invites offers at or about a specified price. In the latter case he is said to make an '**invitation to treat**', and he is not bound to accept the highest or any other offer. He only invites offers which he may accept or reject. It is important to distinguish between preliminary negotiations and the fact of the offer itself. Only an offer is capable of being converted into a contract by the fact of acceptance. Anything other than an offer is termed an invitation to treat which may defined as a statement that a person is ready to receive offers.

Price marked goods, in shop windows and supermarkets, are only invitations to treat. The offer is made by the customer when he/she takes an item to the till for payment. Therefore, his/her offer may be rejected.

Thus in *Fisher* v. *Bell* (1960), a shopkeeper displayed a flick knife for sale in his shop window, and was charged with the criminal offence of 'offering' to sell an offensive weapon. The court held that he was not guilty of the offence since the display of the knife in the window was an invitation to treat and not an offer.

In *Pharmaceutical Society of Great Britain* v. *Boots Cash Chemists Ltd* (1953), the court said that the display of goods only constituted an invitation to treat and that when a customer placed the goods in the basket and presented them at the cash desk they were making an offer to buy at that point.

The same applies in the case of petrol stations advertising the price at which petrol is to be sold; *Esso Petroleum Ltd* v. *Customs and Excise Comrs.* (1976).

Likewise, advertisements in newspapers or in tradesmen's circulars, and price lists, are not effective offers, as they only attempt to induce offers.

Thus, in *Partridge* v. *Crittenden* (1968), Mr. Partridge placed an advertisement, offering wild birds for sale, which was an offence. It was held that the advertisement was an invitation to treat and not an offer and therefore, he was not guilty of the offence charged.

But it should not be supposed that all displays and advertisements are only invitations to treat. A notice displayed at the entrance to an automatic car park has been held to be an offer, presumably because no further act of acceptance on the part of the proprietor is contemplated after the customer drives in; *Thornton* v. *Shoe Lane Parking Ltd* (1971).

For the same reason, advertisements in newspapers for rewards for the return of lost property are commonly held to be offers. Similarly, where in an advertisement a firm manufacturing carbolic smoke balls, promised to pay £100 to any person who caught influenza after using their product as directed, the court held that this advertisement was an offer; *Carlill* v. *Carbolic Smokeball Company* (1893).

An offer does not continue indefinitely; once an offer has come to an end it is no longer capable of being accepted. In this respect, there are three ways by which an offer can be revoked by the offeror:

1 Communication; in order to validly revoke an offer the offeror must communicate the revocation to the other party at any time up until it has been accepted; *Payne* v. *Cave* (1789). In general, the offeror is entitled to do this even if he has promised to keep the offer open for a specified time.

2 Lapse of time; this occurs where an express time limit is placed on the duration of the offer, or where a reasonable time has elapsed since the offer was made; *Ramsgate Victoria Hotel Co. Ltd* v. *Montefiore* (1866).

3 Death; although there is no clear authority on this, it would appear that if the offeror died then the validity of an acceptance by the offeree would depend on whether the offeree has heard of the death of the offeror before purporting to accept the offer or not. If he has, then it would be clear that the offer would not be capable of acceptance, otherwise the acceptance of the offer would be valid.

Acceptance

Once an offer has been made, a contract comes into existence when this offer is accepted. The offeree may express his assent either expressly by words, or by conduct, as in the above example of the car park notice, where the driver accepts by driving into the car park.

The essential feature of acceptance one must remember is that an acceptance must correspond with the offer. If it seeks to qualify or vary the offer, then it is ineffective as an acceptance. In other words, one could say that a qualified acceptance is no acceptance at all.

For example, an offer by A to sell to B 1,200 tons of iron is followed by a reply from B that he will only take 800 tons; *Tinn* v. *Hoffman & Co.* (1873). In such a situation it is said that B's reply is a counter offer. In other words, he rejected A's offer, and he made a new offer to A, which A may accept or reject.

This principle of counter offer is very important because of the modern commercial practice of making quotations and placing orders with conditions attached, the so-called 'battle of the forms', in which each party sends the other a previously prepared form containing the terms on which he is prepared to contract.

As an example, suppose a buyer makes an offer to buy goods on the terms of his 'purchase form' and the seller purports to accept the offer on the terms of his 'sales form'. Since, in most cases the terms of the forms differ, there is no contract. All that has happened is that the seller has made a counter offer. This counter offer may be accepted by conduct when the buyer takes delivery of the goods. In that event, there will be a contract on the terms of the seller's form; *British Road Services* v. *A.V. Crutchley Ltd* (1968). On the other hand, the contract would be on the buyer's terms if the original offer had come from the seller, and had been followed by a buyer's counter offer which had in turn been accepted by the conduct of the seller. Thus victory in the 'battle of the forms' normally goes to the party who fires the last shot!

As a general rule, an acceptance must be communicated to the offeror. This means that it must be brought to the attention of the offeror. If, for example, the words of acceptance are drowned by an aircraft, or the telephone has gone dead, there is no contract. Finally, silence does not amount to acceptance.

Thus, if X sends a letter to Y offering to buy certain property, and he adds in it: 'If I hear no more about it in the next five days, I shall consider this property mine', there will be no contract if Y simply ignores the letter; *Felthouse* v. *Bindley* (1862).

Postal rule

When acceptance is communicated by post, it becomes effective when the letter of acceptance is posted, that is, when the letter is in control of the Post Office, even if the letter is delayed, destroyed or lost in the post; *Adams* v. *Lindsell* (1818). However, the letter of acceptance must be properly posted; if such letter is handed to a postman to post, the acceptance is valid when it is actually received by the offeror, not when it is posted; *Re London and Northern Bank* (1900).

It must be reasonable to use the post as a means of communicating acceptance, and obviously, must not be excluded as a means of acceptance by the terms of the offer; *Henthorn* v. *Fraser* (1892).

A telegram is effective as an acceptance when it is given to an employee of the Post Office such as a counter clerk; *Cowan* v. *O'Connor* (1880).

It has been observed that the postal rule does not apply where its application would lead to manifest inconvenience and absurdity, where for example, both parties have clearly indicated their intention of withdrawing from the contract; *Holwell Securities Ltd* v. *Hughes* (1974).

Furthermore, the postal rule does not apply to instantaneous methods of communication such as telex, facsimile and telephone, where the rule is that the contract is complete when the acceptance is received by the offeror, not when it is transmitted. Thus, in *Entores Ltd* v. *Miles Far East Corporation* (1955) X sent an offer from London to Y in Amsterdam by telex. Y accepted the offer by telex from Amsterdam, the message being received on the machine in London. The question arose whether the contract was made in Amsterdam or in London. The court held that the contract was made when the acceptance was received in London.

Clearly, the postal rule is a potential problem for an offeror, where, for example the letter of acceptance is lost in the post. In such a case the offeror may be unaware that a binding contract has been formed. In order to avoid such problems offerors are advised to protect themselves by specifically stating that the acceptance will only be complete when received on or before a certain date.

If an offer specifies the method of communication, an acceptance would still be effective if sent using a different method, provided is not prejudicial to the offeror, and is as quick and reliable as the method prescribed in the offer.

It should be noted that the postal rule only applies to the communication of acceptances; offers and revocations of offers **must be communicated** to be effective; *Henthorn* v. *Fraser* (1892). There is no clear authority as to revocation of posted acceptance, but one would assume that the postal rule would not permit such a withdrawal. However, a perhaps better view, is to apply the question whether the rule produces, on balance, a convenient result; *Brinkibon Ltd* v. *Stahag Stahl und Stahlwarenhandelsgesellschaft mbH* (1982). This is a particularly good test of the difficult question of whether a posted acceptance can be revoked by the offeree, if he or she manages to communicate the revocation to the offeror before the latter has received the acceptance. However, as mentioned above, there is no clear authority on this question, and therefore, one would tend to strictly apply the postal rule, which would not permit such withdrawal.

Consideration

Consideration is the price for which the promise is bought; *Dunlop* v. *Selfridge* (1915). Consideration is based on the idea of reciprocity – that the person who makes a promise should not be able to enforce this promise, unless something has been given in exchange for it. To put it in simple words, in a contract of sale of goods, both buyer and seller exchange promises: the buyer promises to pay, and the seller promises to deliver the goods. The consideration for the buyer's promise to pay is the seller's promise to deliver the goods; and the consideration for the seller's promise to deliver the goods is the buyer's promise to pay.

If a person makes a promise (to another), and is not to receive anything back, then this is a gratuitous promise, and such a promise, generally speaking, is not enforceable in English law. Examples of gratuitous promises are charities, gifts, etc. Such gratuitous promises, however, are not enforceable in law. If X promises to give Y a gift, and in the end does not give Y anything, there is no way Y can force X to perform the promise.

However, it is possible to make such a promise legally enforceable by the signature of a deed. All that it means is that the person signing it intends to be bound by the deed. This is the essence of a contract in a deed, that is, consideration is not necessary.

X promises to lend Y a car for a week without charge. If X goes back on his or her word, there is no way that Y can enforce X's promise. However, if there is a counter-promise from Y, to the effect that Y will wash X's car, then there is no difficulty in finding consideration and there would be a binding contract; *Bainbridge* v. *Firmstone* (1838).

Past consideration is no consideration. Thus, where services are rendered voluntarily (without any promise of payment), a subsequent promise to pay for them is not supported by consideration.

Where an employer promises to pay an employee a sum of money in recognition of his past services, and the promise is made after the employee has retired, such promise cannot be enforced by the employee, since this is past consideration; *Simpson* v. *John Reynolds* (1975).

The same is true where goods are sold and at some later time the seller gives a guarantee as to their quality. Thus, in *Roscorla* v. *Thomas* (1842), X sold a horse to Y for £30. After the sale, X promised that the horse was sound and free from vice. It was not. Y sued for damages for breach of warranty. It was held that the only consideration which had been given was the purchase price and that it was not given for the promise, since, at the time of the promise, that consideration was already past.

Legal Relations

Even when the parties have reached agreement, which is supported by consideration, there could still be no contract because the agreement was made without any intention to effect legal relations.

However, in the majority of commercial transactions there is no need to prove that the parties had such intention, as there is an automatic presumption that the agreement will be binding. Furthermore, it must be noted that it is for the party denying the existence of a contract to disprove the intention to create legal relations; *Edwards* v. *Skyways Ltd* (1964).

It would be sufficient to know that this topic includes social and domestic agreements, where there is a presumption that the parties do not intend to be legally bound, although the presumption may be rebutted if the facts of the case show an intention to be bound.

For example, where husband and wife draw on a joint bank account normally such an arrangement does not amount to a contract; *Gage* v. *King* (1961). However, if they live apart because of the break-up of their marriage, any agreement between them regulating the terms of separation is likely to be contractual in nature. Also, there is no contract if the intention to be legally bound is negated by an express provision in the agreement. Therefore, if an agreement contains a so called 'honour clause', which usually provides that the relevant agreement is not to be a 'legal agreement', or if it is expressed to be a 'gentlemen's agreement' only, then such agreement will not be enforceable as a contract.

Thus, in *Rose and Frank Co.* v. *Crompton* (1923), the parties signed a written agreement whereby X was given a limited right to sell Y's goods. The agreement contained an 'honourable pledge' clause to the effect that the agreement was not a formal legal agreement and was 'not to be subject to a legal jurisdiction in the law courts'. The wording was held sufficient to rebut the presumption that the agreement was legally binding.

Finally, an agreement for the sale of land 'subject to contract' is not legally binding, since the effect of this wording is to negate contractual intention. However, note that where these words are omitted from the agreement it will amount to a binding contract even though one party subjectively believed that he or she was not to be bound until the usual 'exchange of contracts' had taken place.

Capacity

One of the elements required in order to have a valid contract is contractual capacity. Adult citizens, that is persons over the age of 18 (Family Law Reform Act 1969), and corporations have full capacity to enter into any kind of contract but certain groups of persons and corporations have certain disabilities in this connection. With regard to the element of capacity, infants or minors will be examined. This area of law is now regulated by the Minors' Contracts Act 1987.

Valid contracts are executed contracts for necessaries, and contracts for the minor's benefit. Necessaries are defined in s.3(3) of the Sale of Goods Act 1979, as goods suitable to the condition in life of the minor and to the minor's actual requirements at the time of sale and delivery. If the goods are deemed necessaries the minor may be compelled to pay a reasonable price. This price may or may not be the contractual price. Expensive but useful items may be necessaries provided they are appropriate to the social background and financial circumstances of the minor. However, if the minor is already adequately supplied, the goods will not be classed as necessaries.

Thus, in *Nash* v. *Inman* (1908), a tailor sued an infant Cambridge student for the price of clothes he had supplied. The tailor failed in his action because the student was already adequately supplied with clothes.

A minor is bound by contracts of employment, apprenticeship and education, which are for his benefit. Thus, in *Roberts* v. *Gray* (1913), the minor (Gray), had agreed to go on a world tour with a professional billiards player (Roberts). After the plaintiff (Roberts) had spent much time and money organizing the tour, the infant (Gray) changed his mind and refused to go. The plaintiff sued for breach of contract, and the court held that this was essentially a contract to receive instruction, and therefore, for the infant's benefit.

Trading contracts are not for the minor's benefit and therefore, a minor is not bound by them, but can sue on these contracts; *Cowern* v. *Nield* (1912).

Voidable contracts are leases of land, partnerships, the purchase of shares, and trading contracts in general.

Finally, it should be noted that where a contract is unenforceable against a defendant because (a) of the defendant's age (that is, being a minor), or (b) because the defendant obtained goods by fraud, or (c) obtained a loan by fraud, the principle of restitution could be applied. Section 3(1) of the Minors' Contracts Act 1987, gives the court the power, where they think it is just and equitable to do so, to require a minor to return the goods/proceeds or money.

Legality

Courts will not uphold an agreement which is illegal or contrary to public policy. This is another element required, in order to have a valid contract. Where the contract involves some kind of moral wrongdoing, it will be illegal. In this connection, a court may object to an agreement either because of a rule of common law or because it is contrary to statute.

Contracts illegal at common law

This category includes contracts:

1 to commit crimes or civil wrongs, for example a contract to assassinate someone, or to defraud the Inland Revenue;
2 involving sexual immorality; for example an agreement to pay an allowance to a mistress. Thus, in *Pearce* v. *Brooks* (1866), Pearce let a coach out on hire to a prostitute (Brooks) knowing that it would be used by her to ply her trade. The coach was returned in a damaged state. Pearce was unable to recover the hire charges or for the damage as the court refused to help him enforce a contract for an immoral purpose.
3 tending to promote corruption in public life, for example bribing an official;
4 of trading with an enemy in wartime;
5 directed against the welfare of a friendly foreign state, for example a partnership intending to import whisky into America during Prohibition; *Foster* v. *Driscoll* (1929);
6 prejudicial to the administration of justice; a contract not to prosecute a person for an offence concerning the public, for example.

The consequences of illegality depend on whether the contract was illegal/unlawful on the face of it, or whether the contract was lawful on the face of it.

Unlawful on the face of it

In such cases the contract is void and there is no action by either party for debt, damages, or otherwise; *Dann* v. *Curzon* (1911). Money paid or property transferred to the other party under the contract is usually irrecoverable.

Thus, in *Parkinson* v. *College of Ambulance* (1925), X was a charitable institution and Y was the secretary. Y represented, fraudulently, to Z that the charity was in a position to obtain some honour, probably a knighthood, for him if he would make a suitable donation. Z paid over the sum of £3,000 and said he would pay more if the honour was granted. No honour of any kind was received by Z, and he brought this action to recover the money he had donated to X. It was held that the agreement was contrary to public policy and illegal, thus no relief. There are some exceptions to this last rule:

1 If the plaintiff relies on rights other than those which are contained in the contract. For example, if X leases his land to Z for five years, under an illegal contract and after the lease has expired, no payments of rent have been made, and Z does not return the land to X, then X could not recover any of the rent, since the contract was made for illegal purposes. But he could bring an action for the return of his property as owner (not as a landlord); *Bowmakers Ltd* v. *Barnet Instruments Ltd* (1944).

In other words, in such a case the right of a person to ownership is independent of the illegal contract, and therefore, such person can sue provided he does not rely on an illegal contract, that is, such right does not arise from an illegal contract. So that in the above case, X can sue Z not under the illegal contract for rent, but under the fact that he is the owner of this land.

Therefore, if in *Pearce* v. *Brooks* (1866), mentioned earlier, Brooks had refused to return the coach to Pearce, then Pearce would have been able to bring an action for the return of his property, as such right did not arise from the illegal contract he had entered with Brooks.

2 If the plaintiff is not in equal wrong (*pari delicto*). For example, if in *Parkinson* v. *College of Ambulance* (1925), Y, the secretary, had oppressed Z, or had used undue influence on Z, in order to make him donate the sum of money, then Z would have been entitled to recover the £3,000.

Thus, in *Atkinson* v. *Denby* (1944), the plaintiff (Atkinson) was in financial difficulties and offered to pay his creditors the sum of 5s in the £ as a full settlement. All the creditors except the defendant (Denby) agreed to this. The defendant said that he would only agree if the plaintiff (Atkinson) paid him £50. The plaintiff paid him £50 as demanded. It was held that the plaintiff (Atkinson) could recover this payment of £50 because he had been coerced into defrauding his creditors.

3 If the plaintiff repents. Provided that the repentance is genuine, and performance is partial and not substantial, then money paid by him may be recoverable. Thus, in *Kearly* v. *Thomson* (1908), the plaintiff had a friend who was bankrupt and wished to obtain his discharge. The defendant was likely to oppose the discharge and accordingly the plaintiff paid him £40 in return for which the defendant promised to stay away from the public examination and not oppose the discharge. The defendant did stay away from the public examination but before an application for discharge had been made the plaintiff brought an action claiming the £40. It was held that the claim failed because the illegal scheme had been substantially effected.

Lawful on face of it

If both parties intended the illegal purpose, there is no action by either party, for anything; *Pearce* v. *Brooks* (1866).

Where one party was without knowledge of the illegal purpose, the innocent party's rights are unaffected and he may sue. Thus, in *Clay* v. *Yates* (1856), it was held that a printer who had innocently printed libellous matter could recover his charges.

Figure 1.1: Elements of a simple contract

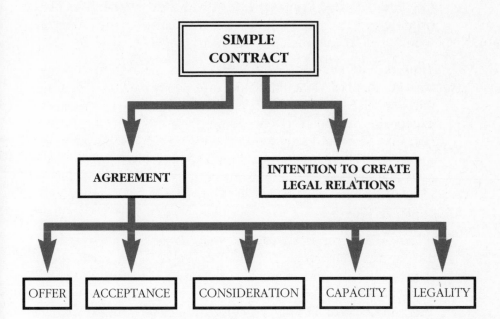

Questions for Discussion

1 Define a contract and its elements.
2 Define the following types of contract: (a) Express; (b) Implied; (c) Simple.
3 What is an offer?
4 What did the *Thornton* v. *Shoe Lane Parking Ltd* (1971) case decide?
5 Briefly state the different ways by which an offer may be revoked.
6 What is the importance of a counter-offer and what is meant by the 'battle of the forms'?
7 Briefly explain the legal principle governing acceptance by post.
8 What is consideration in a simple contract?
9 Briefly state the type of contracts that are illegal at common law.

2

Terms of a Contract

Once a valid contract has been made, it is necessary to see what the parties have actually contracted to do. A contract may be made either orally or in writing or partly orally and partly in writing.

A contract may contain both express and implied terms. Express terms depend on the words used by the parties in reaching their agreement. Implied terms are included even though they have not been expressly stated in words. Therefore, there are two kinds of contract terms: Express; and Implied.

Express

In so far as express terms are concerned, the intention of the parties is of primary importance. The ascertaining of express terms is mainly a question of fact. Problems may arise where a contract incorporates another document, for example, subject to the rules of a trade association, or subject to some set of rules. In such cases, the parties may not be aware of the full contents of the incorporated document, and/or there could be inconsistencies between the terms of the contract and the provisions of the incorporated document. Courts usually try to deal with such inconsistencies as best they can; and where possible put more weight on the drawn terms of the contract, as these are more likely to indicate the main intention of the parties; *Adamastos Shipping Co. Ltd* v. *Anglo-Saxon Petroleum Co. Ltd* (1959).

Implied

These can be divided into: terms implied in fact; terms implied in law; and terms implied by custom or usage.

Implied in fact

This is a term not expressly stated, but which the parties must have intended to include because it was 'so obvious that it goes without saying'.

In other words, if while two parties were making their bargain, an officious bystander were to suggest some express provision for it in the agreement, they would suppress him with a common 'Oh, of course!'; *Shirlaw* v. *Southern Foundries Ltd* (1939).

In one case, A sold some land to B, and he undertook that if he was going to sell some adjoining land in the future, B should have 'the first refusal'. A term was held to be implied in this contract, that A would not defeat B's expectation by conveying the adjoining land to a third party by way of gift; *Gardner* v. *Coutts & Co.* (1967).

However, courts nowadays are reluctant to imply a term in fact under the 'officious bystander' test. In other words, the courts would not 'improve' a contract by adding implied terms in fact; *Liverpool City Council* v. *Irwin* (1977). This is particularly true where the parties have entered into a carefully drafted written contract containing detailed terms agreed between them; *Shell (UK) Ltd* v. *Lostock Garages Ltd* (1976).

Where an estate agent was to receive a commission 'on completion of sale', it did not mean that a term was implied to the effect that the home owner should not sell the property privately; *Luxor (Eastbourne) Ltd* v. *Cooper* (1941).

Implied in law

This category includes terms implied by statutes, and by common law. A person who contracts to supply services in the course of a business undertakes (impliedly) that he will carry them out with reasonable skill and care (Supply of Goods and Services Act 1982).

At common law such implied terms can be excluded, but nowadays the power to exclude such terms has been considerably reduced by statute. Thus a term excluding liability as to the quality of the goods, which is a term implied by the Sale of Goods Act 1979, is invalid in a consumer sale.

Implied by custom or usage

Customs of particular markets may be incorporated in a contract. The thing to remember is that parties to a contract may be bound by such implied term, whether they know it or not.

The important test however, for the application of such implied term, is whether the custom is reasonable, that is whether it is inconsistent with any express or implied terms of the contract. If it is then it is said that the custom is unreasonable. Where persons who are in the business of hiring machinery deal with each other on a regular basis on terms drawn up by a trade association, those terms may be implied in a transaction even though no express reference to them has been made.

Thus, in *British Crane Hire Corporation Ltd* v. *Ipswich Plant Hire Ltd* (1974) X hired a crane from Y who were the owners. The agreement was an oral one, though after the contract was made X received a printed form from Y, the owners, containing conditions. One of these was that the hirer of the crane was liable to indemnify the owner against all expenses in connection with its use. Before X, the hirers, signed the form the crane sank into marshy ground, though not due to Y's fault. Y, the owners, were put to some cost in repairing the crane and sued X, the hirers, for an indemnity under the contract. X, the hirers, claimed that the conditions had not been incorporated in the oral contract of hire. It was held that X knew that printed conditions in similar terms to those of Y, were in common use in the business. Therefore, the conditions were incorporated into the oral contract. The action succeeded.

Importance of the Terms of a Contract

Not all terms in a contract carry equal weight. Failure to perform one of the terms may have a more serious effect on the contract than failure to perform another. The identification of the terms of a contract is of great importance, because, as it will be seen later, the remedies available to the parties are considerably affected.

Traditionally, terms used to be classified as conditions and warranties, a condition being a term, the breach of which goes to the root of the contract and therefore is capable of terminating the contract.

For example, a contract of sale may require that goods be shipped by a particular date; or a charter-party may provide that the shipowner can withdraw the ship if the hire is not punctually paid. Such term has been held to be a condition; *Bunge Corporation* v. *Tradax Export S.A.* (1981); *The Laconia* (1977).

For a term to be held to be a condition at least one of the following three requirements must be fulfilled:

1 The particular term has already been classified as a condition by previous judicial decision. For example if A has entered into a charter-party with B, and the charter-party provides that the ship will be expected ready to load at a particular port, on a particular date. Such term has been held to be a condition; *The Mihalis Angelos* (1970).
2 The term may be a term prescribed by statute as a condition, such as the various implied terms contained in the Sales of Goods Act 1979. Thus, the Sales of Goods Act 1979 provides that it is an implied condition that the seller will have the right to sell at the time when the property is to pass to the purchaser, that is, will have legal ownership.

3 The parties have expressly or impliedly agreed that a particular term should be a condition. The word 'condition' has a number of meanings and is often used in a non-specific sense, for example, standard form 'Terms and Conditions'. If the word is expressly used, the court must be satisfied that it was intended to be used in its technical sense; *Schuler A.G. v. Wickman Machine Tool Sales Ltd* (1974). A provision giving the buyer the right to reject goods if they did not possess a specified quality would be classified as a condition, as this would give effect to the intention of the parties.

Thus, in *Bannerman* v. *White* (1861), X was intending to buy hops from Y and he asked him whether sulphur had been used in the cultivation of the hops, adding that if it had, he would not even bother to ask the price. Y said that no sulphur had been used, though in fact it had. It was held that Y's assurance that sulphur had not been used was a fundamental term of the contract, that is, a condition.

A warranty if breached entitles the innocent party to damages only. For example, the Sale of Goods Act 1979 classifies as a warranty the implied term that the goods are free from charges in favour of third parties. In such case damages, enabling the buyer to pay off the charge, will generally be an adequate remedy. The difference between a condition and a warranty may be illustrated by the following cases:

In *Poussard* v. *Spiers* (1876), Poussard was engaged to appear in an operetta from the start of its London run. Owing to illness, she was not available until a week after the show had opened and the producers were forced to engage a substitute. They refused Poussard's offer to take up the part.

It was held that the obligation to perform from the first night was a condition of the contract. Failure to carry out this term entitled the producers to repudiate Poussard's contract.

In *Bettini* v. *Gye* (1876), Bettini, an opera singer, was engaged by Gye to appear in a season of concerts. He undertook to be in London at least six days before the first concert for the purpose of rehearsals. He arrived three days late and Gye refused to accept his services. It was held that the promise to appear for rehearsals was a less important term of the contract.

Gye could claim compensation for a breach of warranty but he could not repudiate Bettini's contract.

A third category has been added to these, that of 'intermediate' or 'innominate' term. The main difference of this category is that breach of it only justifies rescission if it leads, or amounts, to a serious failure in performance. Thus, in *Reardon Smith Line* v. *Hansen-Tangen* (1976), a ship which was going to be chartered, was described in the charter-party as Osak number 354 (this is the yard where it was built) when it was in fact Oshima number 004. In all other respects the ships were exactly the same. As this is a misdescription, usually considered to be a condition, the charterers sought to terminate the contract. The House of Lords rejected the argument and held that the description was not a condition but an innominate term and that since the injured party had not been deprived of substantially the whole benefit under the contract, the charterers were only entitled to damages and not to rejection of the contract.

Therefore, a term may be classified as any of the above mentioned categories depending on the particular term, its implications and construction. The contract should be examined as a whole and the intention of the parties must be determined at the time the parties entered into it. The court will examine the terms and will have to determine what the parties intended it to function as, that is, a condition, warranty or intermediate term.

Generally speaking, the courts have expressed a preference for innominate terms rather than conditions, mainly because of the flexibility this permits them in deciding the appropriate remedy. The position in so far as remedies are concerned, is broadly speaking, as follows:

1 If the term broken is a condition, the innocent party can terminate the contract usually irrespective of the degree of loss or damage flowing from the breach. In addition if loss or damage has also been caused by the breach of the term, the innocent party may claim for such loss or damage.
2 If the term broken is a warranty, the remedy is one in damages only.

3 If the term broken is an intermediate one the injured party
can terminate the contract if the actual and prospective
consequences of the breach are such as to substantially
deprive him of the benefit of the whole of the consideration
he bargained to receive under the contract. Otherwise,
damages are only awarded.

Figure 2.1: Terms of a contract

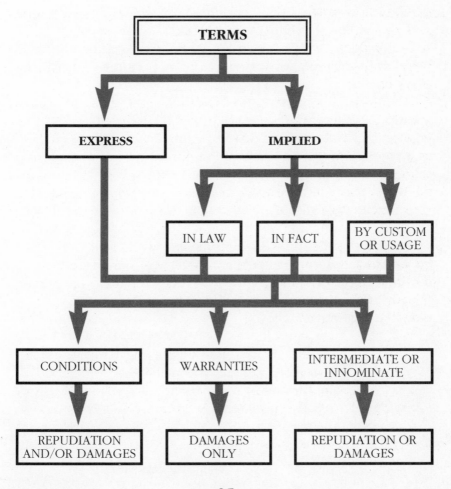

Factors considered by the Courts:

A Statute: If a statute renders the particular term a condition or a warranty, for example Sale of Goods Act 1979.

B Intention of the parties: What the parties intended the particular term to be.

C Previous judgements: If the particular term has been considered by a Court before.

Questions for Discussion

1 Illustrate and explain what is meant by conditions and warranties?

2 What factors should be considered in order to classify a term as a condition?

Misrepresentation

Definition

The term misrepresentation refers to certain kinds of misleading statements, made before a contract is entered into, by which persons may be induced to enter into contracts. In general, in order for a representation to become a misrepresentation, four requirements must be fulfilled. In particular, the statement must be:

1 false;
2 one of fact;
3 addressed to the party misled; and must have
4 induced the representee to enter into the contract.

It must be a false statement of fact. Thus, statements of law are outside the scope of misrepresentation. Parties should not seek advice and rely on statements of the other party, on legal matters – 'ignorance of the law is no excuse'.

Also, statements of opinion are outside the scope of the doctrine of misrepresentation, unless it can be shown that the person making the statements was in a position to know and could not have reasonably held that opinion.

Thus, in *Bisset* v. *Wilkinson* (1927), X was selling some land. Y asked X whether the piece of land on sale could support 2,000 sheep. X had no such knowledge, but he responded in the affirmative, thus stating his belief. After Y bought the land, he realised that the land could not support 2,000 sheep, and sued X for misrepresentation. The court held that as X had no personal knowledge of the facts, and as the buyer, Y, knew this, there was no liability on the seller's part.

Sales talk or puffing, or what is known nowadays as hype, do not come within the scope of misrepresentation. Therefore, statements like 'this is the finest or the best machine on the market' would not amount to misrepresentation.

Silence in general cannot amount to misrepresentation. However, where the statement was true when made but became false before the conclusion of the contract, and the party who made the statement is aware of such a change, his silence would amount to misrepresentation as he is under a duty to disclose the change.

Thus, in *With* v. *O'Flanagan* (1936), X, a medical practitioner, wished to sell his practice to Y. Y was interested and in January X represented to Y that the income from the practice was £2,000 a year. The contract was not signed until May. In the meantime, X had been ill and the practice had been run by various other doctors. In consequence the receipts fell to £5 per week, and no mention of this fact was made when the contract was entered into. Y claimed rescission of the contract. It was held that Y could rescind, as the representation made in January was of a continuing nature and induced the contract made in May. The plaintiff had a right to be informed of a change of circumstances, and the defendant's silence amounted to a misrepresentation.

Remedies

Remedy depends on the nature of misrepresentation. There are three types of misrepresentation: fraudulent; negligent; and innocent.

Fraud means that the representor made the false representation knowing it to be false or without belief in its truth. In *Derry* v. *Peek* (1889), the Plymouth, Devonport and district Tramways Company had power under a special Act of Parliament to run trams by animal power, and with the consent of the Board of Trade by mechanical or steam power. Derry and some other directors of the company issued a prospectus, inviting the public to apply for shares in it, stating that they had power to run trams by steam power, and claiming that considerable economies would result. The directors had assumed that the permission of the Board of Trade would be granted as a matter of course, but in the event the Board of Trade refused permission. Therefore, the directors were sued for fraud. The court held that the directors were not fraudulent but honestly believed the statement in the prospectus to be true.

Note however, that as fraud is a serious charge which must be strictly substantiated, actions under this heading are not commonly brought. The misled party may sue for rescission and/or damages.

Negligent misrepresentation means that the representor made the false statement without having any reasonable grounds for believing that the statement was true. The misled party may sue for damages and/or rescission. The Misrepresentation Act 1967 recognises only a claim for damages.

However, in *Mapes* v. *Jones* (1974) a property dealer contracted to lease a grocer's shop to the plaintiff for 21 years but in fact did not have sufficient interest in the property himself to grant such a lease, the maximum period available to him being 18 years. As no lease was supplied as originally promised, the plaintiff shut the shop and treated the contract as repudiated. It was held that the plaintiff was entitled to rescission for misrepresentation under the Misrepresentation Act 1967.

Innocent misrepresentation is where a false statement is made, but the representor had reasonable grounds to believe that the statement was true not only when he made it but also at the time the contract was entered into; *Oscar Chess Ltd* v. *Williams* (1957).

The misled party may ask the court for rescission only, but remedies under this type of misrepresentation are left at the discretion of the court and thus the misled party may be awarded damages instead; Misrepresentation Act 1967. This provision in effect caters for misrepresentations on trivial matters, as rescission may cause great hardship and inconvenience.

Thus, if A sells his car to B, and he tells B that the previous owner fitted new tyres at 25,000 miles, and this statement is false but A, the seller, was told this by the previous owner, then the court could award damages instead of rescission, thus leaving the contract intact but giving the party misled monetary compensation.

Misrepresentation by Non-Contracting Parties

One of the factors to consider in misrepresentation cases is whether there is a 'special relationship' between representor and representee. Such a relationship may arise where a person in the exercise of his profession gives information or advice to a person other than his own client, such as a banker supplying a bank reference, knowing that person is likely to rely on it.

Thus, in one case a valuer employed by a building society negligently overvalued a house and was held liable to the purchaser to whom his report was shown and who had relied on it in buying the house; *Yianni* v. *Edwin Evans & Sons* [1982].

In general there is a 'special relationship' whenever it is reasonable for one party to rely on the other's skill and judgment in making the statement. For example, in *Esso Petroleum Co. Ltd* v. *Mardon* [1976], the defendant was induced to take a lease of a filling station from an oil company by a statement, made by one of the company's salesmen, as to the potential turnover of the premises. It was held that the company owed a duty of care to the defendant as he had reasonably relied on the salesman's superior knowledge and experience.

The question whether there is a liability for negligent misrepresentation at common law only becomes acute where the misrepresentation does not lead to a contract between the representor and representee. This was the position in the case of the valuer, mentioned above, where the contract which the representee (house purchaser) made was with a third party, viz. with the owner of the house.

In simple words, if X is negligently induced by Y, a banker, to enter into a contract with Z, the contract between X and Z is concluded under misrepresentation. But the misrepresentation is not made by Z, but by Y. Therefore, X in such a case will have an action against Y for negligent misrepresentation under common law. If there was a contract between X and Y, as in the case where Y is a financial adviser, then X would have two actions against Y: one for negligent misrepresentation under common law, and another for breach of the contract between X and Y.

It should be borne in mind that section 2(1) of the Misrepresentation Act 1967 states that damages are paid 'where a person has entered into a contract after a misrepresentation has been made to him by another party thereto'. In other words the Act caters for cases of misrepresentation, whereby the representee enters into a contract with the representor, due to misrepresentation made by the representor.

The following two simple examples may be of assistance in distinguishing the two cases.

A, the buyer, is induced to enter into a contract with B, the seller, due to B's misrepresentation.

Compare this with the case where A, the buyer, is induced to enter into a contract with B, the seller, due to C's misrepresentation.

Figure 3.1: Misrepresentation

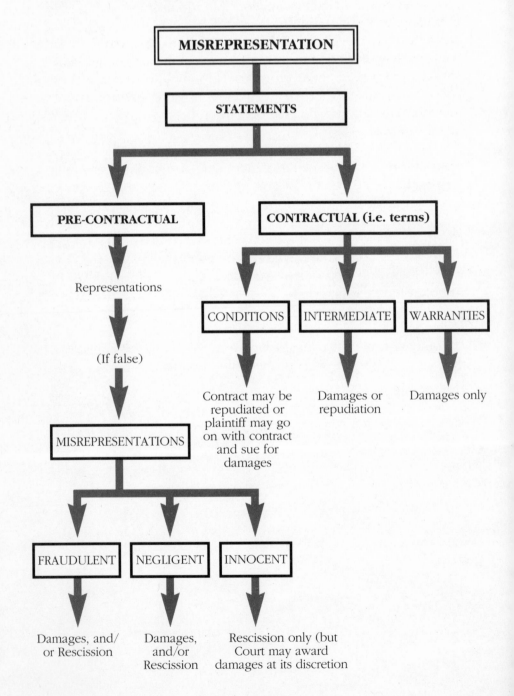

Questions for Discussion

1 What is misrepresentation?
2 Briefly describe (a) Fraudulent misrepresentation; (b) Negligent misrepresentation; (c) Innocent misrepresentation.

4

Mistake

Introduction

It is particularly important to distinguish between mistake and misrepresentation, since a contract affected by mistake may be void, whereas a contract affected by misrepresentation is only voidable. The distinction is very important in so far as third parties are concerned.

If A sells goods to B under circumstances of mistake and B re-sells them to C, then C may get no title and A can recover the goods from him or sue him for damages. If on the other hand, the contract between A and B was voidable for misrepresentation, then if B sold the goods to C who took them *bona fide* before A had rescinded his contract with B, then C would get a good title and A would have a remedy only against B.

For a mistake to be operative it must be one of fact and not of law. Thus, where a landlord and a tenant agree that the rent payable by the tenant must be increased by a certain amount, when in fact, by some legislation it cannot be increased, and this is discovered after the tenant has paid this increase, the tenant cannot recover the extra rent, nor can it be deducted from future payments, as this extra rent is paid under a mistake of law; *Sharp Bros and Knight* v. *Chant* (1917).

Errors of judgement are not mistakes (technical meaning). Thus, if A buys an article thinking it is worth £100 when in fact it is worth only £50, the contract is good and A must bear the loss if there has been no misrepresentation by the seller; *Bell* v. *Lever Bros.* (1932).

Mistakes may be classified into three categories:

1 Mistake as to the nature of the contract itself.
2 Unilateral mistakes, that is, made by one party only.
3 Bilateral mistakes, that is, where both parties make a mistake. This category can be further divided into Common mistakes, and Mutual mistakes.

Mistake as to the Nature of the Contract

If a person signs a contract in the mistaken belief that he is signing a document of a different nature, or contents, there may be a mistake. Such person can plead *non est factum*; it is not his deed.

Thus, in *Lewis* v. *Clay* (1898), Clay was asked by Lord William Neville to witness a confidential document and signed in holes in blotting paper placed over the document by Neville. In fact he was signing two promissory notes and two letters authorizing Lewis to pay the amount of the notes to Lord William Neville. The court held that the signature of Clay in the circumstances had no effect, and he was not bound by the bills of exchange.

However, it must be noted that in order to plead the defence of 'this is not my deed', the person who signed must prove that he made the mistake despite having taken all reasonable care, that is, lack of negligence. Thus, in *Saunders* v. *Anglia Building Society* (1970), Mrs. Gallie, a widow aged 78 years, signed a document which Lee, her nephew's friend, told her was a deed of gift of her house to her nephew. She did not read the document but believed what Lee had told her. In fact the document was an assignment of her leasehold interest in the house to Lee, and Lee later mortgaged that interest to a building society.

In an action by Mrs. Gallie against Lee and the building society it was held that the assignment was void and did not confer a title on Lee, and although Mrs. Gallie had been negligent she was not estopped from denying the validity of the deed against the building society for she owed it no duty. However, as the transaction intended and carried out was the same, that is, an assignment, and as Mrs. Gallie was negligent, (by not reading it) the plea of *non est factum* (it is not my deed), was not available to her. The House of Lords also added that the document which was in fact signed must be 'fundamentally different', 'radically different', or 'totally different', in order for the plea of non est factum to be successful.

Negligence might be avoided where a person was told he was witnessing a confidential document and had no reason to doubt that he was. Thus, in *Lewis* v. *Clay* (1898), mentioned earlier, although Clay was negligent in not taking all reasonable care, that is, reading the document, negligence was negatived by the fact that he had no reason to doubt that he was witnessing a confidential document. Therefore, the plea of *non est factum* (it is not my deed) was available to him.

If however, negligence is proved, and the document happens to be a negotiable instrument (for example, a bill of lading), and has been taken by a third party, then the person who signed it under mistake is liable to the third party. For example, it is usual after goods are loaded on board a vessel, for the charterer to ask the master to sign the bills of lading and add the statement 'loaded in apparent good order and condition', if of course the goods have been so loaded. If the master does not realize that this statement has been inserted (by the chief mate) in the bill of lading, and some goods were actually loaded in a damaged state, and he signs the bill of lading, then when this bill of lading has been endorsed to a third party then this third party can have an effective action for damages against the shipowner. This is due to the fact that the master of the ship, who is the agent of the shipowner, was negligent in not reading the bill of lading.

Unilateral Mistake

This occurs where one of the parties is mistaken as to some fundamental fact concerning the contract and the other party knows, or ought to know this. Thus, in *Legal and General*

Assurance Society v. *General Metal Agencies* (1969), Legal and General were the landlords of General Metal Agencies. They served a statutory notice of termination of the tenancy to General Metal. The latter applied to the County Court for a new tenancy, which Legal and General opposed on the grounds of persistent late payment of rent. The application was dismissed by the Court. However, Legal and General subsequently sent by mistake a computerized demand for the next quarter's rent in advance over the signature of their general manager. General Metal sent a cheque for the rent and this was presented to the bank and was paid. In this action Legal and General claimed possession of the premises and General Metal contended that Legal and General by demanding and accepting the next quarter's rent had by implication created a new tenancy. It was held that Legal and General were entitled to show that the demand was sent and the rent received by mistake. There was no intention to create a new tenancy. Therefore, Legal and General were entitled to possession of the premises.

This case illustrates that when one party to a contract is mistaken and the other party knows or ought, as a reasonable person, to know that this is so, the contract is not enforceable. General Metal knew that their application for a new tenancy had been opposed by Legal and General, and that the latter had no intention to create a new tenancy.

If the other party cannot know that there is a mistake, then this is a valid contract.

In *Higgins Ltd* v. *Northampton Corporation* (1927), Higgins entered into a contract with the corporation for the erection of dwelling houses. However, in arriving at his price Higgins made an arithmetical error. The corporation sealed the contract, assuming that the price arrived at was correct. It was held that the contract was binding on the parties. In this case one party to the contract was mistaken, but the other party did not know, and did not ought to know of this mistake.

The cases under this classification are mainly concerned with mistakes of one party as to the identity of the other party. Two types of mistakes with regard to identity may be put forward: mistakes as to the identity of the contracting party; and mistakes as to the attributes of the contracting party.

Identity

Where X contracts with Y, thinking that Y is another person, Z, and if Y knows that X is under this misapprehension, then such a contract is void. Note that it is important in such a case, that X intended to deal with some other person other than Y; *Lake* v. *Simmons* (1927).

For example, if a person disguises his letter so as to make it appear from a respectable firm, in order to induce the other party to enter into a contract, the mistake will be as one of identity and therefore, will render the contract void.

Thus, in *Cundy* v. *Lindsay* (1878), Lindsay were linen manufacturers with a business in Belfast. A fraudulent person named Blenkarn wrote to Lindsay from 37 Wood Street, Cheapside, ordering a quantity of handkerchiefs but signed his letter in such a way that it appeared to come from Messrs. Blenkiron, who were a well-known and solvent house doing business at 123 Wood Street. Lindsay knew of the existence of Blenkiron but did not know the address. Therefore, the handkerchiefs were sent to 37 Wood Street. Blenkarn then sold them to Cundy, and was later convicted and sentenced for the fraud. Lindsay sued Cundy in conversion claiming that the property had not passed to Blenkarn or to Cundy, as the contract they (Lindsay) entered into with Blenkarn was void for mistake. It was held that there was a mistake as to the party with whom Lindsay were contracting, and therefore the respondents (Lindsay) succeeded in their action. In other words Lindsay were induced to contract with the rogue, due to the rogue's disguise which lead Lindsay to believe that the rogue was Blenkiron.

Attributes

A typical case illustrating a mistake as to the attributes of the contracting party is *Lewis* v. *Averay* (1972). In this case Lewis agreed to sell his car to a rogue. Before the sale took place the rogue persuaded Lewis that he was the actor Richard Green in the 'Robin Hood' serial. He signed a worthless cheque for £450 in the name of 'R.A. Green'. It was held that as Lewis had effectively contracted to sell the car to the rogue he could not recover the car or damages from Averay, who was a student who had bought it from the rogue for £200. The contract was voidable (as to the attributes) but not void (as to identity) for unilateral mistake.

When the parties conclude a contract *inter praesentes*, that is, face to face, there is a presumption that each party intends to contract with the person physically present and identifiable by sight and sound; *Lewis* v. *Averay* (1972). This in turn means that if one of the parties simply misrepresented himself, then this will amount to a mistake as to the attributes of that person rather than his identity. Consequently, such a contract would be voidable for fraud but rarely void for mistake.

Bilateral – Common Mistake

This is where both parties have made the same mistake. Thus, if A buys an article from B thinking it is worth £100, and B also is of the opinion that it is worth £100, when in fact it is worth only £50, the contract is good and A must bear the loss if there has been no misrepresentation by the seller.

In *Leaf* v. *International Galleries* (1950), X bought from Y a drawing of Salisbury Cathedral for £85. Y said that the drawing was by Constable. Five years later X tried to sell the drawing and was told that it was not drawn by Constable. Thus, X sued for rescission of his contract with Y. It was held that the statement that the drawing was by Constable could have been treated as a warranty giving rise to a claim for damages, but it was not possible to award damages because X's appeal was based on his right to rescind. Furthermore, the court treated the statement as a representation, and found it to be innocent. Therefore, no right of rescission was available to X.

There are two exceptions to this rule:

Cases of *res extincta*

When A agrees to sell his car to B and unknown to them both

the car has been destroyed, in such a case the contract is void. Thus, in *Couturier* v. *Hastie* (1856), Hastie dispatched a cargo of corn from Greece and sent the charter-party and bill of lading to his London agents so that the corn might be sold. His London agents employed Couturier to sell the corn and a person named Callander bought it. Unknown to the parties the cargo had become overheated, and had been landed and sold, so that when the contract was made the corn was not in existence. Callander repudiated the contract and Couturier was sued because he was an agent who, for an extra commission, undertakes to indemnify his principal against loss arising out of the repudiation of the contract by any third party introduced by him. It was held that the claim against Couturier failed because the contract presupposed that the goods were in existence when they were sold to Callander.

Cases of *res sua*

When a person makes a contract to buy something which already belongs to him, such a contract is void; *Cochrane* v. *Willis* (1865).

Bilateral – Mutual mistake

This is where both parties have made a different mistake. Thus, if X offers to sell car A and Y agrees to buy, thinking X means car B, there is a bilateral mutual mistake.

The test applicable in these cases is that of the 'sense of the promise', that is, what a reasonable man looking at the dealings of the parties would have thought that the parties were bargaining for; *Wood* v. *Scarth* (1858). In other words, the contract will be enforced. If, however, the court cannot find the 'sense of the promise', then the contract is void.

Thus, in *Raffles* v. *Wichelaus* (1864), Y agreed to buy from X 125 bales of cotton to arrive 'ex Peerless from Bombay'. There were two ships called Peerless sailing from Bombay, one in October and one in December. Y thought they were buying the cotton on the ship sailing in October, and X meant to sell the cotton on the ship sailing in December. In fact X had no cotton on the ship sailing in October. Y refused to take delivery of the cotton when the second ship arrived and was sued by X for breach of contract. It was held that there was a mistake as to the subject matter of the contract and therefore, there was in effect no contract between the parties.

Figure 4.1: Mistake

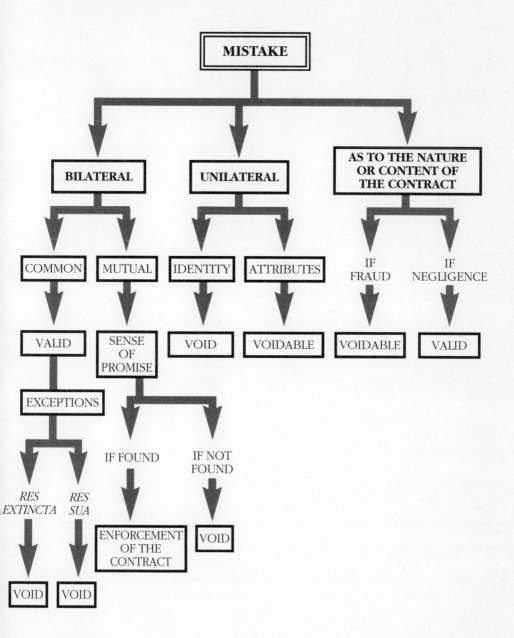

Questions for Discussion

1 How could mistakes be classified?
2 What is meant by *non est factum*?

5

Remedies for Breach of Contract

Introduction

So far we have looked at essential elements of a valid contract and the factors which may affect the validity of an agreement. We now turn our attention to the remedies available to the injured party when a term of the contract has been broken.

Every breach of contract will give the injured party the right to recover damages (financial compensation). Other remedies, such as specific performance and injunction, may be granted at the discretion of the court as part of its equitable jurisdiction.

Damages

In the business world it is quite common for the parties to agree in advance the damages that will be payable in the event of a breach of contract. These are known as liquidated damages. If there is no prior agreement as to the sum to be paid, the amount of damages is said to be unliquidated.

Liquidated damages

It makes sense for the parties to establish at the outset of their relationship (contractual) the financial consequences of failing to live up to their bargain. Provided the parties have made a genuine attempt to estimate the likely loss, the courts will accept the relevant figure as the damages payable. In practice, knowing the likely outcome of any legal action, the party at fault will simply pay up, without argument.

Thus, for example, liquidated damages are usually provided for in holiday bookings, in the event of cancellation (cancellation charges notice): if cancellation is notified six weeks prior to departure the deposit is lost; if notification is made within four to six weeks of departure 30 per cent of holiday cost is charged, and so on.

There is a temptation for a party with stronger bargaining power to try to impose a penalty clause, which is really designed as a threat to secure performance. Therefore, in order to illustrate the distinction between liquidated damages and penalty clauses, the following examples may be useful:

X, a tyre manufacturer, supplied tyres to Y, a motor trader, under an agreement by which, in return for a trade discount, Y agreed to pay £5 by way of 'liquidated' damages for every item sold below list prices. The court held that since the sum was not extravagant, it was a genuine attempt by the parties to estimate the damage which price undercutting would cause X. The £5 was liquidated damages; *Dunlop Pneumatic Tyre Co. Ltd* v. *New Garage & Motor Co. Ltd* (1915).

In another case, X, a retailer, agreed to pay £250 for each Ford car sold below the manufacturer's list price. The court held that the clause was a penalty, and not liquidated damages. Its size suggested that it was not a genuine pre-estimate of loss; *Ford Motor Co.* v. *Armstrong* (1915).

If the court holds that the sum is liquidated damages, it will be enforced irrespective of whether the actual loss is greater or smaller. Furthermore, if the sum is agreed by the parties as liquidated damages it will be enforced even though the actual loss is greater or smaller.

Thus, in *Cellulose Acetate Silk Co. Ltd* v. *Widnes Foundry Ltd* (1933), Widnes were builders of industrial plants, and agreed to build a plant for Silk Co. by a certain date. It was also agreed that Widnes would pay Silk Co. £20 per week for every week they took in erecting the plant beyond the agreed date. In fact,

Widnes completed the erection 30 weeks late, and Silk Co. claimed for their actual loss which was £5,850. It was held that Widnes were only liable to pay £20 per week as agreed.

One must remember therefore, that if the court decides that the 'clause' in a contract is not for liquidated damages but is a penalty clause, then enforcement of the penalty will not be made, but the court will award damages on 'normal' principles. As a general guide, extravagant sums are in the nature of penalties. Also, where the sum provided for in the contract is payable on the occurrence of any one of several events it is probably a penalty for it is unlikely that each event can produce the same loss.

Thus, in *Ford Motor Co.* v. *Armstrong* (1915), X, a retailer, agreed to pay £250 for each Ford car sold below the manufacturer's list price. Furthermore, X agreed (a) not to sell Ford cars to other dealers in the motor trade, and (b) not to exhibit any car supplied by Ford without their permission. The court held that the clause was a penalty, and not liquidated damages. The same sum was payable for different kinds of breach which were not likely to produce the same loss. Furthermore, its size suggested that it was not a genuine pre-estimate of loss.

Unliquidated damages

The aim of unliquidated damages is to put the injured party in the position he would have been in if the contract had been carried out properly. Damages are designed to compensate for loss and not to punish the defendant. Contractual damages are certainly not intended to put the plaintiff in a better position than if the contract had been properly performed.

If no loss has been suffered, the court will only award nominal damages, that is, a small sum to mark the fact that there had been a breach of contract. In general, the principles on which the remedy of damages is based and assessed on, are as follows:

1 The damages can include sums for financial loss, damage to property, personal injuries and distress, disappointment and

upset caused to the plaintiff.

Thus, in *Jarvis* v. *Swan's Tours* (1973), Jarvis paid £63.45 for a two week winter sports holiday in Switzerland. The tour operator's brochure promised a 'house party' atmosphere at the hotel, a bar which would be open several evenings a week and a host who spoke English. The holiday was a considerable disappointment, as in the second week of the holiday Jarvis was the only guest in the hotel and no one else could speak English. Furthermore, the bar was only open one evening and the skiing was disappointing. The court held that Jarvis was entitled to compensation of £125, for 'the loss of entertainment and enjoyment which he was promised'.

2 The injured party cannot necessarily recover damages for every kind of loss which he has suffered.

The consequences of a breach of contract may be far reaching, that is, the breach might have caused a chain reaction of events to occur. The law must draw a line somewhere and say that damages incurred beyond a certain limit are too remote to be recovered. Damages in contract must therefore be proximate. The modern law regarding remoteness of damage in contract is founded upon the case of *Hadley* v. *Baxendale* (1854). The rules relating to remoteness of damage were laid down by the court and in this case, state that the injured party may recover damages for:

(a) loss which has resulted naturally and in the ordinary course of events from the defendant's breach, and

(b) the loss which, although not a natural consequence of the defendant's breach, was in the minds of the parties when the contract was made.

Thus, in *Victoria Laundry Ltd* v. *Newman Industries Ltd* (1949), X, a firm of launderers wished to expand their business and they ordered a new boiler from Y, the defendants. The boiler was damaged during the course of its removal and as a result there was a five month delay in delivery. X claimed (a) damages for £16 per week for the loss of profits X would have made on the planned expansion of their laundry business, and (b) damages of £262 a week for loss of profits they would have made on extremely lucrative dyeing contracts. The court held that X were entitled to (a), but they

could not recover for the especially profitable dyeing contracts of which Y, the defendants, were ignorant.

In another case, X entrusted samples of his products to Y, for
delivery to Newcastle, for exhibition at an agricultural show.
The goods were marked 'must be at Newcastle on Monday
certain'. They failed to arrive in time. Y was held liable for
Y's prospective loss of profit arising from his inability to
exhibit at Newcastle. This was because Y had agreed to carry
the goods knowing of the special instructions of X, the
customer; *Simpson* v. *London and North Western Rail Co.*
(1876).

3 Once breach of contract has occurred, the innocent party is
under a duty to mitigate (minimize) his loss. This means that
the innocent party cannot stand back and allow the loss to
get worse. A seller whose goods have been rejected, for
example, must attempt to get the best possible price for them
elsewhere. The plaintiff (seller) will not be able to recover for
that part of the loss which has resulted from his failure to
mitigate.

Thus, in *Brace* v. *Calder* (1895) X was dismissed (wrongfully)
by his employers but he was offered immediate re-engagement
on the same terms and conditions as before. He refused the
offer and instead sued to recover the salary he would have
received for the remaining nineteen months of his two year
contract. It was held that X should have mitigated the loss by
accepting the employer's reasonable offer of re-employment.
Therefore, X was entitled to nominal damages only.

Equitable Remedies

So far we have seen that the 'normal' remedy for a breach of
contract is an award of damages at common law. There are
some situations, however, where damages would be neither
adequate nor appropriate. Equity developed other forms of
relief to ensure that justice is done. It is important to understand
however, that whereas common law remedies are prescribed by
common law, equitable remedies are discretionary, that is, it is
up to the court to award them. In a very simplistic way, it could

be said that one can be awarded a common law remedy 'by right', that is, the remedy can be demanded, whereas a discretionary remedy cannot be demanded but requested, as it is up to the court to award it if it thinks it is appropriate. The most important of these equitable remedies, are:

Specific performance

A decree of specific performance is an order of the court requiring the party in breach to carry out his contractual obligations. Failure to comply with the directions of the court lays the party in breach open to the imposition of penalties for contempt of court. However, it must be remembered that like all equitable remedies, the grant of specific performance is discretionary.

For all practical purposes this remedy is now confined to contracts for the sale of land. It is not normally granted in the case of contracts for the sale of goods because other goods of a similar kind can be purchased and the difference assessed in money damages.

If, however, there is contract for the sale of a unique item, it would seem that as no sum of money can compensate the disappointed buyer for his lost opportunity, specific performance may be granted.

Furthermore, it appears that each piece of land is regarded as being unique and thus the remedy is available in contract for the sale of land.

Finally, an order for specific performance cannot be made in order to enforce building contracts, or employment contracts. The reason is that the court, in such cases, cannot adequately supervise the enforcement of such contracts. In other words, the court cannot supervise on the day-to-day basis such type of contracts.

Injunction

This is an order of the court requiring the party at fault not to break the contract. Its main use is to enforce the negative promises that can occasionally be found in employment contracts (contracts in restraint of trade).

For example, an employee may agree not to work in a similar capacity for a rival employer during the period of his contract. Thus, in *Warner Bros.* v. *Nelson* (1936) Bette Davis, the film actress, had agreed not to work as an actress for anyone else during the period of her contract with Warner Bros. In breach of this agreement she left the USA and entered into a contract with a third party in the UK. The court held that Warner Bros. were entitled to an injunction to prevent the star breaking the negative provision in the contract.

It should be noted that an injunction cannot be used as a back door method of enforcing a contract of employment for which specific performance is not available. Warner Bros. could prevent Bette Davis working as an actress for anyone else. They could not have obtained a decree of specific performance to force her to return to their studio.

Another example of a prohibitive injunction is the Mareva Injunction. This is granted in order to restrict removal of assets outside the jurisdiction, often by a foreign defendant, where this is a real and serious possibility. However, it must be noted that this remedy will not be granted by courts in order to prevent a person disposing of his property, so that a person suing, for example, for a debt, will be able to recover his money. Mareva Injunction is clearly a valuable addition to existing contractual remedies, particularly when business is now so often conducted on an international scale.

Rescission

This is a further equitable remedy for breach of contract. The rule is the same when the remedy is used for breach as it is when it is used for misrepresentation. In effect, rescission restores the status quo, that is, it puts the parties back to the position they were in before the contract was made. If the contract cannot be completely rescinded, it cannot be rescinded at all.

For example, where X sold 20 bottles of whisky to Y, and Y in exchange sold 10 bottles of wine to X and also paid him £10, under misrepresentation, and the goods have been sold to third parties, the remedy of rescission would not be available.

Limitation of Actions

The Limitation Act 1980 imposes time limits within which an action for breach of contract must be brought. It is obvious that the right to sue does not last indefinitely.

An action on a simple contract must be brought within six years of the date when the cause of action accrued.

An action on a contract made under seal will be statute barred after twelve years from the date when the cause of action accrued.

Where the plaintiff's claims include a claim for damages in respect of personal injuries, the period is three years.

It should be noted that the Limitation Act 1980 does not discharge a contract, it merely makes the contract unenforceable in a court of law. This means that if the defendant does not plead the statutes of limitation, that is, the Limitation Act 1980, the judge will enforce the contract. For example, if X brings an action for money owed to him by Y under a simple contract which was performed eight years ago, unless Y pleads the Limitation Act, that is, puts forward to the court that X's action is time-barred, the court will proceed to decide on the issue of the debt. A right of action 'accrues' from the moment when breach occurs, not from the date when the contract was made. If the plaintiff is the victim of fraud or acts under a mistake, the limitation period will not begin to run until the true state of affairs is discovered or should have been discovered with the exercise of reasonable diligence.

Also, if the extent of an injury only comes to light more than three years after the breach of contract which caused it to take place, the Limitation Act 1980 provides that the plaintiff would have three years from the time he has discovered the effect of his injury. The rules about limitation of actions do not apply to the equitable remedies. Nevertheless, the equitable maxim 'delay defeats equity' will apply to defeat a plaintiff who waits too long before taking legal action.

Figure 5.1: Remedies for breach of contract

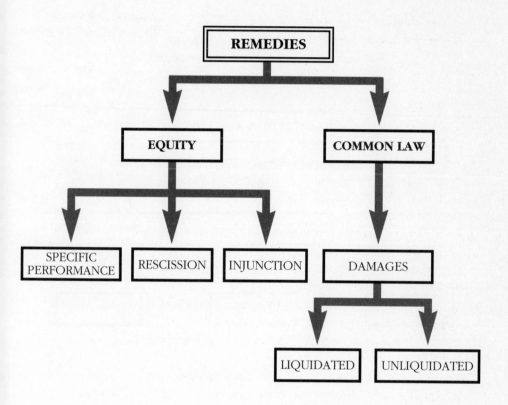

Figure 5.2: Limitation of actions

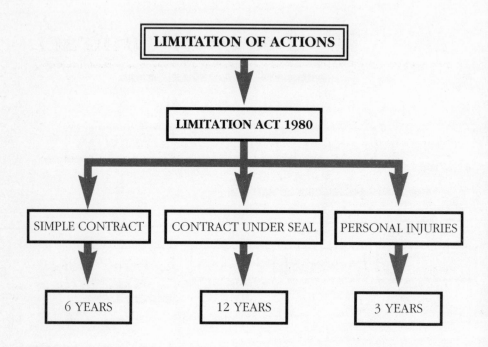

Questions for Discussion

1 What are liquidated and unliquidated damages?
2 Explain the principle founded in *Hadley* v. *Baxendale* on remoteness of damages.
3 What is specific performance?
4 What are the time limits imposed by the Limitation Act 1980?

6

Discharge of Contract

A contract may be discharged in four ways: by agreement; by performance; by breach; and by frustration.

By Agreement

Obviously, a contract may be ended by agreement. Discharge by agreement may arise out of the original agreement or out of a new contract.

Out of the original agreement

The parties, for example, may have agreed from the outset that the contract should end automatically on the expiration of a fixed time. Thus, a lease of premises for a fixed term would come within this category.

Another example is a contract of employment, which can normally be brought to an end by the operation of a provision entitling either party to terminate if they wish, upon giving reasonable notice. Note that in such cases the agreement, between employer and employee, is made at the outset, not when the notice is handed out.

Out of a new contract

Executory contract is a contract for goods or services to be supplied in the future, that is, a promise for a promise. If there has been no performance and the contract is executory, then a mutual bilateral discharge will be adequate. Note that the mutual release of the parties provides the consideration, for example, where there is a contract for sale of goods which have not yet been supplied or paid for, but are to be supplied at a later time, and both buyer and seller agree to end the contract.

Where the contract is executed, as where it has been performed or partly performed by one party, then the other party, that is, the party who wishes to be released, has to provide consideration for the release unless it is effected by deed.

It is important to remember that in order to have a discharge by agreement out of a new contract, it is necessary to have two elements, namely an agreement and a valid or effective new contract, which in turn means that consideration is required.

If consideration in the new contract is non-existent, then this is a gratuitous promise, and therefore the party giving such promise may always go back on the promise at any time and sue. Of course, if this party signs a deed then this is a contract by deed, in which case the party is bound by the promise, even though there is no consideration.

Immediate cash payment by the party which wants to be released would, for example, be good consideration for the other party's promise to end the contract; *Pinnel's Case* (1602).

By Performance

A contract may be discharged by performance when both parties have performed the obligations which the contract placed upon them.

The law cases falling under this heading are instances whereby one of the parties brings an action against the other party, claiming that the other party has not completed or fully completed the performance and therefore the other party is not released from obligation, that is, the contract cannot be discharged.

The general rule is that the manner of performance must comply exactly with the terms of the contract. Thus, in one case, A agreed to serve on a ship sailing from Jamaica to Liverpool. He was to be paid 30 guineas on arrival to Liverpool. Some days after the ship sailed, A died. It was held that his widow could not recover anything for the work A had done before he died. A was obliged to complete the voyage before he was entitled to payment; *Cutter* v. *Powell* (1795).

In another case, X installed a central heating system in Y's house for an agreed price of £560. The work was carried out defectively and it was estimated that it would cost £179 to put matters right. The Court of Appeal held that since X had not performed his side of the contract, he could recover nothing for the work he had done; *Bolton* v. *Mahadeva* (1927).

Therefore, where there is a contract for the sale of a certain quantity of goods, and the contract provides for the goods to be packed in cases containing 30 units each, and in fact the goods are packed in cases containing 28 units each, the buyer is entitled to reject the goods, as this has been held to be a sale by 'description' under the Sale of Goods Act; *Moore & Co.* v. *Landauer & Co.* (1921).

In other words, the manner of performance did not, in this case, comply exactly with the terms of the contract. Unless the degree of this compliance is determined, it is not possible to decide whether the parties in a contract are freed from their obligations, and therefore, whether the contract has been discharged or not. There are some criteria which a court would consider in order to determine whether performance must comply exactly with the terms of the contract. These are:

1 Construction of the contract.
2 Whether partial performance has been accepted by one party.
3 Whether full performance has been prevented by one party.

Construction of the contract

In this connection, a contract may be: divisible; entire; or capable of being fulfilled by substantial performance.

Divisible

This means that the obligations can be split up into stages or parts. Therefore, payment can be claimed for each completed stage, unlike the case of *Cutter* v. *Powell* (1795), where X had an entire contract, that is, he was not entitled to payment until he had completely performed his part of the contract.

An example of a divisible contract can be found in the contracts of carriage of goods by sea where a shipowner is to be paid freight 'pro-rata' – so much per ton delivered. Another example is a contract of employment whereby payment is due every month or week, even though the contract may be for two or three years. If a contract of employment provides for payment monthly in arrear and the employee leaves in breach of contract (or is justifiably dismissed) before the end of the month, he is not entitled to his agreed pay for the month. But if he works for the whole month he may be entitled to his pay.

Similarly, a contract to build a house usually provides for payment to be made in three stages: after the foundations have been laid, when the roof goes on and on completion of the house.

Entire

If an employer has contracted with the employee on a yearly basis, whereby the employer would have to pay his employee, say, £6,000, for a year's work, payable at the end of the year, and in fact he has paid £5,600, then performance has not been complied with, as such a contract is an entire contract, which in turn means that the contract has not been discharged. In such a case, performance must be complete and exact.

Where A has agreed to sell B a certain quantity of canned fruit, which is to be packed in cases of 30 and on arrival it is found that half of this quantity is packed in cases of 24, B (the buyer) is entitled to reject the whole consignment, as this is a sale by description (s.13 Sale of Goods Act 1979), and this is an entire contract; *Moore* v. *Landauer* (1921).

If the contract provided for example that acceptance and payment would be made only for cases arrived packed with 30 cans at destination, then B would not have been able to reject the whole consignment, but only the quantity that did not comply with this provision. Such a contract would be a divisible one.

Thus, where a shipowner contracts to transport some cargo, and freight is to be payable 'on delivery', he is entitled to the full freight, even if some of the cargo was not delivered or it was damaged.

Capable of being fulfilled by substantial performance

In the example of the shipowner above, we assumed that the shipowner delivered substantially the same amount of cargo he loaded on the ship. The reason for this is that the service, the carriage of the goods, in respect of which the freight was contracted to be paid has been substantially performed; *Dakin* v. *Oxley* (1864).

If the court considers that the plaintiff has substantially performed or carried out the terms of the contract, he may recover for the work he has done. The defendant can counter-claim for any defects in performance.

In *Hoenig* v. *Isaacs* (1952), the plaintiff agreed to decorate the defendant's flat and fit a bookcase and wardrobe for £750. On completion of the work the defendant paid £400 but he complained about faulty workmanship and refused to pay the balance of £350. The Court held that the contract had been substantially performed. The plaintiff was entitled to the outstanding £350, less the cost of remedying the defects, which were estimated at £55.

Thus, in the case of the sailor who died on board the vessel, *Cutter* v. *Powell* (1795), the decision of the court might have been different if, for example, he had died a couple of hours before the ship's arrival at Liverpool.

The courts in order to decide whether a particular term must be fully performed or whether substantial performance is enough, will refer to the difference between conditions and warranties. A condition must be wholly performed whereas substantial performance of a warranty is often enough.

For example, in one case an opera singer entered into an agreement to take part in an opera starting from 28th November, and because she was taken ill she could not perform on that date, and therefore the promoters entered into an agreement with another singer for the whole engagement; later, on 4th December, she presented herself and the promoters refused her services thereby treating the contract as discharged. It was held that her failure to perform as from the first night was a breach of condition. Therefore, contract discharged; *Pousard* v. *Spiers and Pond* (1876).

On the other hand, if in the above example, the contract was to the effect that she had to attend for a rehearsal six days before the opera engagement, that is, 22nd November, but she was taken ill and she arrived for the rehearsals on 26th November, then she would have had a successful action against the promoters, since the rehearsal clause is subsidiary to the main purposes of the contract, and this amounts to breach of warranty; *Bettini* v. *Gye* (1876).

Whether partial performance has been accepted by one party

Note that there must be a genuine exercise of the buyer's choice. Thus, if X agrees to deliver 50 bottles of whisky to Y and delivers 40 only, then Y may exercise his right to reject the whole consignment. But if Y accepts delivery of 40 bottles, then he must pay for them at the contract rate; Sale of Goods Act 1979.

Whether full performance has been prevented by one party

This covers cases where X is prevented by Y, both being parties to a contract, from further performance. In such cases, Y is liable to an action based on *quantum meruit* (as much as he has earned) for the value of work done up to the time when performance was prevented; *De Barnardy* v. *Harding* (1853).

Thus, where A made B his agent for the purpose of advertising and selling tickets for a Royal Event, on a 10 per cent commission to be made from the sale of the tickets, and B prepared all the advertising leaflets but before he had sold any tickets, A withdrew B's authority to sell the tickets, and therefore, B was prevented from earning any commission, it was held that B could sue A on *quantum meruit* and his action be successful; *De Barnardy* v. *Harding* (1853).

In another case, *Planche* v. *Colburn* (1831), the plaintiff agreed to write a book on 'Costume and Ancient Armour', on completion of which he was to receive £100. After he had done the necessary research and written part of the book, the publishers abandoned the project. He recovered 50 guineas for the work he had done.

By Breach

There are several forms of breach of contract. In general, they may be classified as follows:

1 Failure to perform the contract. For example, if a seller fails to deliver goods by the appointed time or where, although delivered, they are not up to standard as to quality or quantity.
2 Express repudiation where one party states that he will not perform his part of the contract.
   For example, where A appoints B as his agent, and the appointment is to start being effective in a month's time; after four days A states to B that will not require B's services; *Hochster* v. *De la Tour* (1835).
3 Some action by one party making performance impossible. An example is where X lets his ship to Y for a period of one year and agrees to pay Z a commission on the hire received during the charter period; and X sells the ship free of all liability to another person. X's action was a repudiation of the agreement he had with Y and Z, and entitled Y and Z to damages; *Omnium D'Enterprises* v. *Sutherland* (1919).

In the cases of 2 and 3 above, we have what is called an anticipatory breach. This is a breach which takes place before the time for performance has arrived. In other words this caters for the cases where a party states in advance that he does not intend to carry out his side of the contract or puts himself in a position whereby he will be unable to perform. In the case of anticipatory breaches, the aggrieved party may sue at once for damages.

Alternatively, he can wait for the time for performance to arrive and see whether the other party is prepared to carry out the contract. However, it must be noted that if this option is taken, there is a risk that the contract may become discharged, for example, by frustration, or illegality.

Not every breach entitles the innocent party to treat the contract as discharged. It must be shown that the breach affects a vital part of the contract, that is, that it is a breach of condition rather than a breach of warranty; *Pousard* v. *Spiers and Pond* (1876), or that the other party had no intention of performing his contract; *Hochster* v. *De la Tour* (1835).

By Frustration

In general, for an event to frustrate a contract, it must:

1 occur after the contract is made;
2 not be something which is foreseeable;
3 not be caused by the act or fault of the party claiming not to be liable for breach of contract; or
4 make it illegal to carry out the contract or impossible to carry out the contract or renders performance of the contract radically different from that which was contemplated at the time the contract was made.

In order to examine the doctrine of frustration, it is desirable to classify contracts into two main categories: contracts for personal service and other contracts.

Contracts for personal service may be discharged by:

1 Death. Thus, where A contracted to play the piano at a concert and died before the date of performance, the contract was frustrated, that is, discharged by frustration.
2 Incapacity. Incapacity must affect the contract in a funda-mental manner, as temporary incapacity is not enough. For

example, in one case an opera singer entered into an agreement to take part in an opera starting from 28th November, and because she was taken ill she could not perform on that date, and therefore, the promoters entered into an agreement with another singer for the whole engagement; later, on 4th December, she presented herself and the promoters refused her services thereby treating the contract as discharged. It was held that her failure to perform as from the first night was a breach of condition. Therefore, this affected the contract in a fundamental manner; *Pousard* v. *Spiers and Pond* (1876).

The doctrine of frustration only applies where there is no fault by either party, otherwise we must approach such a problem differently.

Thus, in *Norris* v. *Southampton City Council, The Times*, 27 January, 1982, Norris was a cleaner and he was convicted of assault and reckless driving and was sentenced to a term of imprisonment. His employers dismissed him, and he claimed that his dismissal was unfair. The Tribunal held that the contract of employment was frustrated and that the employee was not dismissed and therefore not entitled to compensation. The Employment Appeal Tribunal added that frustration could only arise where there was no fault by either party. This is because in this case the impossibility of further performance was brought about by Norris's fault.

Other contracts may be frustrated where there is:

1 Government interference, that is, requisitioning of goods under emergency powers; *Re Shipton, Anderson & Co. and Harrison Bros' Arbitration* (1915).
2 Destruction of the subject-matter. Thus, in *Taylor* v. *Caldwell* (1863), the plaintiff hired a music hall for a series of concerts. However, after making the agreement and before the date of the first performance, the hall was destroyed by fire. It was held that the contract was discharged and parties released from their obligations.
3 Non-occurrence of an event. In such cases, the contract must be substantially affected. Thus, in *Krell* v. *Henry* (1903),

Henry hired a room overlooking the route of Edward VII's coronation procession. The procession was cancelled owing to the King's serious illness. Although it would have been possible to come and sit in the room, the main purpose of the contract, to view the procession, had been destroyed. Held, that contract had been frustrated.

4 Commercial purpose of the contract has been defeated (although performance possible). Thus, in *Krell* v. *Henry* (1903), Henry hired a room overlooking the route of Edward VII's coronation procession. The procession was cancelled owing to the King's serious illness. Although it would have been possible to come and sit in the room, the main purpose of the contract, to view the procession, had been destroyed. Held, that contract had been frustrated.

The previous case may be contrasted with the case of *Tsakiroglou & Co. Ltd* v. *Noblee and Thorl GmbH* (1961), where X, the sellers, agreed to deliver the goods to Y, the buyers in Hamburg. The sellers, X, failed to deliver, and their defence to Y's claim was that the contract had been frustrated due to the closure of the Suez Canal. Held, that this was not sufficient to render the contract frustrated.

In other words, mere inconvenience and extra expense would not be sufficient grounds for the doctrine of frustration to operate. The doctrine of frustration will not apply where the parties have made provisions in the contract.

Thus, in *Clark* v. *Lindsay* (1903), the contracts provided that if the coronation procession of Edward VII was postponed the tickets would be valid for the day on which it did take place or that the parties should get their money back with a deduction for the room owner's expenses. Therefore, the cancellation of the procession did not render the contracts frustrated.

The doctrine of frustration will not apply where the frustrating event is self-induced; *Norris* v. *Southampton City Council, The Times*, 27 January, 1982.

Furthermore, it would appear that the doctrine of frustration is not applicable in the cases of leases and contracts for the sale of land. The reason behind it is that the property continues to exist or survives the frustrating event. However, it might be said that the lease of cliff land would be frustrated if the land slipped into the sea. Note that judicial opinion has been divided upon the issue of whether leases and contracts for the sale of land can be frustrated; *Cricklewood Property and Investment Trust Ltd* v. *Leighton's Investment Trust Ltd* (1945); *Hillingdon Estates Co.* v. *Stonefield Estates Ltd* (1952).

Before the Law Reform (Frustrated Contracts) Act 1943 became law, money due and not paid could be claimed and money paid before the frustrating event was not recoverable. Thus, in *Chandler* v. *Webster* (1904), Y agreed to let X have a room for the purpose of viewing the coronation procession, for £141 15s. The contract provided that the money be payable immediately. The procession did not take place and X, who had paid £100 on account, left the balance unpaid. Furthermore, X sued to recover the £100 and Y counter-claimed for £41 15s. It was held that X's action failed and Y's counter-claim succeeded because the obligation to pay the rent had fallen due before the frustrating event.

However, since 1943 and the Law Reform (Frustrated Contracts) Act, money paid is recoverable, and money payable ceases to be payable. Furthermore, the Act provides that the parties may recover expenses in connection with the contract, or retain the relevant sum from money received.

It is also possible to recover on a *quantum meruit*, in respect of part performance before the frustrating event, provided the other party, received 'a valuable benefit'; *B.P. Exploration* v. *Hund* (1982).

In real terms the way this compensation is awarded is two-fold: the court will consider the actual value of the valuable benefit, and the 'just' sum which will include expenses.

The act states that the provision of valuable benefit will apply each part of a divisible contract as if each were a separate contract. Furthermore, the act does not apply to contracts of carriage of goods by sea, and insurance. The reason is that maritime law has well settled rules.

Figure 6.1: Discharge of contract

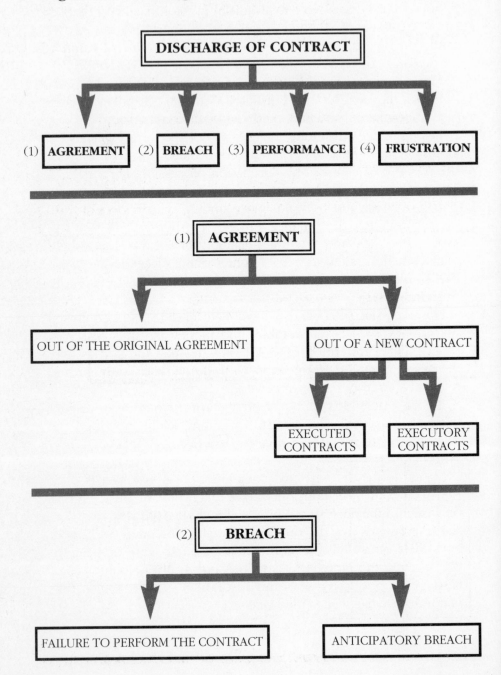

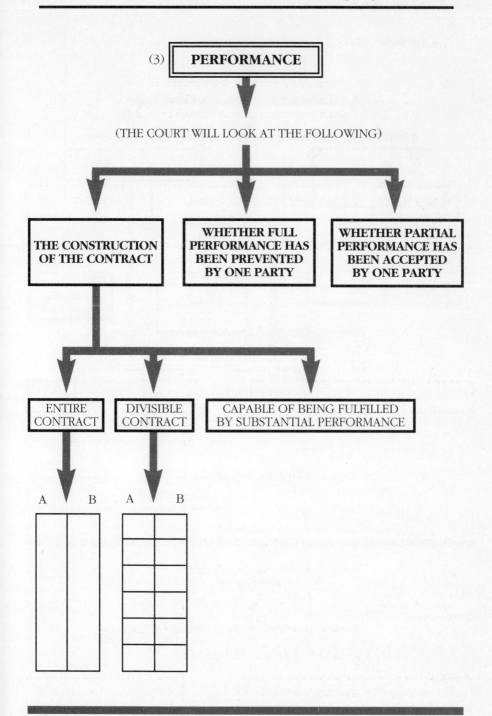

(3) **PERFORMANCE**

(THE COURT WILL LOOK AT THE FOLLOWING)

THE CONSTRUCTION OF THE CONTRACT

WHETHER FULL PERFORMANCE HAS BEEN PREVENTED BY ONE PARTY

WHETHER PARTIAL PERFORMANCE HAS BEEN ACCEPTED BY ONE PARTY

ENTIRE CONTRACT

DIVISIBLE CONTRACT

CAPABLE OF BEING FULFILLED BY SUBSTANTIAL PERFORMANCE

A   B   A   B

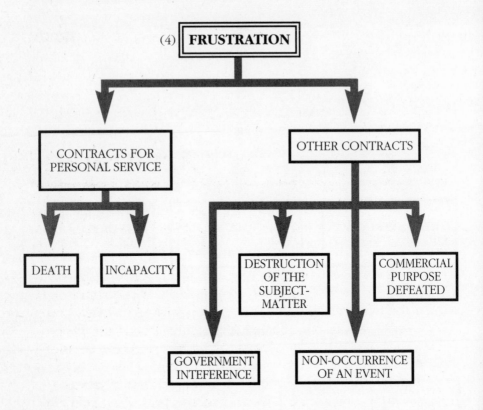

Frustration is not applicable where:
1 The parties have made provisions in the contract.
2 It is self-induced.
3 Sale of land and leases is involved.

Questions for Discussion

1 What is frustration of a contract?
2 Briefly explain in what circumstances a contract will be frustrated.

7

Arbitration

Businessmen and merchants often prefer to refer disputes to arbitration, as an alternative to litigation. The arbitrator is usually chosen by the parties for his specialist knowledge in the field where the dispute lies, and therefore speeds up the process. Furthermore, as most jurisdictions recognize the decisions of arbitrations, the enforcement of arbitration awards is not at a significant disadvantage to judicial decisions. One disadvantage of arbitration is the lack of power on the part of arbitrators to issue an injunction, such as a Mareva Injunction or make an interlocutory award.

The statutory regulation of the law relating to arbitration is found in the Arbitration Acts 1950, 1975 and 1979. The 1975 Act gives effect in the UK to the New York Convention on the Recognition and Enforcement of Foreign Arbitral Awards 1958.

Section 32 of the 1950 Act defines arbitration as 'a written agreement to submit present or future differences to arbitration, whether an arbitrator is named therein or not'.

It is quite usual for arbitration clauses to be framed in such a manner that they prevent any right to court proceedings until an arbitration award has been made; *Scott* v. *Avery* (1856). Such a clause is quite valid on merit, but if a party to the agreement commences court proceedings, contrary to the clause, the courts upon the application of the other party would either:

1 order a stay of proceedings, that is, allow the arbitration; or

2 refuse the application for a stay, that is, breaking the arbitration agreement.

Obviously, the court's decision on whether to break the agreement or not would very much depend on the particular circumstances. One point to note here is that the power of the court to break an arbitration clause is wider in the case of a domestic arbitration. Therefore, it is important to distinguish between domestic and non-domestic arbitration agreements.

Section 3(7) of the Arbitration Act 1979 states that an arbitration agreement which does not expressly or impliedly provide for arbitration in a state other than the UK, that is, in a foreign state, and to which an individual who is a national of or habitually resident in any state other than the UK (a foreign national or foreign resident), is not a party at the time the arbitration agreement is entered into, is a domestic arbitration. In simple words, three requirements are set out, in order for an arbitration agreement to be considered a domestic one.

The individual, or parties, referred to above should reside in the UK or should not be foreign nationals, and should be parties to the arbitration agreement, and the arbitration agreement should not provide for arbitration in any other state. All other arbitrations are non-domestic.

A simple example may be in order here. F and E are both parties to an arbitration agreement which does not specifically state in which state the arbitration is to take place. F is a French national resident in the UK and E a British national and resident. Since F is a UK resident as is E, this is a domestic arbitration. However, if F was a French or American resident, then such arbitration would have been a non-domestic one.

It is usually easier for the parties to exclude judicial review of the arbitration if it is considered non-domestic.

An important point to note is that although an arbitration agreement may be made verbally or in writing, the Arbitration Acts apply only to agreements in writing.

The following is a brief account of some points on the Arbitration Acts:

1 An award under an arbitration agreement may be enforced in the same manner as a judgment or order of court. Thus, the award made by the arbitrator is binding and final.
2 Oral agreements are outside the scope of the Acts.
3 The parties should submit to examination on oath by the arbitrator. Also, witnesses should give their testimony on oath.
4 The arbitrator has discretion as to the award of costs.
5 The arbitrator is not required by the Acts to give his reasons unless specifically requested by either of the parties.
6 Either of the parties may (a) apply to the High Court for leave to appeal, or (b) mutually agree to submit the procedure to judicial appeal.
7 An arbitrator has not the power (*locus standi*) to make a reference to the European Court of Justice; Article 177 of the Treaty of Rome.

Question for Discussion

What factors are to be considered under the Arbitration Act 1979 in order to decide whether an arbitration is a domestic one?

8

Law Governing a Contract

Introduction

It is of great importance for the parties to know what law governs the contract that they have made, because the law for example, of sale and agency, differs from country to country. Even where it is clear that the applicable law is that of another country, the contents of that law still have to be proved to the judge in the ordinary way by expert witnesses or some other admissible evidence.

It is often very difficult to decide whether a particular contract is to be governed by the law of one country or that of another. For example, a contract to work for a French employer in France may be made in England; is French or English law to apply? If the contract states clearly that one or other of the conflicting systems is to prevail, this will be *prima facie* evidence that the system mentioned is to govern the contract; but if no such clause is included, the court will endeavour to ascertain the intention of the parties, and effect will be given to that intention as far as possible. The law intended by the parties is often referred to as 'the proper law of the contract'.

The Contracts (Applicable Law) Act 1990

This Act has brought into force the 1980 Rome Convention on the Law Applicable to Contractual Obligations, and came into force in April 1991. This is now the legislation covering questions of 'applicable law' to govern a contract or 'proper law' as it is best known in the UK.

The Convention applies to contractual obligations in any situation involving a choice between the laws of different countries. Therefore, it applies to any contract with an international flavour not just those which have an EEC connection.

> A contract shall be governed by the law chosen by the parties. The choice must be express or demonstrated with reasonable certainty by the terms of the contract or the circumstances of the case. By their choice the parties can select the law applicable to the whole or a part only of a contract.

Thus, it is clear from the above quoted Article 3(1) that where the intention of the parties is clearly expressed generally no difficulty will arise, but where no definite expression of intention is made it is necessary to presume intention from the attendant circumstances.

There are a number of important exclusions to the application of the Convention:

1 Certain obligations arising under bills of exchange, cheques and other negotiable instruments;
2 Arbitration agreements and agreements on the choice of court, that is, jurisdiction clauses;
3 It does not cover trusts, matrimonial matters and questions on capacity.
4 It does not apply to 'contracts of insurance which cover risks situated in the territories of member states of the EEC', although it does apply to contracts of re-insurance.

If no law has been expressly or impliedly chosen by the parties, Article 4(1) provides that 'the contract shall be governed by the law of the country with which it is most closely connected'. The Convention lays down some rebuttable presumptions in order to determine this close connection between the contract and the country. This is presumed by Article 4(2) as the law of the country of the party making the 'characteristic performance'. In a contract of sale, this will most probably be the seller's country.

The Convention also provides that, in the case of a contract for the carriage of goods, 'if the country in which, at the time the contract is concluded, the carrier has his principal place of business is also the country in which the place of loading or the place of discharge or the principal place of business of the consignor is situated, it shall be presumed that the contract is most closely connected with that country'.

In other words there is a rebuttable presumption that if, for example, X has to effect the performance which is characteristic of his contract with Y, then the law of the state where X's place of business is situated will apply.

However, it should be noted that the presumptions laid down by the Convention should not be applied if 'it appears from the circumstances as a whole that the contract is more closely connected with another country'; Article 4(5).

Since, in broad terms, the Convention continues to recognize the right of the parties to choose the applicable law, it is likely to be even more important than before to ensure that the appropriate governing law is clearly spelt out in the contract.

Under Common Law

It should be noted that in determining the proper law of a contract made before April 1991, that is, before the Act came into force, or contracts which are not covered by the Act, the rules of Common Law would be applicable.

In the absence of contrary evidence it is presumed that the parties intend the contract to be governed by the law of the country of performance. The courts tend to apply as the relevant test of the applicable proper law: 'With which system of law has the contract its closest and most real connection?'

As mentioned earlier, the basic rule is that the applicable law is that stated in the agreement between the parties or, where no such express agreement exists, it may be possible for the court to infer the law intended from the circumstances of the case. The following points should be noted:

1 The proper law is to be decided by reference to a system of law and not to a particular country.
2 The proper law is ascertained in relation to the situation at the time the contract is made.
3 It is possible for different aspects of the contract to be decided by reference to different legal systems. This is called *depecage.*

The law intended by the parties

The parties may choose any law that they wish, even if the contract has no connection with it; *Amin Rasheed* v. *Kuwait Insurance Co.* (1984). However, this choice must be exercised for a *bona fide* purpose and not merely to avoid statutory control. For instance, the mandatory provisions of the Unfair Contract Terms Act 1977 cannot be contracted out of by the parties.

Close connection

The following factors are considered by the court when deciding this issue:

1 The form of the contract.
2 The place where the contract was concluded.
3 The place where the contract is to be performed.
4 The parties place of residence and business.
5 The place where an arbitration is to be held.
6 The personality of the parties.

The form of the contract
Generally speaking, the form of the contract carries as little weight as the language which the parties have used, especially

as English is the recognized language of commerce. The same is also true about the currency of payment. Nevertheless, these factors usually do provide a clue as to the ascertainment of the law of the closest connection; *Whitworth Street Estates* v. *James Miller* (1970).

The place where the contract was concluded

This is a factor of considerable importance, particularly so when the contract has to be performed in the same place, or under the same jurisdiction. As it usually is the case in international trade, a contract is concluded between two parties who are not present in the same country. In this case, note that the contract is supposed to have been concluded at the place where its acceptance is effected.

Thus, if X in Paris receives a shipment order from Y in Japan on CIF terms (Tokyo) and X accepts this order, the likely governing law of the contract will be French, as it is to be performed in France by delivery of the goods on board a ship sailing for the agreed port of destination; *Johnson* v. *Taylor Bros. & Co. Ltd* (1920).

The place where the contract is to be performed

This is a very important factor in deciding which is the law governing a contract. It would appear that it is more weighty a factor than the place where the contract was concluded, therefore, great importance should be attached to it.

Thus, in *Benaim & Co.* v. *Debono* (1924), an offer by X in Gibraltar to sell on FOB terms to Y in Malta was made and accepted. Y rejected the goods and the question arose as to whether the law of Gibraltar or Malta applied to the contract. It was held that although the posting of the acceptance letter took place in Malta and therefore the contract was concluded in Malta, the place of performance was Gibraltar since the goods were shipped FOB Gibraltar. Thus, the applicable law was that of Gibraltar.

The parties place of residence and business

The capacity of the parties to a contract is in general governed by the law of their domicile at the time when the contract was made. A person's domicile is the country in which he has his **permanent home**. Domicile must be distinguished from nationality, which is the political relation that exists between an individual and the State to which he owes allegiance. In order to make the distinction clearer, domicile determines civil rights and obligation, for example right of marriage and succession, whereas nationality determines public rights and obligations, for example the right to vote or to hold political office.

Finally, it must be noted that there is one exception to the rule relating to the capacity of the parties, in an ordinary mercantile contract. In particular, capacity in the case of such contracts (ordinary mercantile) is governed by the law of the country where the contract is made.

The place where an arbitration is to be held
This is another factor which only gives an indication of the intended governing law. It is quite a weighty indication, as it infers that the parties intend to submit the contract to the law of the place of arbitration; *Compangnie Tunisienne* v. *Compagnie d'Armement Maritime* (1971). In this case the charter-party had an English arbitration clause, but a choice of law clause in terms that the contract should be 'governed by the law of the flag of the vessel carrying the goods'. Another clause stated that the ship was to be 'governed or controlled or chartered by French shipowners'. Therefore, it appears that the parties anticipated that ships flying French flags would be employed. In fact, shipments were made on a number of ships flying differing flags. It was held that the two clauses pointed to a choice of French law.

Some Additional Rules Applicable to Foreign Contracts

The following is a more detailed account of the main rules for determining conflicts between English and foreign law in the English Courts.

A contract otherwise valid cannot be enforced in England if

its enforcement is opposed to an English rule of procedure. For example, the English Limitation Act 1980 will apply to foreign contracts sued upon in the English Courts. If X, an Englishman, in France, enters into an oral contract with B, a Frenchman, and the contract is one which by English law must be evidenced in writing, it is unenforceable in the English Courts, even if French law requires no written evidence.

The principle is that the procedure and the rules of evidence to be applied are those in force in the country in which the litigation occurs.

The form of the contract is in general governed by the law of the country in which the contract is made. Obviously, this rule is not applicable where the parties intend the contract to operate in and be subject to the law of some other country.

The validity and construction of a contract is governed by the law of the country to which the parties intended to submit themselves. In connection to this, it should be noted that the sections relating to the avoidance of liability for negligence, unreasonable indemnity clauses, and so on, of the Unfair Contract Terms Act 1977 will not operate as part of the proper law, where the proper law of a contract is the law of any part of the UK only by choice of the parties (and apart from that choice would be the law of some country outside the UK).

In other words, where two parties, say an Italian and an American, have entered into a contract in New York, and the place of performance is to be the USA, under normal circumstances the law of the USA will govern such a contract. If, however, the contract provides that the proper law is to be that of the UK, then the UK law will be the proper law (by choice) and the sections of the Unfair Contract Terms Act 1977 relating to the avoidance of liability for negligence, unreasonable indemnity clauses, etc. will not be applicable. The remaining sections of the Act, of course, will be applicable.

Discharge of contract is governed by the proper law. Foreign law will not receive judicial notice by the English Courts, but must be proved by an expert witness. Note that under the European Communities Act 1972, judicial notice is to be taken of the Treaties referred to in the Act, and of any decision of or expression of opinion, by the European Court.

Figure 8.1: Law governing a contract

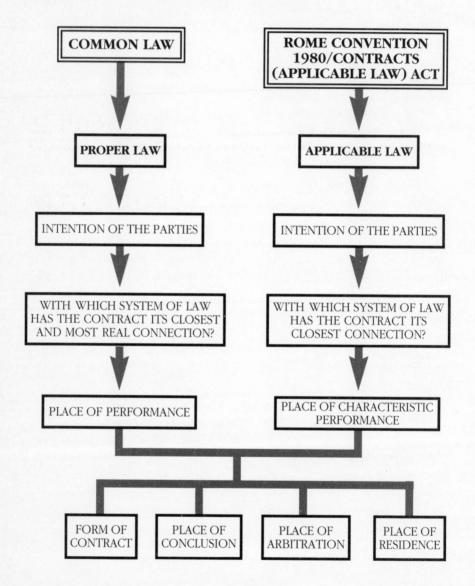

Question for Discussion

What factors are considered by the courts in determining the 'real connection' element of the proper law in a contract?

Part 2

Agency Law

9

Agency

Introduction

An agent is a legal person (either a company or an individual) who is employed by a principal to make contracts on his or her behalf with third parties. An employee who makes contracts on behalf of an employer is acting as an agent. A shop assistant, for example, is in this category. Alternatively, an agent may be an independent contractor who is engaged for specialist skills and knowledge. A person who wishes to sell shares will usually employ the services of a stockbroker to arrange the sale. Agents are given a number of names, the most common being 'broker', 'representative', or 'factor'. The ordinary rules of contract apply to the contract of agency. Therefore, three rules must be considered, in so far as capacity is concerned:

1 The third party must have capacity to contract in order that the contract which the agent makes with the third party on behalf of the principal may be enforceable. In other words, the ordinary rules concerning capacity are applicable.
2 The agent must have capacity to contract if the contract with the principal is to be enforceable; otherwise agent and principal may not be able to enforce the rights and duties arising under the contract of agency. Thus, if a person appoints a minor as his principal, the contract of agency will be unenforceable.

3 However, a person who lacks legal capacity to make a contract does not lose that incapacity by employment of an agent. Thus, a minor who has merely a restricted capacity to contract as a principal, may be appointed to act as agent for any purpose for a principal who has full contractual capacity; but a minor cannot, by appointing another person to contract for him as agent, overcome his own lack of capacity to make certain contracts; *G.* v. *G.* (1970).

Classification of Agents

There are various classifications of agents. For example, they may be divided according to the degree of authority which they possess:

1 Universal agents have unrestricted authority (such agents are rarely met with in practice). The principal is bound by all acts having legal significance done on his or her behalf by the universal agent. This power and authority which these kinds of agents enjoy is called a 'power of attorney'.
2 Special agents are appointed only for a specific purpose or occasion to which their authority is restricted, or in respect of a matter not within the ordinary course of their business or profession. If special agents do anything outside their authority, the principal is not necessarily bound by it; and a third party is not entitled to assume that the agent has unlimited powers, but should make due enquiry as to the extent of the agent's authority. Thus, an estate agent may be appointed to sell a house; once a buyer has been found and the contracts have been exchanged the agent is rewarded and the authority lapses.
3 General agents are appointed to do anything within the authority given to them by the principal in all transactions, or in all transactions relating to a specified trade or matter. (Many of the agencies created in international trade are of this type).

Another classification depends upon the agent's liability:

1 Agents who are not, as a rule, personally liable to their principals in respect of contracts entered into by them on behalf of their principals.

2 *Del Credere* agents, who are answerable to principals for due payment by third parties to whom goods have been sold on behalf of the principal; *Hornby* v. *Lacy* (1817). The agent is liable only if the third party cannot pay, and is not liable, if, say, the third party refuses to take delivery. The agent guarantees that payment will be made by the other party (third party) with whom the agent has contracted on behalf of the principal. A del credere agent is paid an extra commission to compensate for the extra risk undertaken as surety. In other words, the liability of such an agent to the principal, as a surety for the buyer, is limited to cases where there is an ascertained amount or certain sum due as a debt from the buyer to the principal, and the buyer fails to pay, either through insolvency or some other event that makes it impossible to recover payment.

3 Confirming houses, which are mainly involved in overseas trade and arise where an exporter in this country on receiving an order from a customer abroad obtains confirmation from some third person either in the buyer's country or here. This third person, as confirming agent, assumes liability to the supplying exporter, if the buyer fails to perform the contract.

Agents may also be classified according to their functions, for example:

1 Factors or 'mercantile agents': a factor is a mercantile agent, or 'a person having in the customary course of his business as such agent authority either to sell goods, or to consign goods for the purpose of sale, or to buy goods, or to raise money on the security of goods, or to consign goods for the purpose of sale, or to buy goods, or to raise money on the security of goods'; Factors Act 1889. The essential feature of a factor is that he or she holds stock, not as a mere bailee like a carrier, but as a mercantile agent for the purpose of sale.

The above definition is provided by section 1(1) of the Factors Act 1889. In short, a factor is a mercantile agent to whom goods are consigned for sale by the principal. Furthermore, a factor is authorized to sell in his or her own name. From the definition provided by this Act, the following points arise:

(a) Mercantile agent.
   An agent is a factor if, and only if, it is in the customary course of business as such agent
   i) to sell goods; or
   ii) to consign goods for sale; or
   iii) to buy goods; or
   iv) to raise money on the security of goods.
Therefore, a person will normally be considered a factor, or become a factor, if any of the above four requirements is satisfied.
(b) Customary course of business.
   This does not mean that a person has to be normally in business as a factor, nor a known kind of commercial agent. For example, a man who normally sells second-hand furniture which he has previously bought on his own account, becomes a factor if he undertakes to sell a bedroom suite for a principal.
(c) A mercantile agent must be authorized to sell the goods in his own name without saying he or she is an agent.
   Thus, in *Rolls Razor* v. *Cox* (1967), X was a self-employed door to door salesman of washing machines. Y was a company that supplied him with stock and a van. Y went into liquidation owing to X money for commission on goods sold. X wished to keep Y's goods until he was paid in full rather than prove in the liquidation. X alleged he could do this by exercising a factor's right of general lien. X needed to do this because Y did not owe him money on the goods in his hands but on goods already sold. It was held that he (X) was not a factor and not entitled to a factor's lien.
2 Brokers differ from factors in being agents who buy or sell goods on behalf of their principals but without handling the actual goods. They may be agents for either the buyer or the

seller, bringing together parties in opposite situations to their mutual satisfaction in return for a commission called brokerage.

3 Sole distributors: One of the options open to an exporter, when considering securing a steady flow of export orders, is the conclusion of a sole distribution agreement with an importer abroad. This would effectively assist the exporter in achieving intensive exports by establishing a permanent marketing organization overseas, whose duty would be to create and maintain a demand for the goods in question.

Frequently, one hears the expressions 'sole' or 'exclusive' being used in connection to rights of representation by agents and distributors. However, there is no clear meaning attached to these terms, and therefore it is preferable for the parties to make sure that in their agreement they clarify the rights which they intend the representative to have.

Alternatively, it would appear that the following meaning may be attributed to the terms 'sole' and 'exclusive':

(a) Both terms imply that the principal shall not be entitled to appoint another distributor or agent for the territory of the representative.

(b) If the representation is 'sole', the principal himself may undertake sales in the territory of the representative on his own account without any liability to the representative.

(c) If the representation is 'exclusive', the principal is not allowed to compete with the representative in the allotted territory. This interpretation is supported by the definition of the word 'exclusive' in the Patents Act 1977, where the term 'exclusive licence' is defined.

Sole distribution agreements usually provide that the seller grants the buyer sole trading rights within a particular territory with respect to goods of a specified kind while the buyer may undertake to rely on the seller as the sole source of supply whenever he or she requires to buy goods of the specified kind.

Where such a contract is concluded between X, a manufacturer of computers in the UK, and Y, an Indian importer, X is not entitled to appoint another distributor for his computers in India, nor, if that is the intention of the parties, is Y at liberty to buy competitive makes of computers in the UK.

It must be noted that the sole distributor is not an agent of the British manufacturer or merchant in the legal sense. Unlike the agent in the legal sense, the sole distributor does not act on behalf of the British principal and is not account-able for the profits derived from the resale of the goods in his or her own territory. Furthermore, the profit of the sole distributor is normally the difference between the buying and selling price whereas the profit of the agent is usually the commission which is earned when concluding a sales contract on behalf of the principal, or when the principal concludes a sales contract with a customer introduced by the agent.

The sole distribution agreement also differs from an exclusive agency agreement in another aspect; the contracts which are concluded within its framework are proper contracts of sale by which the foreign merchant (the distributor) buys in his or her own name and when the goods are resold in his or her territory no contractual bond is established between the re-purchaser and the British exporter.

A sole distribution agreement might further be concluded between an exporter in the UK and a manufacturer or wholesaler also in the UK. In this case the exporter, who is sometimes referred to as 'export distributor', is granted the exclusive right of distributing the manufacturer's goods abroad, either anywhere or in a specified market. Two types of export distribution agreements are in use and the contract should make it clear which type is intended: under some export distribution agreements the distributor undertakes to place annually orders of a fixed amount with the manufac-turer; and under other agreements the distributor merely undertakes to place such orders if and when they are received from customers abroad.

Finally, note that care should be taken in drafting a sole/exclusive distributorship agreement so that its terms do not infringe the provisions of the Restrictive Trade Practices Act 1976 and Articles 85 and 86 of the EC Treaty of Rome (see page 175).

4 Bankers.
5 Forwarding agents.
6 Servants.
7 Estate agents.
8 Wife, housekeeper, and so on.

Creation of Agency

In this connection there are some points to be noted. Agents may be appointed either expressly or impliedly, agency may be implied from the particular relationship of two persons, and persons who allow a person to act as their agent must have authority to appoint the agent.

Thus, in *British Bank of the Middle East* v. *Sun Life Assurance of Canada (UK) Ltd* (1983), the House of Lords decided that X, a manager of Sun Life, had no authority to bind the company to a transaction concerning life assurance and mortgage protection with Y. The fact that Z, a branch manager, who was X's senior, had held him out as having authority did not affect the decision because Z, the branch manager, had no authority to bind Sun Life in the matters concerned. All matters relating to life assurance and mortgage protection had to be referred to head office.

Therefore, a person without authority himself cannot make representations as to the authority of others.

In other words, assume that you are an employee in a life insurance firm, and the branch manager says 'you now have authority to effect any shipping contracts on behalf of the firm'. You enter into a contract with someone on behalf of the firm to, say, build a ship. If the branch manager had no authority to bind the firm on matters concerning ship building, (as the company is a life insurance company) then you have no authority to bind the firm either, in respect of ship building.

Authority

In this respect, we are concerned with actual authority and ostensible (apparent) authority.

1 Actual authority. This may arise as follows:

   (a) Actual authority by express agreement. This means that the agent is entitled to exercise the powers actually given to him under the contract of agency, and will bind the principal by the exercise of those powers.

   (b) Actual authority by implication. The courts would be prepared to imply powers arising out of a contract of agency, when these powers are ordinarily or necessarily incidental to the performance of his express authority.

   Thus, in *Comber* v. *Anderson* (1808), X instructed his agent, an insurance broker, to insure a cargo of corn, but gave no specific instructions as to the type of policy or with whom it was to be effected. The broker effected a policy with a company which used an exception clause excluding liability for the loss of cargo by the stranding of the ship. The ship was stranded and there was a loss for which X could not recover under the policy. The question arose as to whether the agent was liable as having no authority to effect such a policy. It was held that since the agent was given a discretion, authority to make the sort of policy he had made was implied. There was no suggestion of fraud and the agent was free to elect as between insurers.

   In other words, the court will look at the task undertaken by the agent under the agency agreement and will infer some additional authority arising in the course of the performance of the agency agreement. This authority is implied and dependant on the actual task undertaken.

   (c) Actual authority derived from customary or usual authority. Where the agent is one of a class of agents, for example estate agent, factor, solicitor, the actual authority may be extended to cover the powers which an agent in this class normally possesses.

   Thus, in *Panorama Developments (Guildford)* v. *Fidelis Furnishing Fabrics* (1971), the court held that a modern company secretary was not a mere clerk and must be regarded as having authority to sign contracts connected with the administrative side of the company's affairs, thus binding the company. In this case, the secretary bound the company when he ordered taxis, some of which were used to take customers of the firm to the airport, but some of which he used for his own purposes.

Also, a solicitor has usual authority by the client to compromise a claim. Thus, in *Waugh* v. *H.B. Clifford & Sons* (1982), X sued Y, a firm of builders, for damages for negligence in building a house. Z, who was Y's solicitor, agreed with X's solicitor that Y should purchase the house. Y however, did not wish this compromise but their solicitor did not know this at the time that he made it. The plaintiff, X, asked the court to grant a decree for specific performance, that is, to force Y to buy the house, and he succeeded in this action.

This means that the court will look at the usual or customary authority which an agent of the particular type enjoys.

For example, if you ask a person to find a three bedroom house and buy it for you for a certain price, and in the process of finding a suitable house, and entering into a contract with a house owner, the agent also enters into a contract with a chartered surveyor, you cannot say that there was no such authority. The agent's authority is actual implied. Contrast this with the hypothesis that this person is a house buying agent. Then the agent's authority would be customary. Another example is a stockbroker who acts according to the customs of the stock exchange.

If the agent is found in breach of his or her authority, then this is a breach of warranty, so that the principal is still bound by the contract with the third party, but can claim damages from the agent. Also the agent, in such a case, would not be entitled to any remuneration or commission.

If the third party does not know of the agent's lack or withdrawal of authority, the contract binds the principal. If the third party knows of the agent's lack of authority a contract is obtained not with the principal, but with the agent.

2 Apparent or Ostensible authority (or agency by estoppel).

This arises where the principal holds out a person as his or her agent for the purpose of making a contract with a third party, and the third party relies on that fact. As it was put in *Hely-Hutchinson* v. *Brayhead Ltd* (1968), ostensible or apparent authority is the 'authority of an agent as it appears to the others'.

A wife living with her husband and managing his household is presumed to have authority from her husband to pledge his credit for necessaries for the household.

Thus, in *Spiro* v. *Lintern* (1973) X owned a house which he was considering selling. He agreed with Y, his wife, that she would find a purchaser for the property. However, he did not authorize her to enter into any contract. Y, his wife, however, made a contract with Z to sell the house, and X, knowing of this, allowed Z to have repairs carried out to the house and also to have work done in the garden. In this action for specific performance by Z, it was held that as X knew that Z was acting on the assumption that Y had authority, he (X) was under a duty to tell him she (Y) had no authority, and as X had not done so, he was estopped from denying her (Y) authority to enter into the contract. Thus, Z's action succeeded.

In other words, if a servant, such as an employee, has made purchases on an employer's behalf and the goods have been paid for by the employer, there will be implied an agency for future similar transactions with the same tradespeople; for, if a person has so acted as to lead others to suppose that a certain person is his or her agent, the principal will be 'estopped' from denying the agency. This is known as 'agency by estoppel'.

If a principal gives an agent a certain authority, and later imposes a limitation upon it without notifying third parties who have dealt or are likely to deal with the agent on the faith of the original authority, such third parties can hold the principal bound by acts which are within the original apparent authority, though outside the scope of the limited actual authority.

Agency of Necessity

This type of agency arises without agreement. An agent of necessity is a person who, in an emergency, acquires, by operation of law, presumed authority to act as an agent.

The master of a ship may mortgage the ship and/or the cargo in order to pay for repairs or other expenditure necessary to successfully complete the voyage. Where the ship's master mortgages the ship, he is an agent of necessity for the shipowner and, in the case of cargo, for the cargo owner. If the cargo is perishable, the ship's master can presumably sell it if it is going bad.

In *Springer* v. *G.W. Rly. Co.* (1921), it was held that a carrier may, as an agent of necessity, sell perishable goods entrusted to him for carriage, when a transport strike renders a sale necessary to avoid deterioration of the goods through delay in delivery, and when it is not reasonably possible to obtain the owner's instructions in time to prevent the goods from becoming worthless.

Generally, it must be reasonable for the carrier/master to have acted in the particular way; in addition he must have acted in a *bona fide* manner, that is, having regard to the interests of all parties concerned; *The Winson* (1982).

Subsequent Authority or Agency by Ratification

If an unauthorized person contracts as an agent, the principal for whom the agent intended to contract may afterwards expressly ratify or adopt the contract, and thus be bound by it. Such ratification is retrospective. The principal may alternatively make an implied ratification by his or her conduct.

For example, if the agent makes an unauthorized contract to buy goods, and the principal receives the goods and fails to return them or uses them, the principal has ratified the agent's contract by implication of law.

Thus, in *Bolton Partners* v. *Lambert* (1889), L made an offer to X, the managing director of a company. X accepted the offer on the company's behalf, although he had no authority to do so. L then gave the company notice that he withdrew the offer. The company subsequently ratified X's unauthorized acceptance. It was held that as the ratification dated back to the time of the acceptance, the withdrawal of the offer was inoperative. The following rules govern whether ratification can be valid:

1 The agent must contract expressly as an agent for a principal who must be named or so described as to make it possible to be identified by the third party.
   Thus an undisclosed principal cannot ratify; *Keighley, Maxsted & Co.* v. *Durant* (1901).

2 An agent cannot contract on behalf of a company prior to its registration.
   As was said in *Natal Land & Colonisation Co. Ltd* v. *Pauline Colliery Syndicate* (1904), a company cannot by ratification obtain the benefit of a contract purporting to have been made on its behalf before the company came into existence.
   In other words, as a general rule, if a principal is to make a valid ratification of a contract purporting to have been made on his behalf, he must have been in existence at the time of the making of the contract.

3 A void contract cannot be ratified.
   Thus, if A enters into a contract with T, on behalf of P, his principal, for the improvement of USA's balance of payment, when A knows that P is only a financial adviser, such a contract is void. This is because of the fact that this contract is beyond the reasonable means and power of P, in so far as P's capabilities are concerned. Therefore, P cannot ratify such a contract.
   A voidable contract can be ratified but the principal becomes liable for the fraud or misrepresentation of the agent.
   For example, if A, acting without authority, sells P's house and represents that the drains are in good order when they are not, and P later ratifies the contract, P becomes liable to the buyer.
   Remedies in such a case will depend on whether there was innocent misrepresentation, negligent misrepresentation, or fraudulent misrepresentation. Therefore, if innocent, the

remedy would be rescission; if negligent, then the principal may be sued for damages; and if fraudulent, then the principal may be sued for damages or rescind the contract (rescission). It should be borne in mind that the agent would be liable in damages to the third party for negligence, or fraud at common law, not under the Misrepresentation Act 1967.

4 Ratification must be based on full knowledge of the material facts.

Thus, if the agent tells his principal that he sold his principal's house for £36,000 when he has only sold for £35,000, the principal can cancel the ratification.

5 Ratification must be of the whole contract. The court will not allow ratification of the beneficial parts only.

6 Ratification can only be retrospective.

This means that, for example, a principal cannot say to his or her agent in advance, 'I will ratify all your future contracts'.

Exceptions to retrospectiveness

Ratification is retrospective in its operation, which means that it relates back to the time when the contract was concluded by the agent as if the agent had the authority at the time of conclusion.

Therefore, if an agent accepts an offer by a third party 'subject to ratification' by the principal, the third party is not bound by this acceptance until ratification actually takes place. Note, however, that in such a case we do not have a valid acceptance because acceptance must be unconditional (see page 7). This situation is the only exception where ratification does not relate back to the original acceptance. In short, this rule does not apply where the third party who is dealing with the agent knows that he or she is dealing with an agent who requires the ratification of the principal.

Thus, in *Watson* v. *Davies* (1931), X and Y entered into negotiations, for the sale of X's building to Y's institution. As nothing was agreed on the negotiations, X wrote to Y stating a price of £6,500 for the building. The board of Y's institution met later on and authorized certain members of the board to accept

X's offer, if they thought the building was suitable for the institution's purposes. These members of the board agreed on 11th January to buy the building 'subject to ratification of the full board'. A couple of days later, the full board met and ratified the agreement. In the morning of that day however, X sent a telegraph, which was put forward to the full board at the time of the meeting, wherein he (X) stated that the building was not for sale. The board nevertheless ratified the agreement of 11th January, purporting acceptance of X's offer. It was held that the ratification was ineffective, as an acceptance by an agent subject to ratification by his principal is a nullity until ratification, and being a conditional acceptance, is not binding on X. Furthermore, since X revoked the offer before ratification took place, he was not bound by it.

The rule of retrospectiveness does not apply if it would cause excessive hardship to the third party. Thus, in *Walter* v. *James* (1871), A was acting on behalf of P, and he induced T to accept £60 in full discharge of a liability P had to T. Before the money was paid, P withdrew A's authority, but A nevertheless paid T. When T discovered that the payment had been made without authority, he agreed to return the money to A. T then sued P for the money, and at this stage P purported to ratify A's payment, hoping to prevent T from succeeding on the grounds that the money had already been paid by his agent, A, and that T had handed it back voluntarily. It was held that ratification was not possible here because, if it was allowed, T would lose his action and would suffer undue hardship.

Ratification must be within a reasonable time, and before the time fixed for performance has expired.

Duties of an Agent

The agent must perform his duties in person

This is based on the legal precedent 'a delegate cannot delegate' (*'delegatus non potest delegare'*). The principal, of course, can give the agent authority to delegate, or may ratify the agent's delegation. Delegation is allowed in certain cases:

1 Where delegation of authority is authorized by custom. Thus, if it is the practice of solicitors to employ town agents in matters of litigation, then this delegation is allowed by custom.
2 In cases of emergency, as where the agent is ill.
3 Where the appointment is necessary for properly carrying out the work.
4 Where the appointment involves the sub-agent in purely ministerial acts, for example the signing of a document.

Obedience to instructions

Where an agent has specific instructions he must follow them. Thus, in *Bertram, Armstrong & Co.* v. *Godfray* (1830), an agent was instructed to sell shares at a certain price. He failed to do so as he waited for a higher price. It was held that he was liable for not having acted as instructed.

This rule is subject to the exception of illegality, that is, an agent who has specific instructions may not follow them if they are unlawful.

The agent must carry out his work with ordinary skill and diligence

It seems that both gratuitous and paid agents may be required to exercise the same degree of care and skill whether they act gratuitously or for reward. However, the matter is still unclear and it may be that an unpaid agent will only be required to show the care that would be exercised in his or her own affairs. The basic rule or principle is that a person is bound to use such skill as he or she claims to possess, or such as may be expected or may be implied from their position. For example, a solicitor must use all the skill which is expected of a member of that profession.

Thus in *Keppel* v. *Wheeler* (1927) X employed Y to sell his house. An offer made by N was received and X accepted it 'subject to contract'. A few days later a higher offer for the property was made by Z to Y, but this was not communicated to X, and the written contract between X and N was duly signed. It was held that Y was liable to X for the difference between the two offers.

The agent must not accept a bribe nor must any secret profits be made

A secret profit is a financial advantage over what the agent is entitled to in contract. There need not be conspiracy to defraud. If the agent takes any bribe then he or she is liable under the Prevention of Corruption Acts 1906 and 1916. Furthermore, the principal in such a case may have all or some of the following rights:

1 To dismiss the agent without notice.
2 To refuse the agent remuneration or commission, in respect of the transaction, and the principal may recover any commission which has been paid. If the agent can prove that he or she acted honestly in any matter, remuneration in respect of that matter will not be forfeited.
3 To recover the bribe either from the agent if it has been received, or from the third party if it has not been paid but only promised.
4 To sue the third party for damages. This is independent of whether the amount of the bribe has been recovered.
5 Repudiate the whole transaction, whether or not the offer of the bribe did, in fact, influence the agent or not.

It is notable that the courts will not enquire into the motives of the party giving the bribe, and there is an irrebuttable presumption that the agent was influenced by the bribe. The rules relating to secret profits and bribes apply to an agent who is not receiving payment.

Thus, in *Turnbull* v. *Garden* (1869), an agent who was employed without payment to buy clothing for the principal's son received certain discounts from the seller. The agent tried to charge his principal the full price. It was held that the principal was only required to pay the agent the sum charged by the seller of his son's outfit. The agent could not make a secret profit out of the transaction.

There must be no conflict of interest between principal and agent

The agent must keep his principal duly informed with everything relating to the agency. Furthermore, the agent must not use his or her position for personal benefit to the detriment of the principal.

It is not necessary to show intentional wrongdoing by the agent, and the mere appearance of conflict of interest might suffice. Consequently, agents may not contract, as principals, with their own principals, through themselves as agents.

Thus, if A is employed by P as an agent to sell some property, and he purports to sell it to T, but in reality buys it himself, without informing P, A cannot enforce the contract against P; *Boardman* v. *Phipps* (1967).

Rights of an Agent

There are three main remedies/rights open to an agent, enforceable against the principal.

An indemnity

The agent may in the course of duty incur liabilities or make payments of money for the principal, and the agent has a right to be indemnified against such liabilities and to recover any money paid. The indemnity extends to three main items:

1 Expenses reasonably incurred in the course of employment.
2 Any legal liability for acts or omissions properly authorized.
3 Even illegal acts, if the agent was unaware of their illegality.

The agent must, of course, have acted within his or her authority. Thus, in *Adamson* v. *Jarvis* (1827), a principal instructed an auctioneer to sell goods at auction. The agent (auctioneer) did so, however the principal did not own the goods and as a result the auctioneer had to pay damages. It was held that he (the auctioneer) was entitled to an indemnity from his principal for the damages.

Lien

This is a special right under which the agent may retain the principal's goods which are in the agent's lawful possession (in his or her capacity as an agent) where the principal's liabilities to the agent have not been satisfied. If for example, the agent is owed money by the principal in respect of either remuneration or indemnity, the agent may exercise a lien on any of the principal's goods until the debt is paid. In general, there is no power to sell the goods. Liens may be of two kinds:

1 A general lien. Under this category, the agent may retain goods of the principal even though the principal does not owe the agent money in respect of those goods, but in respect of other goods the agent has dealt with. However, note that the law does not favour general liens.
2 A particular lien. This is a right to retain possession of goods which form part of the transaction in respect of which payment is due. This type is favoured by the law. If the agent surrenders possession of the goods, the lien is lost. Furthermore, the agent must not have waived the right to lien. Finally, such right may be excluded or modified by agreement.

Remuneration

The following principles seem to apply:

1 An agent will be entitled to the agreed commission only in respect of a transaction which he or she was employed to

bring about. The test is: 'has the agent substantially done what he was employed to do?'

Thus, in *Rimmer* v. *Knowles* (1874), the owner of an estate agreed to pay an agent £50 commission if he found a purchaser for the estate. The agent found someone who was prepared to take a lease for 999 years with an option to complete in 20 years. It was held that the agent was entitled to commission.

2 The agent must have been the effective cause of the event which he or she was employed to bring about. Thus, in *Tribe* v. *Taylor* (1876), the agent was employed to introduce someone to P who could provide capital in the form of a loan for his business. Although the agent was entitled to commission for effecting this transaction, it was held that he was not entitled to further commission when that person entered into partnership with P and provided further capital.

3 The terms of the contract should determine precisely when the right to compensation arises. Thus remuneration may be payable even if the principal receives no benefit.

Stoppage in transit

The lien exercised by an agent, as mentioned above, is only a possessory right and is lost when the goods lawfully pass out of the agent's possession. In order for the agent to bring the goods into his or her possession and thus exercise the right of lien, the right of stoppage in transit could be exercised (see also 'stoppage in transit', page 159).

Rights of Third Parties Against Principal and Agent

Once there is a contract between the principal and the third party the agent normally drops out of the transaction and is no longer liable on it.

However, the relationship between principal and third party

is in part dependant upon whether the principal was disclosed or not by the agent, and also on whether a principal did actually exist at the time the contract was made.

A disclosed principal is one whose existence has been made known to the third party at the time of the contract, and may be named or unnamed.

An undisclosed principal is one whose existence the third party is unaware of at the time of making the contract.

Principal disclosed

If the principal is disclosed at the time the contract is entered into, and he or she actually exists, then in the absence of any express statement to the contrary, the contract is with the principal and not with the agent, who is not, therefore, personally liable to the third party. But to this rule there are the following exceptions:

1 Where an agent signs a bill of exchange or cheque without making clear that he or she is signing on behalf of a named principal.
2 Where the agent undertakes personal liability, or the third party has insisted that the agent also accepts liability before making the contract. If the agent has agreed to this, he or she will be liable along with the principal.
3 Where the agent is liable by custom; for example where a broker effects a contract of marine insurance for a principal the broker is liable to the underwriter for the premium.
4 Where the agent enters into a deed on behalf of the principal, it is the agent who must sue and be sued. In other words only the parties to the deed may incur rights and liabilities in respect of the contract.

Where the agent lacks authority
Where an agent exceeds his or her authority the agent is liable to the third party for breach of warranty of authority, if the third party does not know of the lack of authority and the third party suffers loss as a result of lack of knowledge.

The agent's liability is strict and does not depend upon his or her fraud or misrepresentation. Thus, in *Starkey* v. *Bank of England* (1903), X was a firm of stockbrokers. Y and Z were two trustees who held stocks in trust for others. X received authority to sell the stock under a power of attorney purporting to be signed by both Y and Z, but in fact Z's signature was forged. X sold the stock and sent the proceeds to Y who paid them into his private account. Y died 18 months later, and Z on discovering what had happened brought an action against the Bank for replacement of the stock, and the Bank brought in X as liable to indemnify them. It was held that Z succeeded against the Bank, and the Bank in turn succeeded against X for an indemnity, because X had impliedly warranted his authority to the Bank.

Furthermore, where the agent enters into a contract and acts in all respects *bona fide*, without notice that his authority has been terminated, he will nevertheless be liable for impliedly warranting that his authority still exists. Thus, in *Yonge* v. *Toynbee* (1910), X wanted to sue Y for libel. Y instructed Z, a firm of solicitors, to act for him in the matter. Before the action commenced Y was certified as being of unsound mind. However Z, Y's solicitors, not knowing of this, entered appearances in the action. X's solicitors now asked that all proceedings be struck out, and that Z, who acted for Y after his insanity, should be personally liable to pay for X's cost, because they (Z) had acted without authority. It was held that Z had impliedly warranted that they had authority to act when they had not, and that they (Z) were personally liable for X's costs.

In addition, it may be said that an agent's liability in tort (that is, outside or independent of contract) when acting outside authority is threefold:

1 If the agent knowingly acts outside his or her authority he or she is liable in the tort of deceit.
2 If the agent acts negligently he or she may be liable in the tort of negligence.
3 Even if he acts honestly (*bona fide*) he will still be liable for breach of implied warranty of authority; *Collen* v. *Wright* (1857).

Unnamed principal

Where an agent enters into a contract on behalf of an undisclosed principal the agent may or may not be personally liable according to the circumstances.

If the agent clearly contracts merely as an agent, but without naming the principal, and the third party fully realizes that he or she is contracting with some person unknown, the agent will not be personally liable except in the cases described earlier.

In other words, once again the agent is not personally liable, provided he or she contracts as an agent. But if the agent does not make it clear that he or she is contracting as an agent only, liability may be incurred under the rule of principal concealed.

Principal concealed (where the existence of a principal is concealed)

Suppose an agent contracts with a third party on behalf of a principal but does not inform the third party of the agent status and appears a principal, then the doctrine of the undisclosed principal applies. In such a case the third party may, on discovering the existence of the true principal, elect to hold either the principal or the agent liable, provided the contract is within the agent's authority.

Thus, in *Sika Contracts Ltd* v. *Gill, The Times*, 27 April, 1978, X, a Chartered Civil Engineer, made a contract with Y, a building company, on behalf of Z, the owners of certain property. X did not mention to Y the name of the owners (Z) or that he (X) was acting on their (Z) behalf, until after the contract was concluded. He (X) had signed the contract and his (X) letters as 'B.L. Gill BE, MICE – Chartered Civil Engineer'. The question arose as to whether he (X) was personally liable on the contract and it was held that he was. Therefore, he (X) was personally liable to Y upon the contract.

Such choice by the third party, must, however, be exercised within a reasonable time of discovering the real principal, and therefore when the third party has obtained judgment against one party (principal or agent), proceedings cannot then be taken against the other for the third party's right of action is exhausted. Election of this choice is deemed to have been made by any act showing an unequivocal intention of holding only one party liable.

On default by the third party the principal or the agent may sue the third party. Furthermore, if the undisclosed principal intervenes and brings an action against the third party then the agent cannot sue, or must discontinue any action that has begun.

Finally, where there is actual misrepresentation by the agent, the undisclosed principal will not be able to intervene. If the third party asks the agent, 'are you selling for a principal?' and the agent replies in the negative, the contract with the agent can be rescinded (under misrepresentation) and the undisclosed principal cannot intervene.

Principal non-existent (where the principal is non-existent)

Where a person has entered into a contract purporting to be on behalf of a principal who has never existed, he is personally liable on the contract. Thus, in *Kelner* v. *Baxter* (1866), X, who was one of the promoters of P, a company, before the actual formation of P, entered into a contract on the company's behalf. Once P was formed, it ratified the contract. Later, however, it (P) became bankrupt, and X, who had contracted as its agent, was sued upon the contract. It was held that X was liable. The purported ratification by the company (P) was ineffective because at the time when the contract between X and the third party was made, the company (P) did not exist.

In a similar case, *Newborne* v. *Sensolid (Great Britain) Ltd* (1954), P was in the process of forming a company called Newborne Ltd, and he entered into a contract with X. In the contract P signed as 'Newborne Ltd'. X repudiated the contract and it was held that he (X) was entitled to do so because the signature purported to be that of the company itself (Newborne Ltd) which was not yet in existence and technically could not contract.

The principle established by such cases has received statutory support in the European Communities Act 1972:

> Where a contract purports to be made by a company or by a person as agent for a company, at a time when the company has not been formed, then subject to any agreement to the contrary the contract shall have effect as a contract entered into by the person purporting to act for the company or as agent for it, and he shall be personally liable on the contract accordingly. (Section 9(2))

As has been mentioned, where an agent purports to contract as such without authority, or in excess of authority, the agent's acts may usually be ratified by the principal. But if they are not ratified, although the agent cannot be sued as principal, he can be sued by a third party (*ex contractu*) for damages for a breach of an implied warranty of authority, even if the agent *bona fide* believed himself to have authority. This is based on the premise that a person contracting as agent for another is deemed to warrant his authority; *Collen* v. *Wright* (1857).

Furthermore, a person, acting for a company, prior to its incorporation, is not merely liable for breach of warranty of authority to a third party, but is personally liable, to the third party, on the contract, that is, the contract in such a case is between the agent and the third party.

In concluding, one must remember that a person acting for a company prior to incorporation is not merely liable for breach of warranty of authority, but is personally liable on the contract with the third party.

Authority of the Agent to Receive Payment

If a third party pays money to an agent and the agent has no authority to collect it, then the third party will get a good discharge only if the agent has apparent/ostensible authority to receive payment. For example in the course of employment, where the agent is a cashier in a bank or a salesperson in a shop or a rent collector, then he or she would have apparent authority to receive payment. However, note that authority to sell is not necessarily an authority to receive payment.

Termination of Agency

The contract of agency between the agent and the principal may be terminated in the following ways:

1 By mutual agreement.
2 Expiration of time. If an agency is created for a definite period, then on the expiration of that period the agency will be terminated. Accounts, however, may be settled even after the termination of the agency.
3 Performance of contract or destruction of subject matter. If, for example, an agent is employed to sell a horse, the contract of agency is at an end when the horse is sold. Likewise, the agency would terminate if the horse died before the sale.
4 By frustration. This may arise either by impossibility of performance, or by supervening illegality. Thus, where the subject-matter of the agency is destroyed, as where an agent is employed to sell a house and the house is destroyed by fire, the agency is destroyed. Likewise, an agency is terminated by illegality, where the agency involves dealings with enemy aliens.
5 Death or insanity of principal or agent. The authority of the agent is, *ipso facto*, terminated by the death of the principal. Obviously the death of the agent will terminate the contract of agency, since it is one of personal service. If an agent contracts after the principal is dead, the agent will be liable for breach of warranty of authority even if he or she believed the principal to be still alive. Similarly, supervening mental disorder, whether of the principal or of the agent, will terminate the agency; *Yonge v. Toynbee* (1910).
6 Bankruptcy or liquidation. The bankruptcy of the principal terminates the agent's authority. The bankruptcy of the agent, however, does not necessarily terminate the agency.
7 Revocation or renunciation. The principal may terminate the

agent's authority at any time. No special formalities are required for such termination, but notice of such intention must be given to the agent within the period of notice specified in the contract, and if there is no such provision, then such period will have to be reasonable. However, the agent's apparent authority continues until third parties with whom he or she has had dealings are notified of the agent's lack of authority. Renunciation by the agent terminates the agency, but if it is in breach of the contract an action for damages lies at the suit of the principal.

EC Law and Agency Agreements

As from 1st of January 1994, the UK must comply with Directive 86/653. This Directive on the Co-ordination of the Law of Member States relating to Self-employed Commercial Agents, provides a regulatory framework on agency agreement, and it covers matters such as the way in which agents are to be remunerated, the way in which an agency can be terminated, and so on. In effect, this Directive is set to protect commercial agents.

The English Commercial Agents Regulations 1993 which at the time of writing exists in a draft form, is being considered by the Department of Trade, and is expected to give effect to the Directive. It should be noted that all European Community countries, except the UK and Ireland, have enacted legislation implementing the Directive. The Directive contains provisions concerning the duties of agent and principal which cannot be excluded:

Agent's Duties (Art. 3)

1 To look after his or her principal's interest;
2 to act 'dutifully and in good faith';
3 to make proper efforts to negotiate such business as he or she is entrusted by his or her principal;
4 to communicate all information to his or her principal and to comply with reasonable instructions.

Principal's Duties (Art. 4)

1 To provide to the agent all documentation and information necessary for the performance of the agency agreement;
2 to notify the agent as soon as it is anticipated that the volume of business will be considerably lower than the agent could normally have anticipated;
3 to inform the agent of his or her acceptance, refusal and any non-execution of the business the agent has arranged.

Finally, it should be noted that Directive 86/653 specifies a minimum time within which notice to terminate an agency agreement should be given; one month in the first year, two months in the second year, and three months in the subsequent years.

Figure 9.1: Agent's authority

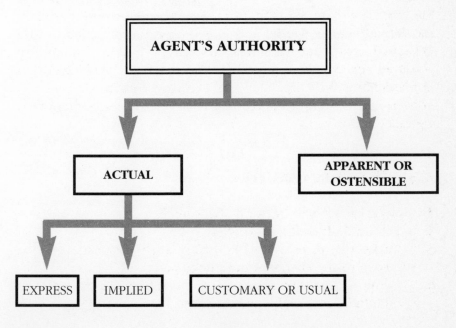

Figure 9.2: Agent's rights

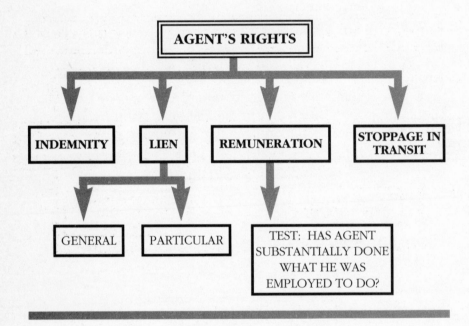

Figure 9.3: Authority or agency by ratification

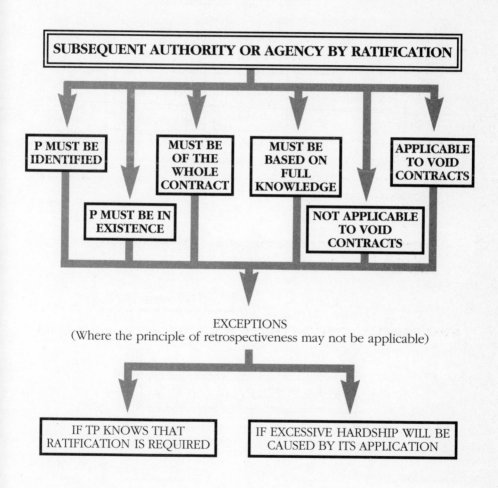

SUBSEQUENT AUTHORITY OR AGENCY BY RATIFICATION

P MUST BE IDENTIFIED

MUST BE OF THE WHOLE CONTRACT

MUST BE BASED ON FULL KNOWLEDGE

APPLICABLE TO VOID CONTRACTS

P MUST BE IN EXISTENCE

NOT APPLICABLE TO VOID CONTRACTS

EXCEPTIONS
(Where the principle of retrospectiveness may not be applicable)

IF TP KNOWS THAT RATIFICATION IS REQUIRED

IF EXCESSIVE HARDSHIP WILL BE CAUSED BY ITS APPLICATION

P   = Principal
TP = Third Party

Figure 9.4:   Agent's duties

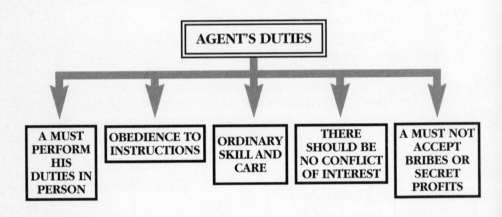

A = Agent

Figure 9.5:   Termination of agency

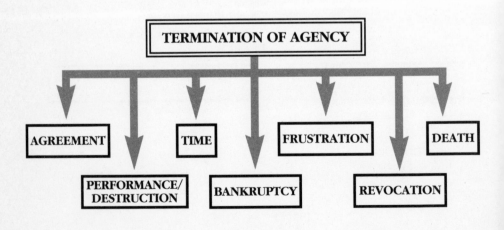

Questions for Discussion

1 What is a *Del Credere* agent?
2 What is usually provided by a 'sole' distribution agreement, and how does a sole distributor differ from an agent?
3 Name the different types of authority that an agent may possess. What is meant by apparent/ostensible authority?
4 What is an agent of necessity? Name the main requirements for a valid ratification.
5 In what circumstances may an agent have authority to delegate?
6 In a contract of agency where the principal is disclosed, what is the liability of the agent towards a third party, if the agent exceeds/lacks authority?
7 State the ways by which a contract of agency may terminate.
8 Briefly describe the agent's and principal's duties under an agency contract, which cannot be excluded, according to Articles 3 and 4 of the European Community Directive 86/653.

10

Exemption Clauses

Background

Exemption clauses are a common feature of business contracts. They are express terms which seek to exclude or limit the liability that might belong to one party in the event of a breach of contract. Such clauses are perfectly fair where they are the result of free negotiations between equals, but, all too often, they are imposed on a weaker party by a stronger party. This abuse of freedom of contract was most commonly practised against consumers. The courts attempted to deal with the problem, but the common law ultimately proved unequal to the ingenuity of those who sought the protection of the exemption.

Over the years, Parliament stepped in to control the use of unfair exemption clauses in particular kinds of contracts and now the overwhelming majority of these clauses are covered by the provisions of the Unfair Contract Terms Act 1977. Statutory control of exemption clauses has been grafted on to the pre-existing common law rules. It is still necessary, therefore, to examine the attitude of the courts to these clauses first, and afterwards consider how Parliament has dealt with the problem.

Judicial Control

The judges based their attack on exemption clauses on two main fronts, namely, incorporation and interpretation.

Incorporation

The person wishing to rely on the exclusion clause must show that it formed part of the contract. In this connection the following rules must be remembered.

Incorporation in signed documents

Where the exemption clause is contained in a document which has been signed, it will automatically form part of the contract. The signer is presumed to have read and understood the significance of all the terms contained in the document.

Thus, in *L'Estrange* v. *Graucob* (1934), X bought an automatic cigarette vending machine for use in her cafe. X signed a 'sales agreement' which provided that 'any express or implied condition, statement or warranty, statutory or otherwise, not stated herein is hereby excluded'. She did not read this document and was completely unaware of the sweeping exclusion clause hidden in the small print. The machine did not work properly but it was held that X was still bound to pay for it because by signing the agreement and in the absence of fraud, X had effectively signed her rights away.

Note that this general rule will not apply where the signer can plead 'this is not my deed' (*non est factum*), or if the other party has misrepresented the terms of the agreement.

Thus in *Curtis* v. *Chemical Cleaning and Dyeing Co.* (1951), X took a wedding dress to be cleaned by Y. She signed a piece of paper headed 'Receipt' after being told by the assistant that it exempted the cleaners from liability for damage to beads and sequins. The 'Receipt' in fact contained a clause excluding liability 'for any damage howsoever arising'. When the dress was returned it was badly stained. It was held that the cleaners (Y) could not escape liability for damage to the material of the dress by relying on the exemption clause because its scope had been misrepresented by Y's assistant.

Incorporation in unsigned documents

The exemption clause may be contained in an unsigned document such as a ticket or a notice. The clause will only form part of the contract if two conditions are met. First, the document must be regarded by a reasonable man as contractual in nature and as such likely to contain exemption clauses.

Thus, in *Chapelton* v. *Barry Urban District Council* (1940), X took a deck chair from a stack near which was a notice which gave the price of hire at so much per session of so many hours and requested the public to obtain tickets from the chair attendant and retain them for inspection. He obtained a ticket which he put into his pocket without reading. Each ticket contained a clause exempting the Council from liability for 'any accident or damage arising from the hire of the chair'. X was injured when the chair he sat on collapsed. He successfully sued the Council. The court held that a reasonable man would assume that the ticket was a mere receipt and not a contractual document which might contain conditions. The Council had not succeeded in incorporating the exemption into their contract with X. Furthermore, the court held that the ticket was a mere receipt for the hire charge.

Even if the document may be regarded as contractual, the person seeking to rely on the exemption clause must show that reasonable steps have been taken either before the contract was made or at the time the contract was made to give notice of the clause to the other contracting party.

Thus, in *Olley* v. *Marlborough Court Ltd* (1949), X booked in for a week's stay at Y's hotel. There was a notice in the bedroom which stated that 'the proprietors will not hold themselves responsible for articles lost or stolen unless handed to the manageress for safe custody'. A stranger gained access to X's room and stole some of his belongings. The court held that Y were liable since X saw the notice only after the contract had been concluded at the reception desk. The exclusion clause could not protect Y because it had not been incorporated into the contract with X.

Previous course of dealings

An exclusion clause may be binding even though it has not

been included in the contract in question, if a previous course of dealings between the parties on the basis of such terms can be established. This principle has been accepted more readily in commercial contracts than in consumer transactions.

Thus, in *J. Spurling* v. *Bradshaw* (1956), X delivered 8 barrels of orange juice to Y who were warehousemen. A few days later X received a document from Y which acknowledged receipt of the barrels. It also contained a clause exempting Y from liability for loss or damage 'occasioned by the negligence, wrongful act or default' caused by themselves, their employees or agents. When X collected the barrels some were empty, and some contained dirty water. X refused to pay the storage charges and was sued by Y. Although X did not receive the document containing the exclusion clause until after the conclusion of the contract, the clause had been incorporated into the contract as a result of a regular course of dealings between the parties over the years. X had received similar documents on previous occasions and he was now bound by the terms contained in them.

Privity of contract

According to the doctrine of privity of contract a person who is not a party to a contract can neither benefit from the contract nor be made liable under it. So while a duly incorporated exemption clause may protect a party to a contract it will not protect servants or agents. They are strangers to the contract and so cannot take advantage of an exclusion or limitation clause.

Thus, in *Scruttons Ltd* v. *Midland Silicones Ltd* (1962), X, a shipping firm, agreed to ship a drum of chemicals belonging to Y from New York to London. The contract of carriage limited the liability of the carrier, that is, X, for damage to $500 (£179) per package. The drum was damaged by the negligence of Z, a firm of stevedores, who had been engaged by X (the carrier) to unload the ship. Y sued Z in tort for the full extent of the damage, which amounted to £593. Z claimed the protection of the limitation clause. It was held that as Z were not parties to the contract of carriage (between X and Y), Y's action succeeded.

Note that the court in this case said that a way in which the benefit of an exemption could be made available to a third party, such as the firm of stevedores, was by fulfilling the following four conditions:

1 a contract of carriage must specifically state that the stevedore is intended to be protected by the exemption clause;
2 the carrier must make it clear that he is contracting both on his own behalf and as agent for the stevedores;
3 the carrier has authority from the stevedore to act in this way; and
4 there is some consideration moving from the stevedore.

Interpretation

Where a clause is duly incorporated into a contract, the courts will proceed to examine the words used to see if the clause covers the breach and loss which has actually occurred. The main rules of interpretation used by the courts are as follows.

Strict interpretation

An exemption clause will be effective only if it expressly covers the kind of liability which has in fact arisen. A clause, for example, which excludes liability for a breach of warranty will not provide protection against liability for a breach of condition. Thus, in *Baldry* v. *Marshall* (1925), X asked Y, who were motor dealers, to supply a car that would be suitable for touring purposes. Y recommended a Bugatti, which X bought. The written contract excluded Y's liability for any 'guarantee or warranty, statutory or otherwise'. The car turned out to be unsuitable for X's purposes, so he rejected it and sued to recover what he had paid. It was held that the requirement that the car be suitable for touring was a condition. Since the clause did not exclude liability for breach of a condition, X was not bound by it.

Contra proferentem

If there is any ambiguity or doubt as to the meaning of an exemption clause the court will construe it *contra proferentem*, that is, against the party who inserted it in the contract. Very clear words must be used before a party will be held exempt from liability in negligence.

Thus, in *Whit* v. *John Warwick & Co. Ltd* (1953), X hired a tradesman's cycle from Y. The written hire agreement stated that 'Nothing in this agreement shall render the owners liable for any personal injury'. While X was riding the cycle, the saddle tilted forward and he was injured. Y might have been liable in tort (for negligence) as well as in contract. It was held that the ambiguous wording of the exclusion clause would effectively protect Y from their strict contractual liability, but it would not exempt them (Y) from liability in negligence.

Repugnancy

Under this rule, a court can strike out an exemption clause which is inconsistent with or repugnant to the main purpose of the contract.

Thus, in *J. Evans & Sons (Portsmouth) Ltd* v. *Andrea Merzario Ltd* (1976), X had imported machines from Italy for many years and for this purpose they (X) used the services of Y, who were forwarding agents. When Y changed over to containers X were orally promised that the containers would be stowed below deck. On one occasion, X's container was stored on deck and it was lost when it slid overboard. It was held that Y could not rely on an exemption clause contained in the standard conditions of the forwarding trade, on which the parties had contracted, because it was repugnant to the oral promise that had been given.

Statutory Control

At first, Parliament intervened on a piecemeal basis to control the use of exemption clauses in specific types of contract. For example section 43(7) of the Transport Act 1962 declared that any clause which purports to exclude or limit the liability of the British Railways Board in respect of injury or death to a passenger 'Shall be void and of no effect'.

However, Parliament truly showed its interest in exemption clauses by the enactment of the Unfair Contract Terms Act 1977, which lays down rules of general application to most contracts.

Unfair Contract Terms Act 1977

(a) The Act came into force in 1978; it does not apply to contracts before that year.

(b) The title of the Act is misleading in two respects. First, it affects the law of tort as well as contract law because it covers non-contractual notices and signs. Secondly, it does not deal with all unfair terms in contracts, only unfair exemption clauses.

(c) Most of the provisions of the Act apply only to 'business liability', that is, liability for things done in the course of business or from the occupation of premises used for business purposes. A business includes a profession and the activities of any government department or local or public authority.

(d) The Act does not apply to international supply contracts (section 26) and ss.2-4 do not apply to certain contracts listed in Schedule 1, which includes:
   (i)   contracts of insurance;
   (ii) contracts in relation to land;
   (iii) contracts of marine salvage;
   (iv) contracts for the carriage of goods by ship;
   (v)   contracts of affreightment (that is, charterparties).

(e) The Act affords the greatest protection to consumers; under section 12(1) a person 'deals as a consumer' if:
   (i)   he neither makes the contract in the course of a business nor holds himself out as doing so, and
   (ii) the other party does make the contract in the course of a business, and
   (iii) if it involves a contract for the supply of goods that are of a type ordinarily supplied for private use or consumption.

(f) Exemption clauses are regulated by the Act in two ways. They are either rendered void and completely ineffective or they are made subject to a test of reasonableness. Although the application of the 'reasonableness test' is a matter for the court to decide in the light of all the circumstances of a particular case, the Act lays down some guiding principles for the judges.

Reasonableness

The following simple rules applicable to reasonableness should be noted.

(a) Reasonableness must be judged in the case of a contractual term in the light of circumstances at the time when the contract was made and in the case of a non-contractual notice or sign, when the liability arose.

(b) It is up to the person who claims that a term or notice is reasonable to show that it is.

(c) Where the exemption clause appears in any kind of contract under which goods are supplied, its reasonableness may be judged according to the criteria contained in Schedule 2, which are as follows:

(i) The bargaining strengths of the parties relative to each other and the availability of alternative supplies. A monopoly supplier, for example, will find it difficult to justify a wide exclusion clause. Thus, in *Waldron-Kelly* v. *British Railways Board* (1981), X placed a suitcase in the care of BR at Stockport railway station for delivery to Haverford West railway station. BR's General Conditions of Carriage limited their liability for non-delivery to an amount assessed by reference to the weight of the goods. The suitcase disappeared and X claimed £320.32 as the full value of the suitcase. BR sought to rely on their Conditions which limited their liability to £27. It was held that BR could not rely on the exemption clause because it did not satisfy the requirement of reasonableness. X was awarded £320.32.

(ii) Whether the customer received an inducement to agree to the term. The supplier may have offered the customer a choice, such as a lower price but subject to an exemption clause or a higher price without the exemption. Provided a real choice is available, the supplier will probably be able to show that the exemption clause was reasonable.

(iii) Whether the customer knew or ought reasonably to have known of the existence and extent of the term. If the customer goes into the contract with his eyes wide open, he may have to accept the exemption clause.

(iv) Where the term excludes or restricts any relevant liability if some condition is not complied with, whether it was reasonable at the time of the contract to expect that compliance with that condition would be practicable. A supplier, for example, may limit his liability to defects which are brought to his attention within a certain time, for example three days. The court will consider whether compliance with such a time limit is practicable. Thus, in *Lally and Weller* v. *George Bird* (1980), X agreed to undertake a house removal for Y for £100.80. The contract contained exemption clauses which limited X's liability for losses or breakages to £10 per article and excluded all liability unless claims were made within three days. It was held that these clauses were unreasonable.

(v) Whether the goods were manufactured, processed or adapted to the special order of the customer. An exemption clause may well be reasonable if the customer has insisted on the supplier complying with detailed specifications.

The reasonableness of exemption clauses in contracts other than for the sale or supply of goods must be judged without the benefit of the above criteria.

The following is a short description of the most important sections of the Unfair Contract Terms Act 1977.

(a) **Section 2: Exemption of liability for negligence**

Under s.2(1) no one acting in the course of a business can exclude or restrict his liability in negligence for death or personal injury by means of a term in a contract or by way of a notice. Liability in negligence for any other kind of loss or damage can be excluded provided the term or notice satisfies the 'reasonableness test'.

(b) **Section 3: Exemption of liability for breach of contract**
Section 3 applies to two types of contract:
   i) where the other party deals as a consumer; and
   ii) where the businessman contracts on his own written standard terms of business.

In both cases, the businessman cannot exclude or limit his liability for breach of contract, non-performance of the contract or different performance of the contract unless the exemption clause satisfies the requirement of reasonableness.

(c) **Section 4: Unreasonable indemnity clauses**
An indemnity clause is a term in a contract between two parties, X and Y, in which Y agrees to indemnify X for any liability that X may be under. X may incur liability in respect of a third party, Z, in which case Y must compensate X for any claim which is made by Z against X. For example a builder may get the owner of a house to agree to indemnify him for any injury or damage that his work on the house might cause to third parties. So if the builder negligently demolishes a wall and injures a next door neighbour, the builder can call on the house owner to make good any award of damages. In some cases, Y is required to indemnify X in respect of a liability that X may be under to Y himself. Such an indemnity clause has the same effect as an exclusion clause. Under section 4, indemnity clauses in contracts where one of the parties deals as a consumer are unenforceable unless they satisfy the requirement of reasonableness.

(d) **Section 5: Guarantees of consumer goods**
At one time, it was common practice for guarantees given with goods to contain a clause exempting the manufacturer from liability in negligence if the product proved defective. Under section 5 a manufacturer or distributor cannot exclude or restrict his liability in negligence for loss arising from defects in goods ordinarily supplied for private use or consumption by means of a term or notice contained in a guarantee.

(e) **Section 6: Exemption of implied terms in contracts of sale and hire purchase**

The original Sale of Goods Act 1893 gave the parties complete freedom to exclude the implied terms contained in sections 12-15. Retailers often used the opportunity to deprive consumers of their rights by getting customers to sign an order form, which included an exemption clause hidden in the small print or by displaying suitably worded notices at the point of sale. This however, was identified as a major defect of the original Act and proposals for the amendment of this provision were made by the Law Commission. The changes were effected by the Supply of Goods Act 1973 and Sale of Goods Act 1979.

(f) **Section 7: Exemption of implied terms in other contracts for the supply of goods**

Terms as to title, description, merchantability, fitness for purpose and sample are now included in contracts for supply of goods by way of hire, exchange or work and materials contracts by virtue of the Supply of Goods and Services Act 1982.

(g) **Section 8: Exemption of liability for misrepresentation**

Section 3 of the Misrepresentation Act 1967 provides that any clause which excludes or restricts liability for misrepresentation is ineffective unless it satisfies the requirement of reasonableness.

The complicated provisions of the Unfair Contract Terms Act 1977 in relation to the exclusion of statutory implied terms (see Sale of Goods, page 133) are summarized in figure 10.1.

Figure 10.1: Exclusion of statutory implied terms

EXEMPTION OF IMPLIED TERMS IN CONTRACTS FOR THE SUPPLY OF GOODS		
IMPLIED TERMS	**CONSUMER TRANSACTION**	**NON-CONSUMER TRANSACTION**
Title	Void	Void
Description	Void	Subject to reasonableness test
Quality and Suitability	Void	Subject to reasonableness test
Sample	Void	Subject to reasonableness test

Figure 10.2: Exemption clauses

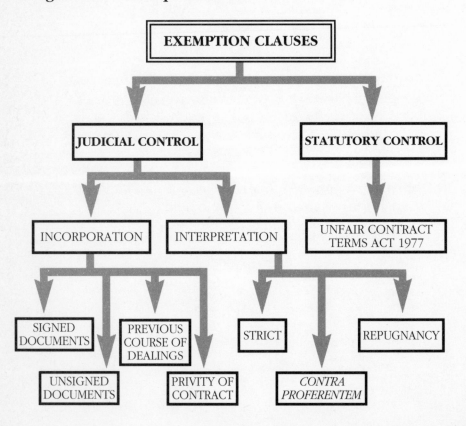

Questions for Discussion

1 Where an exemption clause is duly incorporated into a contract, the courts usually proceed to apply 'strict interpretation' or *'contra preferentem'* rules. Briefly explain the meaning of these two expressions.
2 Under the Unfair Contract Terms Act 1977, when does a person deal as a consumer?
3 How can a businessman exclude or restrict liability in negligence for death or personal injury?

Part 3

Sale of Goods Act 1979

11

Sale of Goods

The law relating to the sale of goods is to be found in the Sale of Goods Act 1979. This Act provides a framework for the relationship between the buyer and seller. However, it would be wrong to think that the Act governs every aspect of a sale of goods contract. Many of the general principles of contract law still apply. Therefore, a contract for the sale of goods, just like any other contract, must possess all the essential elements. The rules relating to the requirements of offer and acceptance, intention, consideration, and so on, are largely untouched by the Act.

Definition

A contract for the sale of goods is defined in section 2(1) of the Act as:

A contract by which the seller transfers or agrees to transfer the property in goods to the buyer for a money consideration, called the price.

A closer examination of this definition is necessary as it will assist you in distinguishing a contract for the sale of goods from other similar kinds of contracts.

1 The definition covers two possibilities: An actual sale and an agreement to sell at some future time.

2 Transfer of property: The essence of the transaction is the transfer of property in the goods from the seller to the buyer.

3 Property: Property in this context means ownership of the goods and not physical possession.

4 Goods: Goods include all tangible items of personal property such as food, clothes and furniture. Land and money are excluded from the definition.

The provisions of the Act only apply to those transactions which fall within the above definition.

Price: The consideration for the goods must be money, (that is, the price) although a part-exchange deal in which goods are exchanged for other goods plus money will be covered by the Act because some money has changed hands; *Dawson* v. *Dutfield* (1936). Section 8 of the Act deals with this, and states in this connection:

1 The price in a contract of sale may be fixed by the contract or may be left to be fixed in manner thereby agreed or may be determined by the course of dealing between the parties.

2 Where the price is not determined in accordance with the foregoing provisions the buyer must pay a reasonable price. What is a reasonable price is a question of fact.

Payment: The price is such a fundamental part of the transaction that it will normally be fixed by the contract. However, it may be ascertained by the course of dealing between the parties or the contract may provide a mechanism for fixing the price, for example by arbitration. The parties may make their own agreement as to the time of payment. The seller may insist on payment in advance of delivery or he may be prepared to extend a period of credit. In the absence of such express agreement, payment is due when the goods are delivered.

Formation of the contract: It is not necessary to observe complex formalities to create a contract for the sale of goods. It may be in writing or by word of mouth, or partly in writing and partly by word of mouth, or even implied from the conduct of the parties.

Capacity to enter into a binding sale of goods contract is governed by the general law of contract, which has already been considered earlier.

Implied Terms

Although the parties are generally free to agree between themselves the details of their contract, the Act automatically includes a number of conditions and warranties in every contract for the sale of goods. These are known as the implied terms and they can be found in sections 12-15. The following is a brief account of each of these implied terms.

Title (s.12)

There is an implied **condition** on the part of the seller that in the case of a sale he has a right to sell the goods, and in the case of an agreement to sell he will have the right to sell when the property is to pass. If the seller cannot pass good title, that is, rights of ownership, to the buyer, the seller will be liable for breach of condition.

Thus, in *Rowland* v. *Divall* (1923), X bought a car from Y for £334 and used it for four months. It was later found that Y had bought the car from someone who had stolen it and it had to be returned to the true owner. X sued Y to recover the full purchase price that he had paid. It was held that Y was in breach of section 12. X had paid £334 to become the owner of the car. Since he had not received what he had contracted for, there was a total failure of consideration entitling him to a full refund.

Furthermore, two implied **warranties** are provided by the same section (s.12(2)):

(a) that the goods are free from any charges or encumbrances not made known to the buyer before the contract; and
(b) that the buyer will enjoy quiet possession of the goods.

Description (s.13)

Where there is a contract for the sale of goods by description, there is an implied condition that the goods will correspond with the description. If the buyer does not see the goods before buying them (for example, from a mail order catalogue), there has clearly been a sale by description. Even where the buyer has seen the goods and, perhaps, selected them personally, it may still be a sale by description, provided the buyer has relied to some extent on a description.

Thus, in *Beale* v. *Taylor* (1967) Y advertised a car for sale as a 1961 Triumph Herald. X inspected the car before he bought it. He (X) later discovered that the vehicle consisted of a rear half of a 1961 Herald which had been welded to the front half of an earlier model. It was held that X was entitled to damages for breach of section 13 even though he had seen and inspected the car. He (X) had relied to some extent on the description contained in the advertisement.

The description of the goods may cover such matters as size, quantity, weight, ingredients, origin or even how they are to be packed. The slightest departure from the specifications would usually entitle the buyer to reject the goods for breach of a condition of the contract; *Moore & Co.* v. *Landauer & Co.* (1921).

A seller may ensure that the transaction is not a sale by description by including such phrases as, 'Bought as seen' or 'Sold as seen' in the contract; *Cavendish-Woodhouse Ltd* v. *Manley* (1984).

Quality and suitability (s.14)

Section 14 starts by stating that there is no implied condition or warranty as to quality or fitness for a particular purpose except as provided by sections 14 and 15. This preserves the idea of *caveat emptor* (let the buyer beware). Section 14 provides two conditions, which are implied only '**where the seller sells goods in the course of a business**', and not to sales by private individuals. So if one buys something privately, and it is defective or unsuitable, there can be no complaint under section 14. These two conditions are the following:

(a) **Merchantable quality** (s.14(2))

Where the seller sells goods in the course of a business there is an implied condition that the goods supplied under the contract are of merchantable quality. This means that a brand new washing machine should wash one's clothes properly, or new shoes should not fall apart on their first outing, or a meat pie bought for lunch should not make one ill. The goods do not have to measure up to an absolute standard of quality. If you buy goods second-hand or very cheaply, you cannot expect perfection.

Thus, in *Bartlett* v. *Sidney Marcus Ltd* (1965) X bought a second-hand car from Y who was a car dealer. X was warned that the clutch was defective and he agreed to a reduction in the price of the car to take account of this. The defect turned out to be more serious and, therefore, more costly to repair, than X expected. He (X) claimed that Y was in breach of section 14(2). It was held that in all the circumstances the car was of merchantable quality. As Lord Denning MR pointed out: 'A buyer should realise that when he buys a second-hand car defects may appear sooner or later.'

Goods are of merchantable quality within the meaning of the Act (s.14(2)), if they are as fit for the purpose or purposes for which goods of that kind are commonly bought as it is reasonable to expect having regard to any description applied to them, the price (if relevant) and all other relevant circumstances.

Thus, in *Cehave* v. *Bremer* (1975) it was held that citrus pulp pellets which had deteriorated in transit but which were still usable for the purpose for which such pellets were normally used, namely, for animal feed, were of merchantable quality.

The buyer can lose his right to complain in two situations:

(i) where the seller specifically points out that the goods are faulty; and

(ii) where he (the buyer) decides to check the goods, but fails to spot an obvious defect.

(b) **Fitness for a particular purpose** (s.14(3))

Where the seller sells goods in the course of a business and the buyer, expressly or by implication, makes known to the seller any particular purpose for which the goods are being bought, there is an implied **condition** that the goods supplied under the contract are reasonably fit for that purpose.

For example, if the buyer specifies shoes suitable for running a marathon in are required, the shoes must be suitable for this purpose. Furthermore, where the buyer purchases goods with only one normal purpose, the buyer makes his or her purpose known by implication. In other words, food must be fit for eating and clothes fit for wearing.

Thus, in *Grant* v. *Australian Knitting Mills Ltd* (1936), X bought a pair of woollen underpants from a shop. The manufacturers neglected to remove properly a chemical used in the manufacturing process. Consequently X developed a skin rash which turned into dermatitis. It was held that the underpants were not of merchantable quality or reasonably fit for the purpose. Although X had not specifically stated the purpose for which he required the underpants, it was clear by implication that he intended to wear them.

If the buyer has any special requirements these must be made known to the seller.

Thus, in *Griffiths* v. *Peter Conway Ltd* (1939), the buyer had a Harris tweed coat specially made for her by the seller. The coat caused her to contract dermatitis. It was held that since the coat would have caused no harm to normal skin and the seller could not have known of the buyer's sensitivity, there was no breach of the implied condition of fitness of purpose.

The only exception to this rule is where the circumstances show that the buyer does not rely, or it is unreasonable to rely, on the seller's skill and judgment. But note, that reliance will normally be assumed from the fact that the buyer has taken his or her custom to that particular shop/agent/merchant. However, if a buyer asks for an item under its brand name or lays down detailed specifications as to what is required, it will be difficult to show that the seller's skill and judgment has been relied upon.

Sample (s.15)

A contract of sale is a contract of sale by sample where there is an express or implied term to that effect in the contract. In the case of a contract for sale by sample there is an implied condition:

(a) that the bulk will correspond with the sample in quality;
(b) that the buyer will have a reasonable opportunity of comparing the bulk with the sample;
(c) that the goods will be free from any defect rendering them unmerchantable, which would not be apparent on reasonable examination of the sample.

Thus, in *Godley* v. *Perry* (1960) X, a six-year old boy bought a plastic toy catapult for 6d. from a newsagent's shop run by Perry, the first defendant. The catapult broke while in use and X lost an eye. He (X) sued Perry for breach of the implied conditions in section 14. Perry had bought the catapults by sample from a wholesaler. He (Perry) had tested the sample catapult by pulling back the elastic, but no defect had been revealed. Perry now brought the wholesaler into the action claiming a breach of the conditions in section 15. The wholesaler had bought his supply of catapults by sample from another wholesaler who had obtained the catapults from Hong Kong. The first wholesaler brought the second wholesaler into the action alleging a similar breach of section 15. It was held that: (1) X could recover damages from the first defendant for breach of section 14, as the catapult was not of merchantable quality or fit for the purpose for which it had been bought; (2) the first defendant could recover damages from the first wholesaler who in turn could recover damages from the second wholesaler, in both cases because there had been a breach of section 15 which was implied in the relevant contract.

Transfer of Property in the Goods

The essence of a contract for the sale of goods is the transfer of property (ownership) in goods from the seller to the buyer. The rules relating to the transfer of ownership depend on whether the goods are classified as **specific** goods or **unascertained** goods.

Specific goods are 'goods identified and agreed on at the time a contract of sale is made'. This includes contracts such as purchasing groceries from a supermarket or buying a coat from a market trader. In other words, if at the time that the contract is made, it is possible to point out the particular goods upon which the parties have agreed, then those goods are specific.

Contracts to supply a certain amount out of a specified bulk are not contracts to supply specific goods as it is not possible to say what part of the bulk will be given. Thus, in *Re Wait* (1927), it was held that a contract to sell 500 tons of wheat out of a bulk of 1,000 tons was not a contract for the sale of specific goods.

The general rule is that property in specific goods passes when the parties intend it to pass and to ascertain the intention of the parties 'regard shall be had to the terms of the contract, the conduct of the parties and the circumstances of the case'. Furthermore, in a CIF contract the intention of the parties would be that passing of property is conditional. If the buyer rejects them upon examination property in the goods reverts to the seller; *Kwei Tek Chao* v. *British Traders* (1954). If the parties do not indicate, expressly or impliedly, when they want ownership to pass, section 18 of the Act sets out various rules to ascertain their presumed intention.

Rule 1: 'Where there is an unconditional contract for the sale of specific goods in a deliverable state, the property in the goods passes to the buyer when the contract is made, it is immaterial whether the time of payment or the time of delivery, or both, be postponed.'

This means that the buyer can become the owner of goods even though he has not paid for them yet and they are still in the seller's possession. Thus, in *Tarling* v. *Baxter* (1827), a haystack was sold but before the buyer had taken it away, it was burned down. It was held that the buyer was still liable to pay the price because he became the owner of the haystack when the contract was made. It was immaterial the he had not yet taken delivery of the goods.

Furthermore, 'unconditional contract' relates to whether the transfer of property in the goods is subject to some contingency. If such contingency is stipulated in the contract then rule 1 would not apply.

Rule 2: 'Where there is a contract for the sale of specific goods and the seller is bound to do something to the goods for the purpose of putting them into a deliverable state, the property does not pass until the thing is done and the buyer has notice that it has been done.'

This means that where the seller agrees to alter the goods in some way for the buyer, ownership will pass when the alterations are completed and the buyer has been informed.

Rule 3: 'Where there is a contract for the sale of specific goods in a deliverable state but the seller is bound to weigh, measure, test or do some other act or thing with reference to the goods for the purpose of ascertaining the price, the property does not pass until the thing is done and the buyer has notice that it has been done.'

If, for example, you agree to buy a particular bag of potatoes, at a price of 10p a pound, you will not become the owner of the potatoes until the seller has weighed the bag and informed you of the price payable. If, however, it is agreed that the buyer will do the weighing, measuring or testing, ownership of the goods will pass in accordance with Rule 1, that is, when the contract is made.

Rule 4: 'When goods are delivered to the buyer on approval or on sale or return ... the property in the goods passes to the buyer:

(a) when he signifies his approval or acceptance to the seller or does any other act adopting the transaction;

(b) if he does not signify his approval or acceptance to the seller but retains the goods without giving notice of rejection, then, if a time has been fixed for the return of the goods, on the expiration of that time, and, if no time has been fixed, on the expiration of a reasonable time.'

Property in goods delivered on approval will pass under part (a) of this rule either when the buyer informs the seller that he or she wishes to buy them or 'adopts' the transaction, for example, by re-selling the goods. Part (b) of the rule may be best understood by the *Elphick* v. *Barnes* (1880) case. Here, the seller handed a horse over to a prospective buyer on approval for eight days. Unfortunately, the horse died on the third day. It was held that ownership of the horse had not passed to the buyer and, therefore, the seller would have to bear the loss.

Unascertained goods can fall into two categories:

(a) Unascertained goods out of a specified bulk, for example 500 tons of wheat from a cargo of 1,000 tons.
(b) Purely generic ascertained goods, for example a Ford Escort car.

One point should be stressed here; it is possible for goods to cease to be unascertained, and to become ascertained by a process of exhaustion. Thus, if in *Re Wait* (1927), mentioned earlier, all the wheat had been delivered save that intended for the buyer, the goods would have become ascertained. In the case of a sale of unascertained goods, the general rule is that the property passes to the buyer only when the goods have been ascertained; section 16. If the parties then fail to mention when they intend ownership to pass, section 18 provides for the application of Rule 5.

Rule 5: '(1) Where there is a contract for the sale of unascertained or future goods by description, and goods of that description and in a deliverable state are 'unconditionally appropriated' to the contract, either by the seller with the assent of the buyer or by the buyer with the assent of the seller, the property in the goods then passes to the buyer; and the assent may be express or implied and may be given either before or after the appropriation is made.'

This rule only applies where there is a sale by description. Goods are 'unconditionally appropriated' to the contract, when they have been irrevocably identified as the goods which are the subject of the contract. In simpler terms this is usually when the goods are separated from the bulk and earmarked for a particular buyer. Delivery to a carrier will amount to an 'appropriation' provided the buyer's goods can be clearly identified.

Thus, in *Healy* v. *Howlett & Sons* (1917), X agreed to sell 20 boxes of fish to Y. He despatched 190 boxes by rail for delivery to various customers but the boxes were not labelled for particular customers. Employees of the railway company were entrusted with the task of allocating the correct number of boxes to each destination. Due to a delay, the fish deteriorated before twenty boxes could be set aside for Y. It was held that the property in the goods had not passed to Y because Y's boxes had not been appropriated to the contract.

Development of Section 16

As mentioned above, a purchaser of unascertained goods which form part of a bulk cannot acquire the property in the goods until they have been ascertained, which will frequently not happen until the goods are delivered, even though the buyer may have paid for the goods and received a document giving a right to delivery (see page 140). If the seller becomes insolvent before delivery of the goods, both the goods and the price may pass to the receiver or liquidator for the benefit of the seller's creditors. Although the present law has the logical basis that a person cannot own goods which have not yet been ascertained, its result does not accord with normal commercial expectations and it is widely regarded as unfair.

The Law Commission proposes (Sale of Goods Forming Part of a Bulk-Law Commission No. 215) to deal with this problem by recommending a solution, viz. that the buyer in such a situation should be able to become the owner, not of any particular goods, but of proportionate part of the bulk. The buyer's share would correspond to the quantity bought and paid for, for example if the buyer has bought and paid for 1,000 tons out of an identical bulk of 10,000 tons, he or she could become the owner of a tenth of the bulk. Whether a pre-paying buyer would become owner of a share in the bulk, and if so when, would depend on the intention of the parties in each case, for example they might wish the title to pass when the price has been paid in exchange for documents relating to the goods. The existing law prevents them from achieving this objective when goods form part of an undivided bulk.

The report is not specifically designed to deal with consumer problems. It will therefore not help consumers who have paid for unascertained goods which the seller can supply out of his general stock or from any source. However, the reform which has been proposed could benefit consumers who have bought and paid for goods forming part of an identified bulk, such as bottles of wine identified in the contract or later as forming part of a lot in a particular store, or a length of carpet forming part of an identified roll.

Figure 11.1: Sale of Goods Act 1979

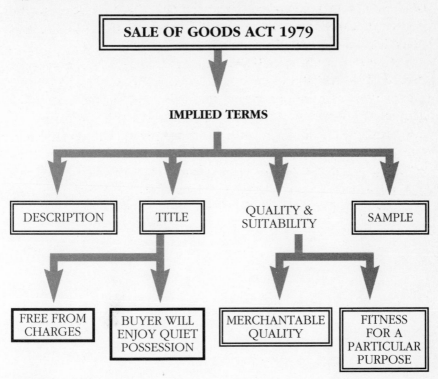

Note:

Implied terms enclosed in double line boxes are **Conditions**.
Implied terms enclosed in single line boxes are **Warranties**.

Questions for Discussion

1 How is a contract of sale defined by the Sale of Goods Act 1979? Does this definition cover barter (that is goods in exchange for goods)?

2 Describe the implied conditions contained in sections 12-15 of the Sale of Goods Act 1979.

3 Does the Sale of Goods Act 1979 provide for any implied warranties?

4 What are 'specific goods'? When will the property in the goods pass to a buyer in the case of (a) 'specific goods', and (b) 'unascertained goods'?

12

Right of Disposal (s.19) [*Romalpa* Clauses]

In the business world sellers are expected to do business on credit terms. If ownership of the goods passes to the buyer before he or she pays for them (see page 141) and the buyer subsequently becomes bankrupt, or, in the case of a company, goes into liquidation, the seller will be treated as an ordinary trade creditor. As such, the seller is unlikely to recover what is owed. The seller can be protected against these considerable risks by stating that the property in the goods shall not pass to the buyer until the contract price has been paid.

Section 19 provides that where the seller has reserved the right of disposal of the goods until some condition is fulfilled, ownership of the goods will not pass to the buyer until that condition is met. The inclusion of such a reservation of title clause in the contract of sale will enable a seller to retrieve the goods and re-sell them if the buyer goes bankrupt or into receivership or liquidation before paying for them.

However, the position becomes much more complicated in the following situations:

1 where the buyer has re-sold the goods; and
2 where the buyer has mixed them with other goods during a manufacturing process and then sold the manufactured product.

The sellers may be able to protect themselves in relation to 1 above by including a carefully worded clause in the contract, allowing them to trace the goods and claim the proceeds of sale. These terms are known as *Romalpa* clauses, after the name of the case in which they achieved prominence.

In *Aluminium Industrie Vaassen B.V.* v. *Romalpa Aluminium Ltd: The Romalpa case* (1976), X, a Dutch company, sold aluminium foil to Y, an English company. A clause in the contract provided that (1) ownership of the foil would not pass to Y until it was paid for; (2) if the foil became mixed with other items during a manufacturing process, X would become the owner of the finished product and property would not pass until Y had paid for the foil; (3) unmixed foil and finished products should be stored separately; (4) Y were authorized to sell the finished product on condition that X were entitled to the proceeds of the sale. Y became insolvent and a receiver was appointed. The court held that X were entitled to recover a quantity of unmixed foil and the proceeds of re-sale of some unmixed foil.

Therefore, Y was accountable to X for the foil and the proceeds of its sale and Y could trace the proceeds into the hands of the receiver. This case was the first case in a series of three which developed this area of law and pointed at the problems which retention clauses might cause in cases involving insolvency; *Borden (UK) Ltd* v. *Scottish Timber Products Ltd* (1979); *Re Peachdart Ltd* (1983).

For the purpose of the topic under consideration, it will be adequate to remember that for a *Romalpa* clause to be effective it should include the following provisions:

1 the ownership of the goods must not pass to the buyer;
2 the buyer must be stated to hold the goods as a bailee;
3 where the goods are used in the manufacture of other products it should be stated that those products are held by the buyer as security for payment of what is owed to the supplier, that is, the clause should create a contractual charge over mixed goods; and
4 the goods and products made therefrom must be identifiable and kept separate.

As long as the clause contains the above provisions, it is thought that it should be effective and on a receivership or liquidation the goods or things made from them or proceeds of re-sale will be held for the supplier unless and until payment is received in full.

Figure 12.1: *Romalpa* **clause provisions**

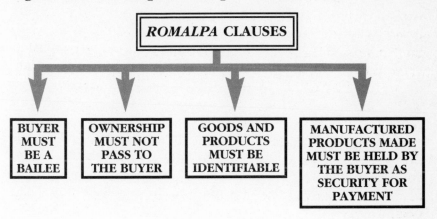

Transfer of Title by Non-Owners (s.21)

As a general rule, a buyer cannot acquire ownership from someone who himself has neither ownership nor the owner's authority to sell. This rule derives from the legal rule which states that 'no one can give what he has not got' (*nemo dat quod non habet*), and it is known as the *nemo dat* rule. This rule is incorporated in section 21 of the Sale of Goods Act 1979:

> Where goods are sold by a person who is not their owner, and who does not sell them under the authority or with the consent of the owner, the buyer acquires no better title to the goods than the seller had . . .

In these circumstances, the buyer will be required to return the goods to their true owner. The buyer's only remedy is to sue the person who sold the item for breach of section 12. In most of these cases, however, the seller is a rogue who disappears before the buyer can take action. The unsuspecting buyer is left to bear the full brunt of the rogue's misdeeds. It is not surprising, therefore, that exceptions to the 'no one can give what he has not got' rule have developed. These exceptions are as follows.

Estoppel (s.21)

If the true owner by his conduct allows the innocent buyer to believe that the seller has the right to sell the goods, ownership of the goods will pass to the buyer because the true owner will be prevented (estopped) from denying that the seller had the right to sell.

Thus, in *Eastern Distributors Ltd* v. *Goldring* (1957), X was the owner of a van. He wanted to buy a car from Y, a dealer, but he (X) could not raise enough money for a deposit. X and Y then devised a scheme to generate the necessary finance. Y would pretend that he owned the van; he would then sell the van and the car to a finance company, who would let both vehicles out on Hire Purchase to X. The proceeds of the sale of the van would raise sufficient money to finance the required Hire Purchase deposits. Unfortunately, the finance company accepted the proposal for the van but turned the car down. Unknown to X, Y proceeded to sell the van to the finance company. It was held that the finance company had become the owner of the van, because the original owner (X) by his conduct had allowed the buyers (the finance company) to believe that the seller (Y) had a right to sell the goods.

Agency (s.21(2))

The law of agency applies to contracts for the sale of goods. An agent who sells his or her principal's goods in accordance with the principal's instructions passes a good title to the buyer because the goods are being sold with the authority and consent of the owner. The buyer may even acquire a good title to the goods where the agent has exceeded his or her **actual** authority, provided the agent is acting within the scope of **apparent** or **ostensible** authority and the buyer is unaware of the agent's lack of authority. Section 21(2) enables the **apparent** owner of goods to dispose of them as if he or she was their true owner.

Sale by a person with a voidable title (s.23)

A person may obtain possession of goods under a contract which is void, for example, for mistake. A void contract is, in fact, no contract at all. A buyer in these circumstances does not acquire title to the goods and, therefore, cannot pass good title on to anyone else. The original owner will be able to maintain an action in tort to recover the goods or their value from a third party who bought them in good faith; *Cundy* v. *Lindsay* (1878).

A person may also acquire goods under a contract which is voidable, for example misrepresentation. In this case, the contract is valid unless and until it is avoided. Section 23 provides that where goods are re-sold before the contract has been avoided, the buyer acquires a good title to them provided they are bought in good faith and without notice of the seller's defect of title; *Lewis* v. *Averay* (1971).

If the original owner acts quickly to rescind the contract and then the goods are re-sold, the seller may be prevented from passing a good title to a purchaser.

Sale by a seller in possession of the goods (s.24)

Where a seller sells goods but remains in possession of them, or any documents of title relating to them, any re-sale to a second buyer, who actually takes physical delivery of the goods or the documents of title, will pass a good title to the second buyer. The disappointed first buyer may sue the seller for non-delivery of the goods.

Re-sale by buyer in possession of goods (with seller's consent) (s.25)

Where a person who has bought or agreed to buy goods obtains possession of the goods with the consent of the seller, any re-sale to a person who takes the goods in good faith and without notice of the rights of the original seller, has the same effect as if the person making the delivery or transfer were a mercantile agent in possession of the goods with the consent of the owner. This exception to the 'no one can give what he has not got' rule was applied in the *Newtons of Wembley Ltd* v. *Williams* (1964) case. In this case X sold a car to a rogue, who paid for it by a cheque which was later dishonoured. X took immediate steps to rescind his contract with the rogue, by informing the police. Some time later, the rogue re-sold the car in a well-established street market in used cars. Y, the buyer then sold the car to another person Z. It was held that Z acquired a good title to the car. When the rogue sold the car at the market, he was a buyer in possession with the owner's (X) consent and he acted in the same way as a mercantile agent would have done. He (the rogue) passed a good title to the purchaser (Y) who in turn passed title to Z.

Figure 12.2:   Transfer of title by non-owners

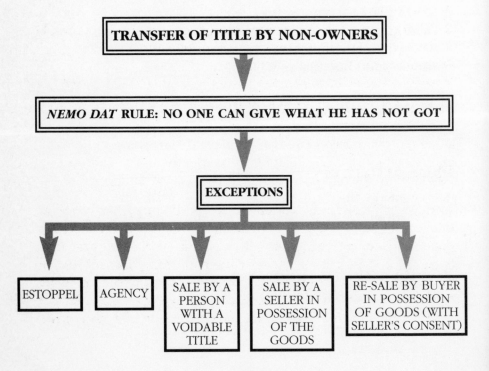

Performance of the Contract

It is the duty of the seller to deliver the goods and the buyer's duty to accept and pay for them. The parties are free to make their own arrangements about the time and place of delivery and payment. The Act sets out the obligations of the seller and buyer, when they have not dealt with these matters specifically in their agreement. Section 28 provides: 'Unless otherwise agreed, delivery of the goods and payment of the price are concurrent conditions ....' This means that the seller can hold on to the goods until the buyer has paid for them.

Delivery

Delivery in the context of the Act means the **voluntary transfer of possession** from one person to another. The delivery may consist of:

1 physically handing over the goods;
2 handing over the means of control of the goods, for example the keys to the premises where they are stored;
3 transferring documents of title; or
4 where the goods are in possession of a third party, an acknowledgement by the third party that he is holding the goods on behalf of the buyer.

Place of delivery

In the absence of any agreement to the contrary, the place of delivery is the seller's place of business; it is up to the buyer to come and collect the goods. If, however, the seller agrees to send the goods and engages a carrier for this purpose, section 32 provides that delivery to the carrier is deemed to be delivery to the buyer. The seller must make the best possible contract with the carrier on behalf of the buyer to ensure the safe arrival of the goods.

Time of delivery

The parties may have fixed a delivery date. Failure to make delivery by that date is a breach of condition, which entitles the buyer to repudiate the contract and sue for non-delivery. Where the seller agrees to send the goods and no time for sending them has been agreed, they must be dispatched within a reasonable time.

A demand for delivery by the buyer or an offer of delivery by the seller will not be valid unless made at a reasonable hour. What is reasonable is a question of fact. If the seller is ready and willing to deliver the goods and requests the buyer to take delivery, but the buyer does not comply with the request within a reasonable time, then the buyer will be liable for any resulting loss and a reasonable charge for the care and custody of the goods.

Delivery of the wrong quantity

If the seller delivers a smaller quantity than ordered, the buyer may reject the consignment, but if the buyer decides to accept the goods, they must be payed for at the contract rate. If the seller sends a larger quantity than agreed, the buyer has the following choices:

1 accept the goods ordered and reject the rest;
2 reject the lot; or
3 accept the whole consignment, paying for the extra goods at the contract rate.

If the seller delivers the contract goods but they are mixed with other goods, which have not been ordered, the buyer may either accept the contract goods and reject the rest, or reject the whole lot.

Thus, in *Shipton, Anderson & Co. Ltd* v. *Weil Bros & Co. Ltd* (1912), X agreed to deliver 4,950 tons of wheat. They in fact delivered 4,950 tons 55lb. It was held that the difference was so trifling that it did not entitle the buyers to reject the whole consignment.

Delivery by instalments

Unless otherwise agreed, the buyer is not bound to accept delivery by instalments. The parties may, of course, agree that the goods are to be delivered in stated instalments. A breach of contract may occur in respect of one or more instalments, for example, the seller may deliver goods which are unmerchantable or the buyer may refuse to take delivery of an instalment. Clearly, the injured party will be able to sue for damages, but the question then arises whether there is also an entitlement to repudiate the contract. The answer depends on whether the contract is **indivisible (entire)** or **severable (divisible)**. A contract is usually treated as being severable if each instalment is to be separately paid for.

Indivisible contracts. A breach of condition in respect of the first instalment will entitle the injured party to repudiate the whole contract. Breaches of condition in relation to the second and subsequent instalments must be treated as breaches of warranty for which the only remedy is an action in damages.

Severable contracts. Whether a breach in relation to one or more instalment will entitle the injured party to repudiate the whole contract depends 'on the terms of the contract and the circumstances of the case'. If the contract is silent on the matter, the courts apply two main tests:

1 the size of the breach in relation to the whole contract, and
2 the likelihood that the breach will be repeated.

Thus, in *Maple Flock Co. Ltd* v. *Universal Furniture Products (Wembley) Ltd* (1933), X agreed to deliver 100 tons of flock by instalments. The first 15 instalments were satisfactory but the 16th was not up to the required standard. Y, the buyers, then took delivery of four more satisfactory loads before refusing further deliveries. It was held that Y, the buyers, were not entitled to repudiate the contract. The defective flock constituted a small proportion of the total quantity delivered and there was little likelihood of the breach being repeated.

Acceptance

The buyer is bound to accept the goods which the seller delivers in accordance with the contract. Acceptance is deemed to have taken place when:

1 the buyer tells the seller that the goods have been accepted; or
2 does anything to the goods which is inconsistent with the ownership of the seller (for example re-sells them); or
3 retains the goods after the lapse of a reasonable time without telling the seller that the goods have been rejected.

Finally, if the buyer exercises the right to reject the goods for breach of a condition, he or she must inform the seller of the refusal to accept them but is not obliged to return them to the seller.

Figure 12.3: Delivery of goods

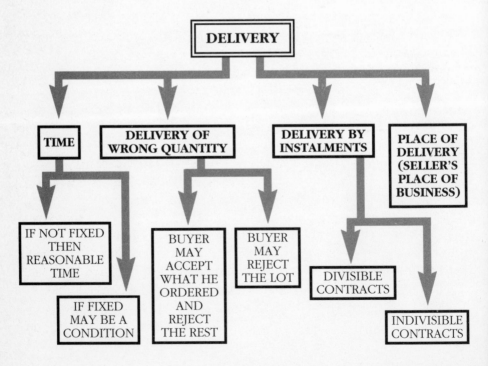

Questions for Discussion

1 What should a *Romalpa* clause provide in order to be effective?
2 What is the *nemo dat* rule?
3 When is delivery and payment supposed to take place under the Sale of Goods Act 1979?

13

Seller's and Buyer's Remedies

Seller's Remedies

Two remedies are open to the seller. He or she can pursue personal remedies against the buyer and real remedies against the goods.

Personal remedies

The seller can sue the buyer for the contract price or for damages for non-acceptance.

(i) **Action for the price** (s.49). The seller can bring an action for the contract price in two situations: (1) where the property in the goods has passed to the buyer or (2) where the buyer has failed to pay by a specified date, irrespective of whether ownership has passed to the buyer.

(ii) **Damages for non-acceptance** (s.50). If the property in the goods has not passed and the buyer will not accept the goods, the seller can sue for non-acceptance. The measure of damages is the estimated loss directly and naturally resulting in the ordinary course of events from the buyer's breach of contract(s.50(2)). If the buyer wrongfully refuses to accept and pay for the goods, the seller is expected to mitigate the loss and sell them elsewhere for the best possible price. Section 50(3) provides guidance as to the measure of damages where there is an available market for the goods. If the market price is less than the contract price, the seller can recover the difference by way of damages. Where the market price is the same or even higher than the contract price, the seller will be entitled to nominal damages only. Finally, the market price is calculated at the time when the goods ought to have been accepted.

In *Thompson W.L. Ltd* v. *Robinson (Gunmakers) Ltd* (1955), Y ordered a new Vanguard car from X, a car dealer, but then Y refused to accept it. X argued that he was only liable to pay nominal damages, since the contract price and the market price were the same. It was held that there was no 'available market' for Vanguard cars because supply exceeded demand and, therefore, s.50(3) did not apply.

In *Charter* v. *Sullivan* (1957), X refused to accept a new Hillman Minx car which he had ordered from a dealer. In contrast to the previous case, the demand for this kind of cars exceeded supply and the dealer would have no difficulty in finding another buyer. It was held that the dealer was entitled to nominal damages only. X's breach would not affect the total number of cars that he (the dealer) would sell over a period of time.

Real remedies

The unpaid seller has three possible remedies in respect of the goods even though the property in the goods has passed to the buyer. These are (i) lien, (ii) stoppage in transit, and (iii) re-sale.

(i) **Lien** (ss.41-43). A lien is a right to retain possession of goods until the contract price has been paid. It does not give the right to the possessor to re-sell the goods. Liens are available in any of the following circumstances:
(a) where the goods have been sold without any mention of credit;
(b) where the goods have been sold on credit but the period of credit has expired;

(c) where the buyer becomes insolvent.

The seller will lose the right of lien if the price is paid or tendered or the buyer obtains possession of the goods. The seller cannot exercise this right to retain the goods if the goods have been handed to a carrier for transportation to the buyer without reserving the right of disposal of the goods or where the seller has given up the right.

(ii) **Stoppage in transit** (ss.44-46). This is the right of the seller to stop goods in transit to the buyer, regain possession of them and retain them until payment has been received. The seller can exercise the right to stoppage in transit in only one situation: where the buyer has become insolvent.

(iii) **Right of re-sale** (ss.47-48). The rights of lien and stoppage in transit by themselves do not give the seller any right to re-sell the goods. The seller is allowed, however, to re-sell the goods in the following circumstances:

(a) where the goods are of a perishable nature;
(b) where the seller gives notice to the buyer of intention to re-sell and the buyer does not pay or tender the price within a reasonable time; or
(c) where the seller expressly reserves the right of re-sale in the event of the buyer defaulting.

The seller can exercise the right of re-sale and also recover damages for any loss sustained by the buyer's breach of contract. The original contract of sale is rescinded and the new buyer acquires a good title to the goods as against the original buyer.

Buyer's Remedies

Various remedies are available to the buyer, where the seller is in breach of contract.

Rejection of the goods (s.11)

The buyer may repudiate the contract and reject the goods where the seller is in breach of a condition of the contract. Most of the implied terms contained in ss.12-15 are conditions, so if the goods are not of merchantable quality or fit for a particular purpose, the buyer is entitled to reject them. This right will be lost as soon as the goods have been accepted: the buyer must treat the breach of condition as a breach of warranty which limits the remedy to a claim for damages.

An action for damages

The following actions for damages may be taken by the buyer:

(i) **Non-delivery** (s.51). The buyer can sue for non-delivery when the seller wrongfully neglects or refuses to deliver the goods. The measure of damages is the **estimated loss directly and naturally resulting in the ordinary course of events from the seller's breach of contract.** Where there is an available market for the goods, the measure of damages is usually the difference between the contract price and the higher price of obtaining similar goods elsewhere. If the buyer has paid in advance and the goods are not delivered, the amount paid can be recovered (s.54) because there has been a total failure of consideration.

(ii) **Breach of warranty** (s.53). The buyer can sue for damages under s.53 in the following circumstances:

(a) where the seller is in breach of warranty;

(b) where the seller is in breach of a condition, but the buyer has chosen to carry on with the contract and claim damages instead; or

(c) where the seller is in breach of a condition, but the buyer has lost the right to reject the goods, because they have been accepted.

The measure of damages is the **estimated loss directly and naturally resulting from the breach.** This is usually the difference in value between the goods actually delivered and goods fulfilling the warranty.

Specific performance (s.52)

The buyer may sue for specific performance but only in cases where the goods are specific or ascertained and where monetary damages would not be an adequate remedy. A court is unlikely to make such an order if similar goods are available elsewhere.

Figure 13.1: Seller's remedies

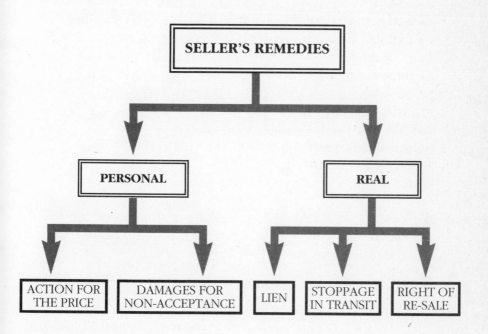

Figure 13.2: Buyer's remedies

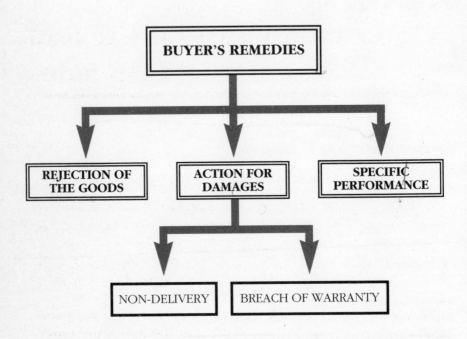

Questions for Discussion

1 An unpaid seller has a right of *stoppage in transit*. What does this mean?

2 Even where the property in the goods has passed to the buyer, an unpaid seller can exercise his right of *lien*. What is a *lien* and in what circumstances may it be available to an unpaid seller?

14

Introduction to CIF and FOB Sales

Certain special clauses have been used over the years in sales where delivery has involved carriage by sea. These clauses have given rise to certain main types of contract, the major terms of which have become largely standardized. The most important quotations in exporting are CIF (Cost, Insurance and Freight) and FOB (Free On Board), although variations of these terms of export contract exist, such as C & F, Ex-Works, and so on.

Under a CIF contract of sale, the seller provides the goods, engages cargo space on the vessel, pays freight to the buyer's port which is normal, for example, CIF Singapore, insures the goods on behalf of the buyer against normal marine and fire risk to that port and pays all charges incidental in getting the goods onto the vessel. The seller is liable for any loss or damage before the goods reach the ship.

FOB implies that the duty of the seller is to present the goods to the port/airport and see they are actually placed on board the vessel/aircraft which the buyer provides. The seller meets all charges incidental to placing the goods on the ship/aircraft such as collection, handling, insurance, but once the goods are on board and the seller has obtained a receipt for the goods, the exporter's (seller's) responsibilities cease. Thereafter, the buyer pays all the charges. Thus, the buyer or an agent would insure the goods from the sea port or airport of departure to the destination and pay the freight.

Under an Ex-Works contract it is the duty of the buyer to take delivery of the goods at the works or store of the seller, as the case may be. The property and risk usually pass when the buyer takes delivery. These sales are almost always of unascertained goods, the appropriation taking place when the goods are selected or handed over at the works or store.

C & F (named port of shipment) is another cargo delivery term under which the seller pays the cost and freight necessary to convey the goods from the port of shipment to the port of destination. The buyer will be responsible for any damage or loss to the goods when the goods pass the ship's rail at the port of shipment and for the unloading costs. The seller bears the costs of freight from the port of shipment to the port of destination including cost of packing, and loading in port of departure.

FOR means 'free on rail', and an FAS (free alongside ship) contract is one in which the goods are delivered alongside the ship free of expense to the buyer; after that the charges incurred are to be met by the buyer.

Incoterms

In a sale of goods contract it is important that there is no ambiguity in the interpretation by either party of the delivery terms quoted, particularly in the area of cost and expenses. If such problems arise, much goodwill is lost, the exporter (seller) could lose the prospect of a repeat order in a competitive market and in addition costly litigation could arise. It is essential, therefore, that buyer and seller agree on the terms of delivery and their interpretation. Such a situation could be overcome by quoting the provisions of Incoterms.

In order to overcome any difficulties in interpreting the chief delivery terms used in foreign trade contracts, a set of international rules have been agreed by the member countries of the International Chamber of Commerce (ICC). These rules eliminate the possibility of varied interpretation of the same terms in the same countries. If the buyer and seller wish to use these rules it must be specified in the contract that it is governed by the provisions of *Incoterms 1990.*

FOB Contracts

The main characteristics of this type of contract have already been mentioned. The goods must be delivered on board by the seller, free of expense to the purchaser, and they are not at the buyer's risk until actually delivered on board, when the property in them passes to the purchaser. So it may be said that in this type of contract risk and transfer of property pass simultaneously. The buyer on the other hand, must name a ship or authorize the seller to select one. The seller cannot sue for the price (see page 157, Seller's and Buyer's Remedies) until the goods are actually loaded, and if the inability to load was caused by the buyer's failure to name an effective ship, the seller's only remedy lies in damages, not an action for the price; *Petraco Ltd* v. *Petromed International S.A.* (1988).

Section 32(3) of the Sale of Goods Act 1979 provides that, unless otherwise agreed, where the goods are sent by the seller to the buyer by a route involving sea transit, under circumstances in which it is usual to insure, the seller must give such notice to the buyer as may enable the buyer to insure them during their sea transit, and, if the seller fails to do so, the goods shall be deemed to be at the seller's risk during such sea transit. Thus delivery to the carrier will not necessarily pass the risk in FOB contracts, as a rule.

Nowadays, under what is called an FOB contract with additional services, the seller often makes the contract of carriage. It must be reasonable in terms of the nature of the goods and other circumstances. If not and the goods are lost or damaged in the course of transit, the buyer may decline to treat the delivery to the carrier as a delivery to himself or may hold the seller responsible in damages; section 32(2).

The duties of the parties to an FOB contract expressly subject to the Incoterms may be summed up as follows:

The seller must
1 Provide the goods and the invoice.
2 Obtain at his risk and expense any export licence and carry out all customs formalities.
3 Deliver the goods on board the named vessel and port of

shipment, both of which will have been named by the buyer, and within the stipulated period.

4 Bear all risks of loss of or damage to the goods until the goods have passed the ship's rail at the named port of shipment.

5 Pay all costs relating to the goods until the goods have passed the ship's rail; for example costs of customs formalities.

6 Give the buyer sufficient notice that the goods have been delivered on board.

7 Provide the buyer with the usual document in proof of delivery in accordance with (3) above.

8 Provide at his own expense packaging and mark the goods appropriately.

9 Render the buyer every assistance in obtaining any document or equivalent electronic messages, which the buyer may require for the importation of the goods.

The buyer must

1 Pay the price.

2 Contract at his own expense for the carriage of the goods from the named port of shipment.

3 Take delivery of the goods.

4 Bear all risks of loss or damage to the goods from the time they have passed the ship's rail.

5 Pay all costs relating to the goods from the time they have passed the ship's rail.

6 Give the seller sufficient notice of the vessel name, loading point and required delivery time.

7 Pay the costs of pre-shipment inspection except when mandated by the authorities of the country of export.

8 Pay all costs and charges incurred in obtaining the documents or equivalent electronic messages and reimburse those incurred by the seller in rendering his assistance.

CIF Contracts   *No delay*

Duties of the seller

1 To ship goods of the description contained in the contract

under a contract of affreightment which will ensure the delivery of the goods at the destination contemplated in the contract.

As mentioned previously undertakings in the contract as to time and place of shipment are nearly always treated as conditions.

Thus, in *Aruna Mills v. Dhanrajmal Gobindram* (1968), a contract for sale of cotton provided for a variation in price if the prevailing rate of exchange should vary between the contract date and the date when the price was payable. The sellers, in breach of contract, failed to ship the cotton until 27th June, 1966, although the last permitted date for shipment was 31st May, 1966. The rupee was devalued on 6th June, 1966, and the buyers paid the additional price on receipt of the shipping document which was received after 6th June, 1966. They (the buyers) sued to recover that additional price by way of damages for late shipment, alleging that if the goods had been shipped on or before 31st May, 1966, they would have received the shipping documents and made payment on or before 5th June, 1966, that is, before devaluation. It was held that the loss due to the devaluation was not too remote, for the parties had contemplated it as likely to result from late shipment.

2 To arrange for insurance which will be available to the buyer.
3 To make out an invoice for the goods.
4 To tender the documents to the buyer in exchange for the price, so that the buyer will know the amount of the freight he must pay, and so that he can obtain delivery of the goods if they arrive, or recover for their loss if they are lost on the voyage.

Incoterms 1990 provide a slightly different set of duties and obligations for the seller and buyer under a CIF contract. These can be summarized as follows:

The seller must
1 Provide the goods and the invoice, in accordance with the contract of sale.
2 Obtain at his own risk and expense any export licence and

carry out all customs formalities necessary for the exportation of the goods.

3 Contract on usual terms at his own expense for the carriage of the goods to the named port of destination.

4 Obtain at his own expense cargo insurance as required by the contract, and provide the buyer with insurance policy or other evidence of insurance cover.

5 Deliver the goods on board the vessel at the port of shipment on the date or within the period stipulated.

6 Bear all risks of loss of or damage to the goods until they have passed the ship's rail at the port of shipment.

7 Pay the freight and costs of loading the goods on board and any charges for unloading at the port of discharge, and the costs of customs formalities necessary for exportation.

8 Give the buyer sufficient notice that the goods have been delivered on board the vessel.

9 Provide the buyer without delay with the usual transport document for the agreed port of destination.

10 Provide at his own expense packaging and mark the goods appropriately.

11 Render the buyer every assistance in obtaining any documents or equivalent electronic messages required for the importation of the goods.

The buyer must

1 Pay the price as provided in the contract of sale.

2 Obtain any import licence and carry out all customs formalities for the importation of the goods.

3 Accept delivery of the goods when they have been delivered and receive them from the carrier at the named port of destination.

4 Bear all risks of loss of or damage to the goods from the time the goods have passed the ship's rail at the port of shipment.

5 Whenever he is entitled to determine the time for shipping the goods and/or the port of destination, give the seller sufficient notice thereof.

6 Accept the transport document.

7 Pay the costs of any pre-shipment inspection, except when

mandated by the authorities of the country of exportation.

8 Pay all costs and charges incurred in obtaining the documents or equivalent electronic messages and reimburse the seller in rendering his assistance.

9 Provide the seller, upon request, with the necessary information for procuring insurance.

Refusal of buyer to accept goods

In a CIF contract the buyer or his agent may repudiate the contract by:

1 refusing to accept the documents if they do not conform with the contract; and

2 rejecting the goods on delivery if following inspection they do not comply with the contract.

Passing of the risk

As a general rule, the risk passes when the goods are shipped. The buyer will still have to pay for the goods if they are lost on the voyage. Note however, that although the risk passes when the goods are shipped, the property in the goods is not transferred to the buyer until the seller transfers the documents to the buyer and the latter has paid for them. Therefore, it appears that a CIF contract is a 'sale of documents', since it is the delivery of these documents that transfers the property to the buyer.

In order to simplify the above mentioned process involved in a CIF contract, consider the following examples.

X, agrees to sell to Y some goods, under a CIF contract. X has to fulfil the above mentioned four duties, that is, (1) to ship goods of the contract description, at the port of shipment, within the time named in the contract and to contract for their carriage; (2) to arrange for insurance which will be available to the buyer; (3) to make out an invoice for the goods; and (4) to tender the documents to the buyer in exchange for the price.

If the contract does not provide for a particular time of delivery then a reasonable time will be assumed.

As mentioned earlier, the risk passes when the goods are shipped. Assume that X ships the goods. Therefore, the risk has passed to Y and he will have to bear any loss or damage that might happen to the goods.

However, as mentioned above, the property in the goods (that is, ownership) does not pass to Y until X has transferred the documents (for example bill of lading, invoice) to Y. Therefore, one may anticipate the situation where the goods have been shipped, as in the example, but the documents have not been transferred. In other words, the buyer (Y) has not got owner-ship of the goods, but nevertheless, the risk of the goods being lost or damaged in transit is for him (Y) to bear. (However, bear in mind that the buyer (Y) has the benefit of the insurance). Under such circumstances it could be said that there is a conditional appropriation of the goods to the contract which will not become unconditional until the buyer (Y) takes up the documents and pays for them. This is the reason why it was mentioned earlier in this chapter that a CIF contract is effectively a 'sale of documents'; because it is the delivery of those documents which transfers the property to the buyer.

In the above example of a CIF contract, let us assume that the documents arrive and are delivered to the buyer (Y). However, Y suspects that the goods he ordered have been damaged/or are not up to his expectations, and therefore, he decides to wait until the goods have arrived (so that he can inspect them) and pay for them after inspecting them. It must be remembered that he is not entitled to take this action; he must pay the agreed price within a reasonable time after tender of the docu-ments; he is not entitled to withhold payment until he has examined the goods.

Clauses such as 'payment on arrival of goods' and 'payment x days after arrival of goods' are ambiguous and their meaning has to be ascertained from the intention of the parties.

The parties may have intended that the arrival of the goods shall be a condition for the payment of the price. In this case it would seem that the contract is not a CIF contract. However, the better view would be that this interpretation should only be adopted if this intention of the parties can clearly be gathered from the contract; *Dupont* v. *British South Africa Co.* (1901).

Alternatively, the parties may have intended that the clause shall only refer to the time at which payment has to be made. In short, if the goods do not arrive, payment shall be made on tender of the documents at the date at which the goods would normally have arrived. In this case the clause refers only to the incident of payment and not to that of delivery and the contract is a proper CIF contract.

Summary of Important Points on Sale of Goods

1   The law of sale of goods was codified by the Sale of Goods Act 1893, and was later consolidated by the Sale of Goods Act 1979.

2   A contract of sale of goods is a contract by which the seller transfers or agrees to transfer the property in goods to the buyer for a money consideration, called the price.

3   It is the duty of the seller to deliver the goods, and of the buyer to accept and pay for them, in accordance with the terms of the contract of sale.

4   The property in the goods passes when the parties intend that it shall pass.

5   The general rule is that 'no one can transfer a better title than that which he has' (*nemo dat quod non habet*) but there are some important exceptions.

6   Sections 12 to 15 of the Sale of Goods Act provide for the implication of terms which are much to the advantage of the buyer. The implied terms are with regard to seller's title (s.12), correspondence of the goods with description (s.13), quality and fitness for purpose (s.14) and correspondence of bulk with sample in quality (s.15).

7   Liability under s.12 cannot be excluded. Liability under sections 13, 14 and 15 cannot be excluded as against a person dealing as a consumer: as against a person dealing otherwise than as consumer, the same liabilities can be excluded only

in so far as the exclusion clause satisfies the requirement of reasonableness.

8 Where the buyer wrongfully refuses to accept and pay for the goods the seller may claim damages. Where the buyer does not pay, the seller may claim the price of the goods; in some circumstances the seller may have a remedy against the goods themselves.

9 Where the seller wrongfully fails to deliver the goods the buyer may sue for damages or, in appropriate circumstances, he might be entitled to specific performance. Where the seller is in breach of condition the buyer may reject the goods and treat the contract as repudiated. Where the seller is in breach of warranty the buyer is left with his right to claim damages.

10 It is not unusual for a contract of sale to include a clause which provides that the property in the goods remains in the seller until payment of the price has been made in full by the buyer. Such clauses are known as 'retention of title clauses' or '*Romalpa* clauses'.

11 *Incoterms 1990* are international rules for interpretation of terms frequently used in foreign trade (export sales) contracts. These rules are drawn up by the International Chamber of Commerce.

Questions for Discussion

1 What are Incoterms?
2 Briefly describe the general provisions of a CIF and a C & F contract.

Part 4

Competition Law

15

Restrictive Trade Practices

In the UK competition law is dealt with by the following statutes:

1 the Fair Trading Act 1973;
2 the Restrictive Trade Practices Act 1976;
3 the Resale Prices Act 1976 (price fixing); and
4 the Competition Act 1980 (large-scale anti-competitive practices).

For the purposes of this book, only the Restrictive Trade Practices Act will be fully considered.

Restrictive Trade Practices Act 1976

Under this Act, collective agreements between two or more persons designed to fix prices and/or regulate supplies of goods must be registered with the Director General of Fair Trading. Unless the parties can prove to the Restrictive Trade Practices Court that the agreement is in the public interest, such agreement would be presumed void.

Any agreement is registrable under the 1976 Act, (1) if made between persons carrying on business in the UK concerned with the production or supply of goods and (2) if they accept the following restrictions of agreements:

1 Agreements relating to the production, supply, processing or manufacture of goods which restrict any of the following: prices, terms or conditions, quantities or descriptions, manufacturing processes, persons who may obtain the goods, and areas in which the goods may be obtained.
2 'Information agreements' relating to goods which concern the furnishing of information on matters relating to, for example, prices, quantities and descriptions of goods, costs of production and supply, and persons to whom and areas in which they are supplied.
3 Agreements relating to the supply of services and restricting charges for, terms and conditions of, form of those services and the persons or areas who or which can supply or obtain these services.
4 'Information agreements' relating to the supply of services which provide for the furnishing of information on, for example, charges for, extent of, terms or conditions of, or costs of provision of, those services.

If the parties attempt to operate the agreement although it has not been approved by the Restrictive Practices Court, the Director General of Fair Trading may ask for an injunction to prevent the operation of the agreement.

However, it is rare that such action has to be taken because in most cases the firms concerned have not attempted to operate an agreement if it has been rejected by the Court.

In general, the Act does not apply to agency agreements, but it can apply to distribution agreements. As it can be seen there are some exceptions to the categories of agreements to which the Act applies, but these are beyond the scope of this work.

Finally, note that the Act is due to be replaced by new legislation, however, no firm date for this has been set.

Restrictive Trading Agreements and the Treaty of Rome

In addition to the above statutes, there are also basic principles of EC competition law which are applicable to individual commercial agreements. It must be borne in mind that these EC competition law principles have direct effect in the UK. Furthermore, EC law in general takes precedence over UK law, and wherever there is a clash, EC law must prevail.

Under Articles 85 and 86 of the Treaty of Rome all agreements between firms which operate to prevent or restrict competition in the Market (EEC) are void. Under s.5 of the Restrictive Practices Act 1976 the Director General of Fair Trading and the Restrictive Practices Court are to take Articles 85 and 86 into account:

(a) on the issue of registration of a particular agreement; and

(b) if the agreement comes before the Court for adjudication.

The two Treaty Articles (85, 86) should be considered in order to assess the position of restrictive trading agreements under Community Law.

Article 85

In general the effect of Article 85 is to prohibit any agreements, decisions or practices which have or may have an effect on trade between Member States. Such agreements, decisions or practices are void. The basic test is whether the relevant agreement affects considerably trade within the common market. However, this provision of Article 85 does not only apply to an agreement between two parties based in different EEC countries, but also if (a) both parties are based in the same EEC country, and (b) one party is based in a EEC country and the other is not.

It must be noted however, that the same Article allows the EC Commission to grant exemptions if the agreement is essentially pro-competitive, for example if it benefits consumers and is not unnecessarily restrictive. In this respect, it is important to note that Regulations 1983/83 of the EC Commission exempts exclusive distribution agreements to which only two parties are involved, provided that the terms of the agreement do not

177

impede parallel trading. Furthermore, agency agreements are not generally within the scope of application of Article 85, because agent and principal are likely to be counted as one undertaking; Article 85 would not apply where the parties to an agreement cannot be described as two separate undertakings. For example Article 85 would not apply to an agreement between a parent and a subsidiary company.

Article 85 may be considered under three headings:

1 Use of trade marks to restrict competition. This may be illustrated by the *Consten and Grundig* (1966) case. Grundig set up a network of exclusive distributors for its products throughout the Community and appointed a French firm, Consten to be its exclusive distributor in France. Consten, in common with all other Grundig distributors, was not permitted to sell either directly or indirectly outside France, and, to make certain that none of the other distributors violated Consten's exclusive territorial rights, Consten was permitted to register the trade mark GINT (which stands for Grundig International) as its French trade mark. A third party imported Grundig products into France and Consten brought an action against the importer for infringement of trade mark. The case went to the European Court of Justice and it was held that the purpose of the trade mark agreement between Grundig and Consten was to guarantee complete territorial protection to Consten in the sale of Grundig products in France. That agreement was prohibited by Article 85 as its purpose was to hamper the importing into France of Grundig products by other firms and in these circumstances the agreement was void.

2 Cartel arrangements. An illustration of cartel arrangements is to be seen in the *Dyestuffs* cartel (1969). In this case the Commission's investigations were commenced on the basis of information which they received from trade organizations of industrial users. These investigations revealed that the ten major manufacturers of dyestuffs had made uniform, and for all practical purposes, simultaneous price increases between 1964 and 1967 on the sale of their goods. This price fixing agreement led to the imposition of fines of $50,000 on the companies involved.

3 The use of patent rights to restrict competition. An illustration of the attitude of the European Court on this issue is to be found in *Parke-Davis* v. *Probel* (1968). Parke-Davis was a company based in Detroit. It held certain Dutch patents for an antibiotic. Another company imported the drug into Holland without the permission of the patent holder, Parke-Davis, and they (Parke-Davis) brought an action against this other company for breach of the patent. It appeared that the defendant company had purchased the drug in Italy, where there was no patent protection in medicines, and had then imported it into Holland. Thus Parke-Davis had been unable to take out patents in Italy in order to protect their rights because there was a gap in Italian law as regards patents. In these circumstances Parke-Davis took the only action they could by suing the defendant company. The defendant company pleaded that the action was in breach of competition rules and the Dutch court referred the matter to the European Court of Justice. The European Court recognized the existence of the patent rights and that the exercise of those rights to prevent goods being imported into Holland from a country where such patent rights did not exist was a wholly proper action and did not constitute a restriction to competition. Note however, that if the goods had been imported from another country where patent rights were in existence, an attempt to prevent their importation would probably have constituted an infringement of Article 85.

Article 86

In general this Article prohibits the abuse of a dominant position within the common market. Here the activities of one undertaking could infringe the Article, unlike Article 85 where it is necessary to have an agreement between undertakings. Three requirements must be fulfilled in order to make Article 86 applicable. It must be shown that:

1 a dominant position is held by some undertaking;
2 there has been an abuse of that domination; and

3 the abuse has had an effect on trade between member states.

Thus, in the *Continental Can* case (1972), X was an American company producing packing materials such as fish tins, meat tins, and in 1969 it (X) took control of company Y which was the largest German producer of packaging. In 1970 X acquired a majority holding of company Z which was one of the few leading European (Dutch) manufacturers of packing materials. In the opinion of the European Commission the situation arising from this concentration within the market of light packing in the North-West region of the Common Market constituted the necessary conditions for an abuse of dominant position within Article 86. However, the finding of the Commission was set aside by the European Court on a technical ground that the European Commission had failed to define which market was abused, whether it was that of meat tins, fish tins etc. However, the important point is that the Court stressed that Article 86 would have been infringed on a definition of the market abused so that the mergers would have been void.

English Courts would appear to use or interpret Article 86 slightly differently. Thus, in *Garden Cottage Foods Ltd* v. *Milk Marketing Board* (1982), X was a middle-man transferring butter from Y (Milk Marketing Board) to traders in the bulk market in Europe and the UK. In 1982 following some packaging problems which X appeared to have overcome, Y (Milk Marketing Board) refused to supply direct to X. Y (Milk Marketing Board) further stated that supplies must be obtained from one of four independent distributors nominated by them (Y). However, these distributors were X's competitors, and as X would have to pay more to them for its supplies than if it bought direct from Y, could not compete on price, and would be forced out of business. Therefore, X alleged that Y (Milk Marketing Board) was in breach of Article 86 of the Treaty of Rome. The Court of Appeal granted an injunction, that is, an injunction until the trial, restraining Y (Milk Marketing Board) from refusing to maintain normal business relations contrary to Article 86.. The House of Lords said that damages were an adequate remedy and therefore the injunction had to be withdrawn. This is a somewhat odd decision as it is uncertain whether an infringement of Article 86 gives rise in English law to an action for damages.

Figure 15.1: Restrictive Trade Practices and Competition

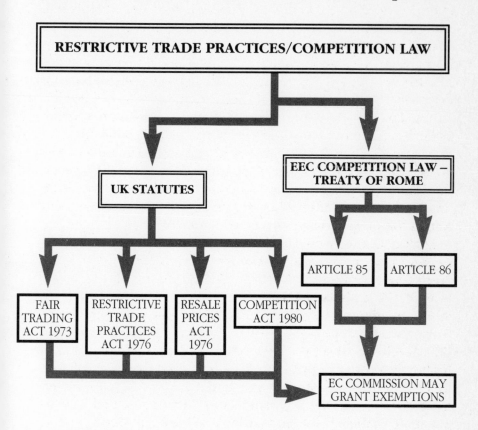

Questions for Discussion

1 Briefly describe the scope of the Restrictive Trade Practices Act 1976.
2 Briefly describe the scope of Article 85 of the Treaty of Rome.
3 Briefly describe the effect of Article 86 of the Treaty of Rome.

16

Free Movement of Goods in the European Community

Since its inception, the European Community has set up four principles: the free movement of goods; persons; services; and capital. The purpose of the free movement of goods principle is to promote efficiency in production by removing barriers to trade between member states. This principle, together with the EC competition law provisions and policies, constitute the essential element for the creation of a true common market. Articles 30-36 of the EC Treaty form the framework of the legal regime for the free movement of goods. Articles 30 and 36 deal with import and export restrictions on the free flow of goods around the common market, and so are relevant to competition.

Article 30

This prohibits between member states measures which impose total or partial restraint on imports, such as rules requiring import licences. A quantitative restriction or quota is a national measure which restrains the volume or amount of imports or exports, by placing direct or indirect limits on the physical actual quantity of goods/commodities/products/raw materials that may enter or leave a country. Article 30 in effect prohibits the re-introduction of such restrictions or other measures having an equivalent effect to quantitative restrictions. However, this prohibition under the Article is sometimes violated by member states, thus resulting in litigation in the European Court; for example in 1978 France imposed an embargo on sheep-meat from the UK; *EC Commission* v. *France (Re Sheepmeat from the United Kingdom)* (1979).

According to Directive 70/50/EEC, 'measures' means 'laws, regulations, administrative provisions, administrative practices, and all instruments issuing from a public authority including recommendations'. However, the concept of 'measures having an equivalent effect' is not confined to legislation, regulations or administrative practices within the ambit of national authorities. It also includes rules enacted by agencies such as professional bodies where these agencies exercise special powers; *R* v. *Pharmaceutical Society of Great Britain* (1989). Finally, it should be noted that Article 30 is not an absolute prohibition, since, as we shall see, Article 36 provides derogation.

Article 36

This sets out circumstances in which such controls may be permitted, for example because of public security reasons. In particular this Article in setting out the various exceptions states:

> The provisions of articles 30 to 34 shall not preclude prohibitions or restrictions on imports, exports or goods in transit justified on grounds of public morality, public policy or public security; the protection of health and life of humans, animals or plants; the protection of national treasures possessing artistic, historic or archaeological value; or the protection of industrial and commercial property.
> Such prohibitions or restrictions shall not, however, constitute a means of arbitrary discrimination or a disguised restriction on trade between Member States.

In summarizing therefore, one could conclude that there are four exceptions by which a member state may impose quantitative restrictions:

1 In order to protect public morality, public policy or public security. Thus, for example a restriction imposed by the UK on the imports of pornographic materials was considered by the European Court justified, in *R* v. *Henn and Darby* (1979), since the materials could not legitimately be manufactured within the UK.

2 For the purpose of protecting the health of life of humans, animals or plants; *Schumacher* v. *Hauptzollamt Frankfurt-am Main* (1990).

3 In order to protect the artistic, historic or archaeological treasures.

4 The protection of industrial or commercial property. This would include copyright, patents and other intellectual rights.

Although the above four exceptions are those derived from Article 36, it would appear that the European Court has derived a number of other exceptions in the *Cassis de Dijon* Case (1979). In this case the German authorities imposed a restriction on the sale of fruit liqueurs which contained less than 25% alcohol. Cassis contained 15%, and the ECJ held that this restriction was prohibited under Article 30, that is, a measure having equivalent effect to an import quota. In reaching its decision the Court considered that a Member State may impose some types of 'mandatory requirements' on the free movement of goods:

(a) Fiscal supervision requirements; this in effect means rules imposed by a state in order to ensure that its currency is not undermined; and

(b) Fairness of commercial transactions; the objective of this would be the protection of consumers from misrepresentations etc.

Finally, it should be noted that Articles 30, 36, 85 and 86, do not as such alter the notion of rights (for example patent rights, ownership rights and so on) which exist within a national jurisdiction; rather they affect the way in which such rights are exercised. Thus, Article 222 states that the treaty (of Rome) 'shall in no way prejudice the rules in Member States governing the system of property ownership'. Or again, as has been seen,

Article 36 allows restrictions on imports.

Cases such as *Deutsche Gremmophon* v. *Metro* (1971) and *Parke, Davis* v. *Probel* (1968) dictate that the owner of a right cannot prevent parallel imports of products sold by himself, his agent or his licensee in another Member State.

In simple words, Articles 85 and 30 recognize the legitimate existence of a right, as it is conceived or understood in each Member State, and this is the reason the Articles contain exceptions to the prohibitions they impose. In the case of Article 85, as we have seen, a right, such as a patent right in the UK, may be granted an exemption from the Commission, if its exercise is essentially pro-competitive, for example if it benefits consumers and is not unnecessarily restrictive. Or an exclusive distribution agreement would not be void under Article 85 provided only two parties are involved, and the terms of the agreement do not impede parallel trading; Regulations 1983/83 of the EC Commission. This is what is meant by Article 222, that is, that the treaty does not prejudice the rules in Member States governing the system of property ownership.

However, the test in all the above cases, and the philosophy of Articles 85 and 30 is that:

(a) although the exercise of such rights is recognized,
(b) if the enforcement of such exercise becomes or is 'illegal', which means contrary to the aim and provisions of the Articles, then
(c) there is an infringement of Community Law, and therefore such right cannot be enforced/exercised.

Figure 16.1: Free movement of goods in the EC

```
┌─────────────────────────────────────────┐
│    FREE MOVEMENT OF GOODS IN THE EC      │
└─────────────────────────────────────────┘
                    │
        ┌─────────────────────┐
        │      ARTICLE 30      │
        └─────────────────────┘
                    │
   ┌──────────────────────────────────┐
   │ PROHIBITION OF QUANTITATIVE       │
   │ RESTRICTIONS BY MEMBER STATES     │
   └──────────────────────────────────┘
                    │
        ┌─────────────────────┐
        │      ARTICLE 36      │
        └─────────────────────┘
                    │
               EXCEPTIONS
```

| TO PROTECT PUBLIC MORALITY, PUBLIC POLICY OR PUBLIC SECURITY | TO PROTECT THE ARTISTIC, HISTORIC OR ARCHAEOLOGICAL TREASURES | TO PROTECT INDUSTRIAL OR COMMERCIAL PROPERTY | 'MANDATORY REQUIREMENTS' |

| TO PROTECT THE HEALTH OF LIFE OF HUMANS, ANIMALS OR PLANTS | | FISCAL SUPERVISION | FAIRNESS OF COMMERCIAL TRANSACTIONS |

Questions for Discussion

1 What is the scope of Article 30 of the Treaty of Rome?
2 How may an EEC state impose quantitative restrictions under
   Article 36 of the Treaty of Rome?

Part 5

Legal Aspects of the Finance of Exports

17

The Law Relating to Export Finance

Bills of Exchange

Negotiability

The concept of a 'negotiable' instrument is very important in overseas trade. Among instruments now legally recognized as negotiable are Bills of Exchange, Promissory Notes, Cheques, Exchequer Bills, Bank Notes, Dividend Warrants, Share Warrants, Banker's Circular Notes and Debentures Payable to Bearer.

Post Office Orders, Money Orders, and Share Certificates and Transfers are not negotiable. Nor are letters of credit.

Negotiability is the property that some business instruments have of transferring a good title to the receiver of them irrespective of the title of the giver, provided that the receiver takes them in good faith, for value.

Definition

Section 3(1) of the Bills of Exchange Act 1882, defines a bill of exchange as follows:

A bill of exchange is an unconditional order in writing, addressed by one person to another, signed by the person giving it, requiring the person to whom it is addressed to pay on demand or at a fixed or determinable future time a sum certain in money to or to the order of a specified person, or to bearer.

Every word of this definition is important, for an instrument is not a bill of exchange unless it fulfills every condition given in the legal definition.

Cheques are bills of exchange, but remember the following differences:

1 A cheque is payable on demand.
2 The drawee is always a bank.
3 There is no indication on the face of a cheque as to the date on which it is payable.

A table outlining the differences between cheques and bills of exchange appears on page 207. The usual form of a bill does not differ materially from the following example.

Specimen 17.1: Ordinary form of inland bill of exchange

£84.00

297 London Wall
London, EC2
1st *January*, 19....

Thirty days after date [*or* On Demand] pay **X** or Order [*or* Bearer] the sum of *Eighty-four* pounds for value received.

Y.

To **Z**,

87b Chancery Lane,
London, WC2

In the above specimen, **Y** is the '**drawer**' of the bill; **Z** is the '**drawee**'; and **X** is the '**payee**'. If the **drawee** (Z) agrees to pay the bill on the due date, he (Z) '**accepts**', that is, he (Z) writes the word 'Accepted' and his (Z) signature across the face of the bill. He (Z) is then termed the '**acceptor**'. Until he (Z) does this he is not a party to the bill, and is in no way liable thereon.

It is possible to explore the definition with reference to the specimen bill of exchange. The essentials of a bill are therefore that:

1 It must be an 'order in writing'. It can be seen in the specimen that the bill is in writing, and it tells Z (the drawee) to pay £84.

2 The order must be 'unconditional', that is, there must be no conditions attached to the making of the payment. As in the example, there are no conditions attached to the payment.

3 It must be 'addressed by one person to another'. Again it can be seen that the order is addressed to Z (the drawee) from Y (the drawer). The drawer (Y) and drawee (Z) are usually a different person, for example the customer (drawer) and a bank (drawee) but they may be the same person. The commonest example is a banker's draft.

4 It must require payment to be made to a specified person or his order, or to bearer. Payment may be made to X and Y, as where X and Y are partners. Furthermore, a cheque may be payable in the alternative, that is, pay X or Y.

5 If the order is not to pay on demand, the time of payment must be fixed or determinable. In the example above, the order is not to pay on demand but at a fixed or determinable future time, because it says 'thirty days after date'. That is 30 days after 1st January 19 . . . ', that is, the bill is payable on 31st January 19. . . .

6 It must order payment of a certain sum of money only. The main relevance in practice of this is where the words and figures on a cheque are different (s.9(2)). In such a case the words prevail and are taken to be the sum payable. In practice, however, bankers usually return such cheques with the comment 'words and figures differ'.

7 It must be signed by the drawer (Y). A 'signature' is not defined in the Bills of Exchange Act 1882. However, the writing may be in ink or in pencil, and may be printed in whole or in part.

It must be understood from the outset that no one is liable on a bill unless he or she is a party to it and that a party to a bill is the drawer, acceptor or indorser, that is someone who has signed or authorized the signing on his behalf, of the bill in one of those capacities.

The payee and drawee of a bill are sometimes loosely called 'parties'. They do not become parties unless and until they sign as indorser and acceptor respectively.

Impersonal payees

Cheques made payable to impersonal payees such as 'Cash or order', 'Wages or order', had often been regarded as payable to bearer. But in *North & South Wales Bank* v. *Macbeth* (1908), it was held that an instrument so expressed does not fall within the definition of a bill because it does not order payment to a 'person'.

Fictitious payee

If the payee is a fictitious, or non-existing person, the bill is treated as being payable to bearer; *Bank of England* v. *Vagliano* (1891); *Clutton* v. *Attenborough* (1897); *Vinden* v. *Hughes* (1905). These cases further added the 'test' applicable in order to discover whether a payee is fictitious or not; in particular:

(a) if the drawer intends that an existing person whose name is inserted as payee shall actually be paid, the payee is not 'fictitious';
(b) if the drawer does not so intend, then the payee is 'fictitious';
(c) if the payee does not exist, then he is 'fictitious'.

Payee blank

An instrument made payable to '_____order', the blank not being filled in so as to specify a payee, is not a legal bill of exchange, but it was decided in *Chamberlain* v. *Young* (1893) that it will be construed as payable to the order of the drawer, and if the drawer indorses it, it becomes a valid bill of exchange.

Time of payment

A bill is payable at a 'determinable future time' within the meaning of the Act when it is expressed to be payable at a fixed period after date or at a fixed period after the occurrence of a specified event which is certain to happen, though the time of happening may be uncertain.

For instance, a bill payable seven days after the death of X would be a valid bill, as the specified event is bound to happen, and therefore the 'future time' is 'determinable'. But a bill payable seven days after the marriage of X would not be valid, as although the event may happen, yet it may not, and thus there is no certainty. The marriage spoken of is a possibility; *Korea Exchange Bank* v. *Debenhams* (1979).

Finally, where a bill is payable at a fixed period after date, after sight, or after the happening of a specified event, the time of payment is determined by excluding the day from which the time is to begin to run and by including the day of payment.

Negotiation of a bill

Negotiation is a transfer of a bill from X to Y in such a way as to make Y the holder (s.31).

Acceptance

Acceptance is the 'signification by the drawee of his assent to the order of the drawer' (s.17(1)). Note that presentment for acceptance is not necessary, but it is advisable that a bill should be presented for acceptance as soon as possible. The reason for such a suggestion is that if acceptance is refused, the parties to the bill, other than the drawee, become immediately liable (even though the bill has not yet matured), while if the bill is accepted, it becomes a more valuable security, by reason of the fact that the drawee, who has now become the acceptor, has acknowledged liability upon it.

Furthermore, the wrongful omission of an agent to present a bill for acceptance would render the agent liable to the principal for any loss resulting from neglect.

Restrictive indorsements

A restrictive indorsement makes the indorsee a holder, but for certain limited or restricted purposes only. There are two types of restrictive indorsements:

1 Where further negotiation is prohibited, that is, 'pay X only'.
2 Where negotiation is permitted but with mere authority to deal as directed.

For example, X, the payee of a bill/cheque for £600, owes £1,000 to Y, an overseas supplier, and he (X) wants to indorse the cheque to Y's agent, A, who is in England but he (X) wishes to make it clear that A is not the beneficial owner of the cheque/bill. In such a case, X can indorse the cheque/bill by stating 'Pay A for the account of Y'. A therefore, can obtain payment but must then account to Y, though A cannot transfer the bill/cheque.

Dishonour of a bill

When a bill is presented for acceptance, the drawee should accept it. If he refuses to do so, claiming perhaps that he has not authorized the bill to be drawn and knows nothing about it, the bill is dishonoured by non-acceptance.

A bill is dishonoured by non-payment when it is duly presented for payment and payment is refused or cannot be obtained. Usually, when a bill is dishonoured by non-payment, an immediate right of recourse against the drawer and indorsers accrues to the holder, but in order to preserve this right the holder must give notice of dishonour to those parties.

Thus, if a bill is presented for payment on the due date, and the acceptor refuses to pay it, then the bill is dishonoured by non-payment. It is now necessary for the holder to take certain action to protect himself. He must give notice of dishonour to the drawer and all other indorsers of the bill. In practice he usually gives notice of the dishonour to the person from whom he obtained the bill, who gives notice to the person from whom he obtained it and so forth, until the drawer is found. Eventually the drawer must honour it, and he will bring an action against the acceptor.

Thus, on a cheque, B is the drawer and C is the payee. C has negotiated the cheque to D, D to E, and E to F. Suppose that F is the holder at the time of dishonour and that he gives notice to E and to C but not to D. The result would be that F could claim on E and C because he gave notice. E could claim on C by reason of being a prior indorser who had a right of recourse against C. Finally, indorsers subsequent to F can also claim on E and C by reason of F's notice to them being subsequent holders. Furthermore, D can sue C because he is a prior indorser who has a right of recourse against C.

Specimen 17.2: Specimen notice of dishonour

TO .... ADDRESS AND DATE

....

Please take notice that a bill, particulars of which are given below, upon which you are liable as drawer [*or indorser*] has been dishonoured by non-acceptance [*or non-payment*]. I request immediate payment of the amount of the said bill, £ .... *plus* expenses.

.... (Signature)

PARTICULARS:

Amount £ .... Date .... Tenor ....

Due ....

Drawer .... Acceptor .... Payable at ....

Indorsers ....

Answer given ....

Holder of the bill

A holder of a bill is not necessarily the person who is legally entitled to it. Thus, a thief who steals a bearer cheque is a person in possession and therefore a holder, though obviously he has no title to the cheque and cannot sue upon it.

However, if he delivers it to X who takes it in good faith and for value, then X will get a good title. If however, X knows of the theft and is not in good faith then his title is no better that the thief's. This arises because where there is a 'defect' on the cheque as where it has been stolen or obtained by fraud, then no one can sue upon it and obtain its face value, unless he has taken it without knowledge of previous defects and in good faith.

Finally, note that where X sells goods to Y a debt comes into being when the contract is made, so that when X decides to pay Y by cheque/bill the cheque is based on a previous or past debt or liability and is therefore for past consideration, which according to the basic elements of the law of contract, is not good consideration.

Does this mean that X and Y have not a simple contract, but all there is between them is a gratuitous promise? Do they need to 'seal' the contract? Section 27(1)(b) of the Bills of Exchange Act 1822 answers these questions by providing that a form of past considerations is enough.

Section 27(1)(a) furthermore provides that any consideration sufficient to support a simple contract will support a bill of exchange. This is the section under the Act (s.27) that most text books refer to and classify as 'holder for value'. This is simply because what is required for a person to be termed as a holder for value is consideration, in the context of the Act.

Holder in due course

Section 29(1) provides that a holder in due course is a holder who has taken a cheque, complete and regular on the face of it, under the following conditions:

1 that he became the holder of it before it was overdue and

without notice that it had been previously dishonoured if such was the fact;

2 that he took the cheque in good faith and for value; and

3 that at the time that the cheque was negotiated to him he had no notice of any defect in the title of the person who negotiated it to him.

Therefore, it could be said that the Act requires a person to have fulfilled the following six requirements, in order to become a holder in due course:

1 that the bill will be complete and regular on the face of it; and

2 that he took it before it was overdue; and

3 in good faith; and

4 for value; and

5 without notice of any defect in title of the person who indorsed it over to him; and

6 without notice of any previous dishonour of the bill.

If a cheque drawn in favour of X has been negotiated by X to Y as a result of fraud or misrepresentation or duress or undue influence on Y's part or for an illegal consideration, there is a 'defect' on the bill. Suppose that Y negotiates it for value to Z. Ordinarily, Z will be a holder for value, but because there is a 'defect' on the cheque Z can only take it free from the defect in the title of Y and successfully sue on it if he is a holder in due course, which means amongst other things that he (Z) took it without notice of any defect in the title of Y.

However, thanks to section 29, if it is established that Z is a holder in due course (that is, show that the holder for value of the bill is either a holder in due course as defined under section 29(1), or a person who has taken the bill through a holder in due course), then the defect is said to be 'cured' and Z can sue the various parties to the cheque for its full face value.

In other words, it could be said that when a bill is negotiated to a holder in due course, he obtains a good title to it, notwithstanding any defect in the title of his transferor or previous holders.

'Notice' means actual, though not formal notice, that is to say, either knowledge of the facts, or a suspicion of something wrong, combined with a wilful disregard of the means of knowledge. Therefore, an original payee of a bill is not a holder in due course, as the bill has not been negotiated to him; *R.E. Jones Ltd* v. *Waring & Gillow Ltd* (1926).

Defective title

When the person who negotiates the bill has obtained the bill by fraud, duress, or force and fear, or other unlawful means, or an illegal consideration, or when he negotiates it in breach of faith, or under such circumstances as amount to a fraud.

'A holder in due course is a holder'

This implies that no-one can be holder in due course after forgery of an essential signature.

'Bill, complete and regular on the face of it'

If the bill is not complete, then no-one who takes it can be a holder in due course. Thus, a person who takes an instrument, even though he may have authority to complete it, cannot be a holder in due course. If the bill is not regular on the face of it then again no-one can be a holder in due course. For example, a bill marked 'Not Negotiable' or 'Not Transferable' is not regular on the face of it although quite valid.

'Before it was overdue'

If a bill is due and payable on 31st October then, on and after 1st November it is overdue and anyone taking the bill then cannot be a holder in due course though he may be a holder for value.

'Without notice that it had previously been dishonoured if such was the fact'

Although this provision of the Act might appear at first unnecessary, since if a bill had been dishonoured it would be overdue, note that this is not always true. If, for example, a bill is drawn on 1st October payable three months after date it is due on 1st January. Yet a holder might present it for acceptance on 15th October and find acceptance refused by the drawee. This would be dishonour of the bill by non-acceptance, yet the bill would still be current and not overdue. A person taking such bill with the knowledge that it has already been dishonoured in this way cannot be a holder in due course.

Liability of acceptor

The acceptor of a bill, by accepting it, undertakes that:

1 He will pay it according to the tenor of his acceptance.
2 He is precluded from denying to a holder in due course:
  (a) the existence of the drawer, the genuineness of his signature, and his capacity and authority to draw the bill;
  (b) in the case of a bill payable to drawer's order, the then capacity of the drawer to indorse, but not the genuineness of validity of his indorsement;
  (c) in the case of a bill payable to the order of a third person, the existence of the payee and his then capacity to indorse, but not the genuineness or validity of his indorsement.

Subsection (2)(b) means that the acceptor cannot refuse payment to a holder in due course on the excuse that the drawer does not exist, or the drawer's signature is a forgery, or the drawer had no capacity or authority to draw the bill.

Liability of the drawer

The drawer is responsible for payment should the bill be dishonoured by the drawee (or acceptor). Before the bill is accepted he is primarily liable for payment; after acceptance, the acceptor takes on the primary liability and the drawer becomes second in the order of liability or, in other words, becomes surety for the acceptor. If the drawer is called upon by a holder in due course to pay the bill, he cannot escape liability merely because the payee does not exist or has no capacity to indorse.

Liability of the indorser

The indorser is responsible to all who became parties subsequent to himself and also to the holder. He agrees to pay the bill, should the drawee (or acceptor) dishonour it. Furthermore, his (indorser's) indorsement acts as a guarantee to any subsequent holder in due course that all the indorsements prior to his own are genuine. Where the drawer's signature is forged the possessor of the bill has the rights of a holder in due course against all indorsers.

In the case of a forged indorsement the possessor of the bill has the rights of a holder in due course, though no actual title to the bill, against all parties who indorsed subsequent to the forgery.

All this could be illustrated by the following example. A draws a bill payable to B. B transfers it to C by indorsement. The bill is stolen from C by Z. Z forges C's signature to a special indorsement and transfers the bill to D. By further indorsements the bill passes to E and thence to F. Under section 24, F has no title to the bill since he is not a holder, the bill being payable to C. A and B will not recognize anyone else but C as having any right to the bill. C, in his turn, can compel F to restore the bill to him or pay him its equivalent. F, consequently, would be in a very poor position but for this section which says that those who indorsed the bill after the forgery (D and E) guarantee the genuineness of all indorsements prior to their own, which includes the forgery purporting to be C's indorsement. In this case they cannot escape their liability that they undertake in subsection (2)(a). Thus, F can recover from E and E from D. D, the victim of the forgery, will bear the loss unless he can recover from Z, the forger.

Forgery

Where a signature to a bill is forged or placed on the bill without the authority of the person whose signature it purports to be, such signature is wholly inoperative and no right can be acquired thereunder. Therefore a forged indorsement on an order bill would give no title to a transferee; he is not a holder in due course, even though he took the bill for value and with no knowledge of the forgery, as the bill has not been negotiated to him, negotiation requiring indorsement (which means a **valid** indorsement) and delivery.

The following example will clarify the issue of the effects of a forged or unauthorized indorsement. A cheque is drawn by X in favour of C and indorsed by C to D. It is then stolen from D by a thief who forges D's indorsement and negotiates the cheque to E who indorses it to F, who indorses it to G. G has no knowledge of the forgery and in all respects complies with the definition of a holder in due course (s.29). G has no title to the cheque because it rests on a forgery. He (G) cannot sue D or C and he (G) has rights against E or F by virtue of section 55(2) which provides that an indorser gives a 'guarantee' to the transferee with regard to the validity of a cheque. This means that when E indorsed the cheque to F he impliedly guaranteed that it was a valid cheque and the signatures of the drawer and previous indorsers were valid signatures. F made a guarantee to the same effect when he indorsed the cheque to G.

Claused bills

Sometimes bills are 'claused' with phrases which require the drawee to pay more than the actual value of the bill. The reasons why these 'claused' bills were introduced are:

1 In order to throw the burden of any exchange risk on to the foreign drawee, so that the UK drawer received the full sterling amount due.

2 To enable the drawer to provide for the payment of interest by the drawee, in order to compensate the drawer for the time taken for the drawee's payment to reach him.

3 A clause was often helpful in permitting the banker to act as an arbiter in deciding what rate of exchange to use when the drawee paid in local currency.

An 'exchange clause' may be defined as a clause included in the wording of a bill which fixes the method of arriving at the rate of exchange to be used when the drawee pays the bill.

Inland and foreign bills

An inland bill is a bill which is or on the face of it purports to be (i) both drawn and payable within the British Islands, or (ii) drawn within the British Islands upon some person resident therein.

Any other bill is a foreign bill. British Islands are defined in the Act as any part of the UK of Great Britain and Northern Ireland, the Islands of Man, Guernsey, Jersey, Alderney, and Sark, and the islands adjacent to any of them being part of the dominions of the Queen.

Documentary bills

Where a bill has attached to it the bill of lading, invoice, and policy of insurance relating to the goods against which it is drawn, so that they are available in case the bill is not honoured, it is termed a Documentary Bill.

The bill of lading constitutes the title to the goods, and, to enable the drawee/buyer to obtain the goods which he has purchased, arrangements are made whereby the documents are handed to him against either his acceptance or his payment of the bill, the method adopted depending on his credit and standing. The bill is generally marked accordingly, that is, 'Documents to be surrendered on Acceptance', known as a 'D/A' bill, or 'Documents to be surrendered on Payment', known as a 'D/P' bill, as the case may be. The documents are attached to the bill in the first place by the drawer/seller, when he has shipped the relative goods. A banker who purchases or discounts the bill retains the documents as security, and, through his correspondents abroad, collects the bill when due.

In simple words, the seller would normally arrange for the presentation of the documents by a bank which would be under instructions not to part with the documents except against payment or acceptance. It would be this collecting bank which presents the documents to the buyer and which would receive payment, to be remitted to the seller.

When bills of exchange are to be passed to a bank for collection, as described above, the process is usually controlled by the 1978 Uniform Rules for Collections, published by the International Chamber of Commerce.

The term 'collections' refers to the handling by banks of documents (financial documents or commercial documents, or both) in order to obtain payment or acceptance, or to deliver documents against payment or acceptance.

The term 'documents' is applied to two types of remittances: 'clean' remittances; and 'documentary' remittances.

A clean remittance is simply a bill of exchange or similar document which is not supported by any other document. The holder of this bill passes it to the bank for collection in the normal course of events as the due date approaches, and the bank has only this simple duty to perform.

With 'documentary' bills there are other duties involved, such as handing over the documents against payment or acceptance.

The Uniform Customs and Practice for Documentary Credits (UCP)

This is a standardized code of practice formulated by the International Chamber of Commerce regarding the processing of documentary credits. These Rules regulate the implementation and operation of the documentary credit, and are published by the International Chamber of Commerce (ICC). The 1983 edition of the Rules have been revised by the ICC and a new set were published in January 1994. The 1983 rules are divided into six sections lettered A-F, dealing with the operations of the credit. Thus, for example section A deals with the general provisions and definitions. The following is a brief account of those sections:

Section	Reference
A	General provisions and definitions
B	Form and notification of credits
C	Liabilities and responsibilities
D1	Transport documents
D2	Insurance documents
D3	Commercial invoice
D4	Other documents
E	Miscellaneous provisions
F	Transfer

An important point to remember is that these rules do not apply to a credit unless they are expressly incorporated therein. The parties to a documentary credit arrangement are:

1 The applicant for the credit; this is usually the buyer under the contract of sale. The instructions given by the buyer to his bank should reflect the contract of sale. Such instructions must be strictly complied with by the bank (Art.15 of 1983 UCP).
2 The beneficiary; under a documentary credit, this is the seller.
3 The issuing bank; this is the buyer's bank, that is the bank which receives instructions by the buyer. As soon as this bank receives these instructions, it will issue notice to the seller as to the opening of the credit and its terms. Thus, it is referred to as the issuing bank.
4 The correspondent bank; this may play the role of either (a) the adviser, that is, merely to advise the beneficiary of the terms of the credit, or (b) the confirmer, by giving the beneficiary an undertaking/confirmation that it will make payment if the correct documents are tendered to it.

The UCP 500

As mentioned above, the new version of the ICC's Uniform Custom and Practices for Documentary Credits came into effect from 1st January 1994. The most important changes in the new version may be summarized as follows:

1 Under the Transport section of UCP 500 seaway bills are now covered – such a document was not specifically covered by the 1984 version.
2 The new edition also allows transhipment – the absence of a specific clause in a credit frequently leads to unnecessary rejection of documents.
3 Reasonable time for the acceptance of documents has been set to seven banking days.
4 The word 'negotiation' is defined in UCP 500 so that exporters can refer to the definition in order to find out what it actually means.
5 Under the new version a bank can accept an invoice which is for less than the full amount of the credit, provided that (a) the goods have been shipped and (b) the difference does not exceed five per cent of the original amount.

Figure 17.1: Differences between Cheques and Bills of Exchange

CHEQUES	BILLS OF EXCHANGE
A cheque must always be drawn on a banker and always be payable on demand.	A bill may be drawn on anyone and may be payable on demand or at a fixed or determinable time.
A cheque is never accepted. Therefore the drawee banker is never liable to the holder of a cheque. His liability is to his customer, the drawer, and to him only.	A bill of exchange payable other than on demand is accepted and after acceptance the acceptor is primarily liable to the holder.

CHEQUES

The drawer is not discharged on a cheque for six years unless, through delay in presentation, the position of the drawer has been injured by the failure of a banker who had sufficient funds of the drawer in his hands. The holder of the cheque must then prove in the winding up of the bank in a liquidation.

When a cheque is returned for any reason, no notice of dishonour is necessary. Want of assets is sufficient in itself as regards the drawer, and mere return of the cheque is in point of form deemed to be sufficient notice of dishonour as regards the holder, but in practice an answer is always written on the cheque.

A banker who pays a cheque to order bearing a forged, unauthorized or irregular indorsement or lacking an essential indorsement is not liable to the true owner or to his customer, if he pays in good faith and in the ordinary course of business.

Cheques may be crossed in several ways.

Drawee's authority to pay is void by death, notice to stop, or bankruptcy.

BILLS OF EXCHANGE

A bill must be duly presented for payment or the drawer will be discharged.

Upon dishonour for non-acceptance or non-payment of a bill, notice must be given in accordance with the provisions of the Bills of Exchange Act.

Bankers obtain no protection if they pay a bill bearing a forged indorsement.

Bills cannot be crossed.

Drawee's authority to pay cannot be countermanded if the bill has been negotiated.

CHEQUES

Cheques are drawn on special forms supplied by a banker.

BILLS OF EXCHANGE

No special form is used.

Figure 17.2: Bills of Exchange

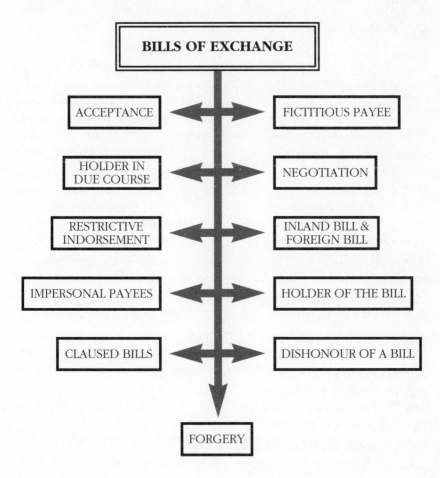

Cheques

After looking at bills of exchange, we continue with a brief examination of cheques and the basic duties of bankers and customers.

The banker must obey his customer's mandate

A bank has no right to debit a customer's account for the amount of a cheque on which the customer's signature has been forged because the bank then has no mandate from the customer to pay. However, the customer may be estopped in some cases from denying the validity of his signature and in these circumstances the bank may debit his account even on the basis of a cheque on which the customer's signature was forged.

Thus in *Greenwood* v. *Martins Bank Ltd* (1933), X opened an account (joint) with bank Z, in the names of X and Y, his wife. Cheques drawn on this account were to bear the signatures of them both, that is, X and Y. Later on X opened a further account with bank Z in his own name, that is, X, though his wife kept the pass books and cheque books in respect of both accounts. A few months later, X asked his wife to give him a cheque, saying he wanted to draw £20 from his own account. His wife then told him that there was no money in the bank, and that she had used it to help her sister who was involved in legal proceedings over property. He (X) asked her (Y) who had forged his signature but she would not say. However, she did ask him not to inform the bank of the forgeries until her sister's case was over. X complied with this request for the next 10 months. Then he (X) discovered that there were no legal proceedings instituted by his wife's sister and that his wife had been deceiving him. He (X) told his wife that he intended to go to the bank (Z) and reveal her forgeries, but before he actually made the visit to the bank she (Y) shot herself. X claimed £410 from the bank (Z) on the grounds that this sum had been paid out of his own account and the joint account by means of forged cheques. The bank (Z) pleaded ratification, adoption or estoppel.

It was held that there could be no ratification or adoption in this sort of case, but the essential elements of estoppel were present. X's failure to inform the bank (Z) was a representation that the cheques were good.

Furthermore, note that if a bank pays a cheque on which the signature of its customer as drawer has been forged the bank can sue the person to whom payment was made for restitution of the amount paid out, for the money with which payment was made was the property of the bank.

It should also be noted that the bank has no right to debit a customer's account where the mandate requires two signatures and only one signature in fact has been used; *Ligget (Liverpool) Ltd* v. *Barclays Bank* (1928).

Finally, note that where one joint account-holder, say A, forges the signature of the other, say B, the bank in effect agrees with both, that is, A and B, jointly that:

1 it would honour cheques signed by them both; and
2 with A separately that it would not honour cheques unless signed by him; and
3 with B separately that it would not honour cheques unless signed by him.

This in effect means that where the bank honours a cheque on which B has forged A's signature, A should be able to sue the bank because it is in breach of the separate agreement with him. Therefore, joint account-holders have separate actions against the bank; *Jackson* v. *White and Midland Bank* (1967); *Catlin* v. *Cyprus Finance Corporation (London) Ltd, The Times*, 27th October, 1982.

A banker must honour his customer's cheques

The general rule is that a bank is bound to honour its customer's cheques to the extent that the customer is in credit or to the extent of any agreed overdraft.

If a cheque is 'referred to drawer' although the customer is in funds or has an agreed overdraft the matter is treated as follows:

1 If the customer is in business or practice as a profession it is assumed that his credit-worthiness has been affected and damages will be awarded without proof of actual loss; *Davidson* v. *Barclays Bank Ltd* (1940).
2 Where the customer is not in trade or practising a profession damage to credit is not assumed and nominal damages will

be awarded unless a particular loss is proved as where, for example, the customer can show that a particular creditor has refused to do business with him again; *Gibbons* v. *Westminster Bank Ltd* (1939).

The bank's duty to honour cheques ceases on the customer cancelling payment. In this connection it should be noted that notice to the bank must be actual, not constructive; *Curtice* v. *London, City & Midland Bank Ltd* (1908).

A bank which overlooks its customer's instructions to stop payment of a cheque and consequently pays the cheque when it has been presented, can recover the money from the payee because it has been paid under a mistake of fact; *Barclays Bank* v. *W.J. Simms Son and Cooke (Southern)* (1979).

Banker's duty to observe secrecy

A bank must not disclose the financial affairs of a customer. This is based on an implied term in the contract between the banker and his customer, and continues even after the account is closed; *Tournier* v. *National Provincial and Union Bank of England* (1924).

However, there are four exceptions:

1 *Where disclosure is required by law.* For example, under the Taxes Management Act 1970, a bank must report to the Revenue authorities any case where interest of £25 or more is paid per year. In practice, only accounts showing £150 per annum interest or more are sent automatically, though the Revenue may request a statement to be made in respect of interest in excess of £25 per annum or more.
2 *Where there is a public duty to disclose.* As where a banker can see that a customer is trading with the enemy in time of war, or where information is given to the police to protect the public against crime.
3 *Where disclosure is required in the interest of the bank.* As where the bank is suing to recover an overdraft, since the amount of the overdraft is stated on the face of the writ.

4 *Where the customer gives permission.* As where a corporate customer of the bank gives the bank permission to disclose the state of its account to the company's auditors.

Banker's duty to collect cheques paid in by a customer

A bank is under a duty to collect for its customer's account cheques paid in by the customer. The bank then acts as a collecting bank and has certain protections if its customer has a defective title to the cheque (see page 205, Uniform Rules for Collections 1978).

Miscellaneous Points on Cheques

Where a cheque contains an addition of the words 'and Co.' or any abbreviation thereof (for example 'A/C Payee only', 'Not negotiable', 'Barclays Bank plc') between two parallel transverse lines, the cheque is said to be **crossed** generally.

Such a cheque will only be payable by the bank on which it is drawn through another bank, and not over the counter. It is therefore a hindrance for someone who obtains the cheque wrongly because he could only obtain payment through a bank and the loss may be discovered meanwhile and the cheque stopped. In addition, collection through a bank may help trace a thief. The following is a brief explanation of the usual expressions used today, in crossing cheques.

If the words used are 'Not negotiable' then no other person apart from the previous holder can claim to have a better title. Even where a person satisfies the definition of a holder in due course such person will not take the cheque free from defects.

The crossing 'A/C Payee' is an instruction to the collecting banker, addressed to him by a person who has no contract with him, and it would be negligence in a banker if he collected the money for some other account, for a person with no title. The crossing does not prevent the cheque from being transferred or indeed from being negotiable; *National Bank* v. *Silke* (1891). If a cheque is issued uncrossed a holder can cross it generally or specially, and if it is issued crossed generally a holder may turn the crossing into a special crossing.

The safest crossing is a combination of 'Not negotiable' and 'A/C Payee only'. The 'Not negotiable' crossing takes the cheque out of the category of negotiable instruments. The 'A/C Payee' crossing warns the collecting banker that if he collects the cheque for someone other than the payee who is not entitled to it, the banker may be liable to damages to the true owner.

Figure 17.3: Banker's duties

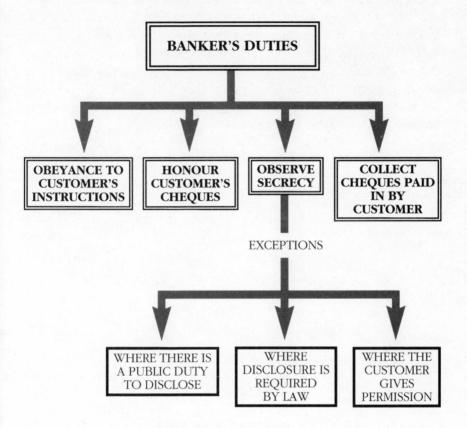

Questions for Discussion

1 What is a bill of exchange?
2 Under the definition provided by section 3(1) of the Bills of Exchange Act 1882, a bill of exchange is payable at a 'determinable future time'. Explain the meaning of this expression.
3 What is a holder in due course, under the Bills of Exchange Act 1882?
4 What is a documentary bill?
5 Briefly state the basic duties of a banker towards his/her customers.
6 In a cheque, what is the effect of a crossing 'A/C Payee'?

18

Letters of Credit

A Documentary Letter of Credit is an instrument by which a bank undertakes to pay the seller (exporter) for goods providing the conditions laid down in the credit are complied with. Whilst ensuring that the exporter receives payment for the goods it also gives the buyer (importer) the confirmation that he or she will not have to part with money until presented with documents evidencing that the stipulated conditions have been fulfilled. The credit specifies when payment is to be made. Usually this is either when the documents are presented to the paying bank or at some future date, usually within 180 days of receipt of the documents by the paying bank. Such a method of payment is common in export sales contracts. Overall it is a letter issued by a bank authorizing credit to a correspondent.

The buyer's (importer's) bank (issuing bank) undertakes, or authorizes its correspondent bank in the seller's (exporter's) country, to pay the seller (exporter) a sum of money (normally the invoice price of the goods) against presentation of shipping documents which are independent of the sales contract. It is a mandatory contract and completely independent of the sales contract. It is concerned only with documents and not the goods to which the documents refer.

Types of Documentary Credit

The usual form of these credits is the '**irrevocable**' credit, which means that it cannot be cancelled or amended without the agreement of the beneficiary (the seller/exporter) and all other parties. Such a credit, opened by a reputable bank in a 'sound' country, means that the exporter/seller can rely on payment being made as soon as the goods have been shipped and the documents called for in accordance with the terms of the credit have been produced.

The security provided by an irrevocable credit may be further enhanced if the bank in the exporter's/seller's country (advising bank) is requested by the buyers's/importer's bank (issuing bank) to add its '**confirmation**'. The exporter/seller then has a '**confirmed irrevocable credit**' and need look no further than the local bank for payment.

Besides the basic irrevocable credit (confirmed or not), there are **revocable** credits which, as the name implies, can be cancelled or amended at any time without notice to the beneficiary. As Article 9(a) of the UCP 1983 states:

> A revocable credit may be amended or cancelled by the issuing bank at any moment and without prior notice to the beneficiary.

These do not constitute a legally binding undertaking by the banks concerned, and the value of such credits as security for payment is plainly doubtful. They are used, however, for parent and subsidiary companies, where a continuing series of shipments is concerned or as an indication of good intent.

It should be noted that under Article 7(a) of the UCP 1983, all credits should clearly indicate whether they are revocable or irrevocable. Furthermore, Article 7(c) provides that in the absence of a clear indication, a credit will be deemed to be revocable. Finally, a credit may be irrevocable without being confirmed, but a confirmed credit is always irrevocable.

Another type of credit is the **transferable** one, which is usually found when the seller (the first beneficiary) is not the manufacturer/original supplier of the goods, so that in effect the sale is performed by someone other than the seller. The credit is established in favour of the seller (prime beneficiary), and authorizes the advising bank, that is, the bank in the seller's/ exporter's country, to accept instructions from the prime beneficiary to make the credit available, to one or more parties (second beneficiaries). The credit is then advised to the second beneficiary in the terms and conditions of the original, except that the amount and unit price are reduced and the shipment and expiry dates shortened.

In simple words, when the credit is transferred, a second beneficiary steps into the shoes of the original first beneficiary, and is entitled and bound to perform the obligations of the first beneficiary, but by using his or her own shipping documents. A documentary credit can be transferable only if it is expressly designated as such by the issuing bank; Article 54(b).

Unfortunately, the UCP give no guidance as to the legal effect of the transfer of a letter of credit. However, there appear to be two schools of thought with regard to this transfer: the transfer operates as an assignment of the documentary credit; or the transfer operates as a contract of novation, that is, it creates a 'new' contract.

As this is still a debatable issue, and no clear legal precedent exists, the merits of the above two possible views will not be dealt with in this book.

Companies with surplus liquidity in one currency may wish to obtain funds in another currency, for investment or expansion, by employing their own surplus without conversion or incurring increased interest costs by borrowing unmatched funds. This may be arranged by means of a parallel, or **back to back**, loan or credit, a form of financing whereby money borrowed in one country or currency is covered by the lending of an equivalent amount in another. Back to back credits arise in circumstances similar to those of the transferable credit and particularly where the supplier as well as the buyer is overseas.

Revolving credits arise where there are shipments in a series at intervals and the parties wish the programme to proceed without interruption. Accordingly a credit is established for a certain sum and quantity of goods with a provision that, when a shipment has been made and documents presented and paid, the credit automatically becomes available as the documents are presented for subsequent payment to the exporter/seller for the goods.

Another type of letter of credit is what is known as '**red clause**' credit. This allows the seller/beneficiary to obtain an advance on the price before the goods are shipped, which is conditional upon the presentation of documents such as a warehouse receipt; *Bank Melli Iran* v. *Barclays Bank* (1951). Consequently, the buyer takes a risk in that he would be liable to reimburse the issuing bank even if the seller disappears with the amount advanced.

A letter of credit will set out in detail a description of the goods, price per unit and packing, name and address of the beneficiary, the voyage, that is port of shipment and port of destination, whether the price is FOB, C & F or CIF, and whether part shipments and transhipment are allowed. In some cases, the ship will be nominated. Details of insurance, if CIF, and the risks to be covered will also be shown. The credit will specify a latest date for shipment and an expiry date which is the latest date for presentation of documents. The basic documents which are usually called for are:

Invoice

Under Article 41(a) of UCP 1983, this must be made out in the name of the applicant for the credit/buyer. The amount must not exceed the credit amount. If terms such as 'about' or 'circa' are used, a tolerance of ten per cent is allowed; Article 43. The description of the goods on the invoice and the packing must be exact and agree with the credit. An essential part of the description is the marks and numbers on the packages; Article 41(c).

Transport document

This is the document 'indicating loading on board or dispatch or taking into charge'; Article 25 of the UCP 1983. Usually, this document would be a bill of lading, without which the buyer will not be able to obtain delivery from the shipping company. If the buyer has specifically requested the seller to tender a bill of lading, then Article 26 of the UCP 1983 would be relevant. If that is the case, then the credit will call for a full set; bills of lading are usually issued in a set of three. They must be 'clean', that is, bearing no superimposed clauses derogatory to the condition of the goods such 'inadequate packing', 'used drums', 'on deck', and so on. Unless the credit has specifically permitted the circumstances contained in the clause, the negotiating bank will call for an indemnity. The bills of lading must show the goods to be 'on board', as 'received for shipment' bills of lading are not generally acceptable under Article 26.

However, if the buyer has not specifically requested the seller to tender a bill of lading, then any other transport document fulfilling the requirements of Article 25, for example 'received for shipment' bill of lading, will be adequate. Article 25(a) requires that banks will accept a transport document if it:

1 appears on its face to have been issued by a named carrier or the agent; and
2 indicates dispatch or taking into charge of goods as the case may be; and
3 consists of the full set of originals issued to the consignor, if issued in more than one original; and
4 meets all other stipulations of the credit.

Insurance certificate

The document must be as stated in the credit and issued by an insurance company or its agent. Cover notes issued by brokers are not acceptable; Article 35. The details on the policy must match those on the bills of lading/transport document. It must also be in the same currency as the credit and endorsed in blank. The amount covered should be at least the invoice amount.

Short-Circuiting of Letter of Credit

Where the parties to the contract of sale have arranged for payment by a letter of credit, they must abide by such agreement and cannot short-circuit the credit by making direct claims connected with the payment of the price against each other. Thus, if there is an agreement to make payment under a documentary credit, then the seller does not have the right to present the documents to the buyer direct; *Soproma* v. *Marine & Animal By-Products Corp.* (1966).

Sometimes however, the short-circuiting of the letter of credit arrangement may be admissible. For example, if the bank whom the parties have interposed as intermediary becomes insolvent, the seller normally can claim the price from the buyer directly, making a direct tender of documents to the latter. The implied condition is discharged by the insolvency of the intermediary.

Autonomy of the Letter of Credit

The contract of international sale is independent of the functions/ workings of a letter of credit, and consequently it is said that as the issuing and advising banks are not involved in the commercial transaction of the sale, a letter of credit is autonomous; Article 3 of the UCP 1983. It follows, that if the bank makes payment against conforming documents then it is entitled to be reimbursed by the credit applicant/buyer; Article 16(a).

Finally, it must be noted that although there is no reference in the UCP to the existence of any exception to the principle of the autonomy of credit, an exception arises in the case of fraud under common law; *United City Merchants (Investments) Ltd* v. *Royal Bank of Canada* (1983).

Fraud Affecting Letters of Credit

Two possibilities exist in respect of fraud:

1 Where it is clearly established to the satisfaction of the bank

that a fraud has occurred, but there is no evidence before the bank which shows that the beneficiary (the seller) knew of the fraud, then the bank must pay!

Thus, in *United City Merchants (Investments) Ltd* v. *Royal Bank of Canada* (1983) the bills of lading were antedated, that is, they showed as date of shipment December 15, 1976, which was the latest date of shipment required by the credit, but the goods were, in fact, loaded a day later, which was out of time. The Royal Bank of Canada, which had confirmed the credit, knew of this fraud because in the first tender of the bills of lading the date was blanked out and the date of December 15, 1976 was superimposed, but later, before the expiry of the credit, a second tender of unamended bills of lading was made which showed the date of December 15, 1976. The documents were thus correct on their face. The false date was inserted by an employee of the loading brokers and the sellers knew nothing about it. It was held (by the House of Lords) that the bank was obliged to pay, in spite of its knowledge of the fraud, since not only the bank and the buyers, but also the sellers were deceived by the fraud of the third party.

2 Where the bank has positive proof that a fraud has been committed and that the beneficiary (the seller) knew of this fraud, then the bank must not honour its obligation under the credit. Such a case may arise, for example, where the beneficiary (seller) tenders documents which, to his or her knowledge, are false or if somebody else does so with the seller's knowledge or connivance.

The Doctrine of Strict Compliance

As it is known, in a commercial transaction the buyer's bank operates the documentary credit as the buyer's agent. If the bank exceeds its principal's (that is, the buyer's) instructions, then according to the law of agency, it would have acted without authority; consequently the loss would fall on the bank in question. The doctrine of strict compliance dictates that a bank will refuse documents tendered by a seller, if such documents are not strictly compliant to the instructions. *Equitable Trust Co. of New York* v. *Dawson Partners Ltd.*

If the documents are correct and the bank delays in making payment against them, it may find itself liable in damages to the seller; *Ozalid Group* v. *African Continental Bank* (1979).

Strictly speaking, the law would justify a bank in rejecting documents evidencing a short shipment of 0.06 per cent, as not complying with the terms of the credit; *Soproma* v. *Marine & Animal By-Products Corporation* (1966). However, UCP 1983 allows for some margin of error – a tolerance of five per cent or less would be permitted if the credit does not stipulate otherwise; and if the words 'about' or 'circa' are used in connection with the quantity the permitted tolerance would be ten per cent (Article 43(a)).

Obviously the above would not be applicable in a case where the quantity is stipulated as a number of packing units or individual items; it would be preposterous to permit this in, for example, container transport.

Besides stating an expiry date for presentation of documents, credits should also stipulate a specified period of time after the issuing of the bills of lading within which the documents must be presented for payment. If such period is not stipulated in the credit, banks will refuse documents presented to them later than 21 days after the issuance of the bills of lading.

Other Methods of Payment

Sight Payment

This type of credit is usually used when the seller does not allow any period of credit to the buyer. It is a credit which provides for payment of a sight bill of exchange drawn on the issuing bank, or some other bank when presented with the specified documents.

Factoring

Factoring is an American idea which was introduced to the UK in the 1970s. The underlying function of the factoring service is the maintenance of the supplier's sales ledger. It provides an administration service based on the copy invoices received from the supplier. It does not make sales or even raise invoices at the time of delivery of the goods. These functions are performed by the supplier against the background of the factor's credit approval. The factoring of export sales provides a comprehensive package of export services to short term exporters. Generally speaking, factoring implies a company which administers the sales ledger and collects payments on behalf of an exporter/ seller once the goods have been shipped.

Nowadays, it would appear that more and more businesses use factoring. This seems to be evident by the increase in the work of the Association of British Factors and Discounters (ABFD); between 1991–92 there was a 15 per cent growth in factoring and invoice discounting in the UK.

Forfaiting

This is a method of international trade finance involving the discounting of bank-guaranteed overseas trade bills or notes. It provides no recourse to the exporter/seller who surrenders or relinquishes his or her rights in return for cash payment from the forfaiter. In such circumstances the seller/exporter agrees to surrender rights to claims for payment on goods or services which have been delivered to the buyer/importer. Any type of trade debt can be forfaited, that is, surrendered for cash, but the most common is trade payee, bills of exchange accepted by the buyer/importer or promissory notes from the buyer/importer. A forfaiter can provide finance for any type and duration of trade transaction but usually credit is provided for the export of capital goods which require finance for periods of between three and seven years.

Open account scheme

Under this scheme, the exporter/seller issues a promissory note to the bank for the invoice value of the goods exported/sold and falling due for payment in any one month. The bank advances the face value of the promissory note at once and the note must be paid at maturity, whether or not the proceeds of the invoice have been received.

In other words, an open account is an agreement whereby the seller/exporter agrees to dispatch the goods to the buyer/importer on the understanding that the goods will be paid for after receipt, usually on a monthly basis.

This method of arranging payment carries, however, considerable risk since the buyer/importer may withhold or delay payment, or the transfer of funds might be delayed as a result of exchange control regulations in the buyer's country.

There are various ways in which the buyer/importer can send money to the seller under open account and the seller/exporter may wish to stipulate the method to be used, for example banker's draft or buyer's cheque. Open account business is transacted on credit terms where no security in the form of bills of exchange or promissory notes is obtained from the buyer/importer. This is a most popular method of payment within the EEC and the most common method of payment is by cheque, banker's draft, and telegraphic transfer.

Figure 18.1: Letters of credit

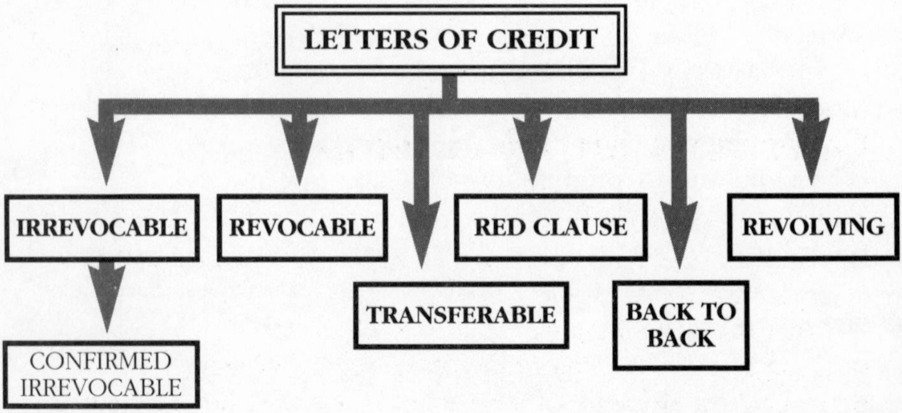

Figure 18.2: Other methods of payment

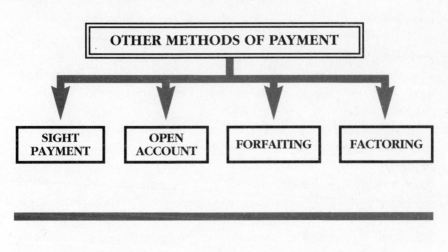

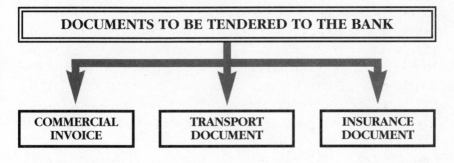

Questions for Discussion

1 What is a *revolving credit*?
2 What are the basic documents which are usually called for under a letter of credit?
3 What is 'short-circuiting' of a letter of credit?
4 What is meant by autonomy of the letter of credit?
5 Explain the doctrine of strict compliance in letters of credit.

Part 6

Export Insurance

19

Marine Insurance

Since the origins of marine insurance can be traced to the mercantile practices in London during the 16th century, it is not surprising that the development of marine insurance as a business took place in London so that, by the middle of the 17th century many financiers were specializing in the underwriting of marine adventures. Nevertheless, each underwriter acted strictly on his own, using his personal fortune and resources to back the outcome of the adventures he chose to underwrite. These underwriters eventually formed the community which founded Lloyd's and many of their traditional practices exist today. The London market contains many insurance companies but it was much later that the Company market as we know it came into existence and adopted many of the usages and customs of Lloyd's.

Lloyd's

The 17th century underwriter was a person of sound financial reputation. His personal fortune had to be adequate to meet his commitments and his integrity had to be beyond reproach. Consequently, there was little documentation involved in underwriting transactions. Details of the cover required were written on a slip of paper and the underwriter simply entered the amount he was prepared to underwrite and initialled it.

At first, transactions would be negotiated in the private residence of the underwriter but, as business grew, this method became inconvenient and, following the practice of the day, the underwriter would spend his time in one or other of the many coffee houses which were becoming popular as meeting places in London in the 17th century.

Edward Lloyd owned such a coffee house which was situated in Tower Street close to the Pool of London. At the time the Pool, that part of the Thames just below London Bridge, was the part of the river where all ships visiting London moored to discharge and load cargoes. Due to its proximity to the river and the world of shipping, the coffee house became a favourite meeting place for underwriters and their associates, and was soon well known as the centre for marine insurance. Edward Lloyd was quick to realise the advantage of a reputation which would attract custom and so went out of his way to encourage association of underwriters on his premises. He provided his patrons with writing materials and set up a rostrum in one corner of the coffee house. From this rostrum a boy, called the Kidney, would make announcements of importance to the customers. To increase the facilities he had to offer, Lloyd published a news sheet in 1696 in which he included details of shipping movements and other matters of interest.

Lloyd's of London is an association of insurers specializing in the insurance of marine and similar risks. The Corporation of Lloyd's of today is an organization/institution which provides facilities to the underwriters to carry out their insurance business. The building of Lloyd's contains an underwriting room with a surrounding gallery floor. Marine, motor and aviation business is conducted on the ground floor while other non-marine business is mostly transacted on the gallery floor.

It is important to note that the Corporation of Lloyd's does not underwrite insurance contracts but merely provides facilities for its members to conduct their own business. Following the traditions of Lloyd's each underwriting member is responsible up to his or her full personal fortune to meet his or her commitments.

The London Company Market

The first major steps towards establishing a Company market took place in 1720 when, following a campaign launched in 1717 by men with marine interests and a discontent for Lloyd's system, two Companies 'The London Assurance' and 'The Royal Exchange' were incorporated by Royal Charter and for the next 100 years or so these two Corporations held a monopoly of the London Company market in marine insurance.

The insurance company of today is a Joint Stock Company with a liability limited to its assets as declared to the Department of Trade and Industry. It must be remembered that the Lloyd's Underwriter has no such limit of liability.

The Company may be part of a group of Companies or it may stand by itself. The majority of Companies each have a board of directors which appoints an underwriter to accept business on behalf of the Company.

The title 'underwriter' is given out of courtesy for the Company Underwriter does not, in fact, have any personal liability for the risks he writes. He is a salaried employee of the Company, and it is the Company which is liable for the commitments undertaken by the Underwriter.

Apart from these differences, the Company and Lloyd's Markets work very well together using similar systems. Several Companies have underwriting rooms in Lloyd's building and others are situated in the same area of London, thus providing a compact market for the broker on his daily rounds.

The Insurance Broker

A broker, in general is not entrusted with the possession or control of the goods, nor with the documents of title thereto. Not having possession of goods the broker has no lien thereon: an exception exists, however, in the case of an insurance broker who has a lien on the policy for any general balance due to him or her. An insurance broker is an agent who effects policies of insurance. The insurance broker fills a very important role in marine insurance practice. His or her knowledge of insurance and the insurance market available is invaluable to the client.

It is a distinct advantage to the underwriters at Lloyd's that the public are not admitted to the 'Room' to negotiate the insurance cover they require. Instead, a member of the public, whether a merchant, shipowner or other proposed assured, must employ the intermediary of a Lloyd's broker and the underwriter finds he or she is negotiating with a person well versed in the laws, customs and practices of marine insurance.

Not all brokers are Lloyd's brokers but any other broker may engage the services of a Lloyd's broker to place business at Lloyd's. Before admission to Lloyd's the broker, wishing to become a Lloyd's broker, has to satisfy the Committee of Lloyd's that he or she is a suitable and satisfactory person to become an authorized Lloyd's broker.

Once admitted, the broker describes him(her)self as such by using the term 'and at Lloyd's' on notepaper and on the name plate identifying his or her premises. The broker is issued with a 'ticket' authorizing entry to the 'Room', upon payment of the necessary subscription, and may arrange for employees to represent him or her in the actual negotiations.

The Contract of Insurance

A contract of insurance comes into being when one party, say X, makes an offer and the other party, say Y, makes a valid acceptance. A better definition, however, would be that where a person, corporation or firm, called the 'insurer' or 'assurer', in consideration of a sum of money, called the 'premium', agrees to pay a certain sum of money to another person, called 'insured' or 'assured', upon the happening of an uncertain event, there is a contract of insurance; *Department of Trade and Industry* v. *St. Christopher's Motorists Association* (1974); *Medical Defence Union* v. *Department of Trade* (1979). The premium may consist of a lump sum or of periodical payments. The instrument evidencing the contract is called a 'policy' of insurance. The insurer in marine insurance is usually termed an 'underwriter'.

In most cases, the would-be insured fills in a proposal form inviting the insurer to provide cover for certain risks, and when the insurer accepts this proposal, the contract of insurance comes into being.

While writing is essential in the case of marine insurance, since oral evidence of its existence is not admissible in case of dispute, there is no legal necessity in other cases, and if the insurer accepted the proposal and a premium without qualification, he or she would probably be held bound after a reasonable time had elapsed.

The essential feature of an insurance contract is that a physical object is exposed to perils and that the assured stands in some relation, recognized by law, to that object, in consequence of which the assured either benefits by its preservation, or is prejudiced by its loss or mishap to it. In simple words, the assured must have something to lose and something to gain from the successful transportation or non-arrival of the insured property. It follows that if the assured has no interest in that object he or she cannot be prejudiced by its loss and there is nothing to reimburse. This is called an insurable interest, and it is absolutely necessary to exist in relation to the assured. Interest is not confined to rights in the nature of property or arising out of contract, for example a shareholder in a submarine cable company has an insurable interest in the successful laying of a cable, although he has no property in the cable; *Wilson* v. *Jones* (1867).

Any interest may be insured which is dependent on the safety of the subject matter exposed to the risks insured against, provided in all cases that at the time of the loss it is an interest legal or equitable; *Moran, Galloway & Co.* v. *Uzielli* (1905). Thus, where a charterer pays freight in advance to a shipowner, for the carriage of goods, from one port to another, such money is usually non-returnable, even if the goods are lost and never arrive at their destination. Such charterer has got an insurable interest in the money paid since it may be lost if the goods are lost. But the shipowner has no such interest in the freight, since earning it does not depend on the successful completion of the adventure.

However, where the charterer agrees to pay freight upon delivery of the goods at destination, then it is the shipowner who has an insurable interest in earning the freight, that is, in the safe arrival of the goods at destination; *Weir & Co.* v. *Girvin & Co.* (1899).

Finally, it should be noted that if a person attempts to insure property in which he or she has no insurable interest, the contract is not one of insurance and is void as being contrary to public policy; section 4 of the Marine Insurance Act 1906.

The proposal

When issuing a blank proposal form an insurer is not making an offer of insurance even if premium rates are quoted on the form. The blank proposal form is an invitation to treat.

The duty of the proposer to make full disclosure of all material facts means that he or she must scrutinize the proposal form with great care. Neglect to do this may mean that, if the insurer accepts the proposal and the loss actually occurs, the insured may find that the insurer can avoid the contract and have no liability beyond the return of the premiums paid; *Reselodge Ltd* v. *Castle* (1966).

As mentioned earlier, the contract of insurance is normally preceded by a proposal form, the answers to which are more than representations, namely warranties. It is important to note that in insurance law warranties are treated as equivalent to conditions in any other type of contract, and therefore, as a general rule a breach of condition gives rise to the right to repudiate.

Thus, in *Dawsons Ltd* v. *Bonnin* (1922), it was held that the inaccuracy of the answer (in the proposal form) as to the place at which the lorry to be insured would be garaged, entitled the insurers to avoid liability on the score of breach of warranty; it made no difference that the answer was not material in the sense of affecting the rate of premium or that the inaccuracy was purely innocent and inadvertent.

The line between what is a material disclosure and what is immaterial is not always easy to draw. Therefore, it would be advisable for a proposer to amplify the information specifically requested.

The slip

Once the broker has got the proposal, he or she will accumulate the facts of the insurance to be effected and will set these down on a piece of stiff card. This document is termed the 'slip' and it occupies a very important position in the negotiation of a marine insurance contract. The slip is used to obtain the agreement of one or many insurers to underwrite the insurance. The number of insurers anticipated depends on the monetary value of the subject-matter of the insurance and the amount of cover required.

Having prepared the slip, the broker will select the section of the market in which it is anticipated the type of risk involved will be readily acceptable. Many insurers specialize in particular types of insurance and thereby achieve considerable knowledge of the peculiarities of such risks. This specialist underwriter is known in the market as a 'Lead' or 'Leader' and it is part of a broker's duty to know the recognized market 'Leads'.

The broker takes the slip to the 'Lead' and negotiates the insurance contract. This practice of negotiation is called 'broking', and it is at this point that the rate of premium is decided. The 'Lead' agrees the rate with the broker and impresses the Syndicate line stamp on the slip (if the Lead is at Lloyd's). Within the line stamp the underwriter will insert his or her 'line'. This 'line' is the amount or percentage of the risk that the underwriter is prepared to accept on behalf of the Syndicate. The impression of a line stamp on the slip has the same effect as if the underwriter had initialled the slip. At this point the contract is concluded between the 'Lead' and the assured. The broker offers the slip to other insurers, until the required percentage of cover has been reached.

The initialling of the slip by an underwriter is deemed to be the acceptance of the contract, thus providing direct evidence as to the conclusion of the contract; *Eagle Star* v. *Spratt* (1971). However, until the contract is embodied in a policy the 'slip' is only evidence of an intended contract and is binding in honour only; section 22, Marine Insurance Act 1906.

Once the policy is actually issued the slip does have a degree of importance in that it may be used in evidence for certain purposes, for example the date of the conclusion of the contract. Thus the slip may be produced in evidence in order to rectify mistakes which may have appeared on the policy.

Section 89 of the Marine Insurance Act 1906 specifically permits the slip to be used in legal proceedings once there is a properly issued policy. Therefore, no action against the insurer can be brought by the insured until the policy is issued, that is, the slip cannot be sued upon.

Uberrimae Fidei

As mentioned earlier, the insured must disclose all material facts. Furthermore, it should be noted that a contract of insurance is *uberrimae fidei*, that is, a contract based on the principle of utmost good faith.

Thus either party may avoid a contract of insurance if he can establish that the other party failed to disclose a material fact or made a misrepresentation, even if innocent, of such a fact. This means that the insurer cannot, for example, take advantage of a misstatement if he is really aware or ought to be aware of the true facts of the case; *Re Universal Non-Tariff Fire Insurance Co., Forbes & Co.'s* Claim (1875).

The insured must disclose every material circumstance which is known, and is deemed to know every circumstance which, in the ordinary course of business, ought to be known to him/her. A circumstance is material if it would influence the judgment of a prudent insurer in fixing the premium, or determining whether to take the risk. However, in the absence of inquiry by the insurer, the insured need not disclose any circumstance:

1 which diminishes the risk;
2 which is known or presumed to be known to the insurer;
3 regarding matters of law;
4 which it is superfluous to disclose because it is already covered by an express or implied warranty, for example a policy for burglary insurance may be subject to a warranty that a certain form of lock be fitted, but it is superfluous to disclose whether they are or are not fitted since the policy

operates only if they are;

5 which the insurer's representative fails to notice on a survey (provided there is no concealment).

It is a question of fact whether a circumstance which is not disclosed is material or not; *Ionides* v. *Pender* (1874).

The duty of disclosure continues throughout the negotiations, and where circumstances alter, previous statements should be corrected.

The policy

The policy is not the contract but merely written evidence of it. Nevertheless, a court will regard it as containing the expressed intentions of the parties in the absence of proof to the contrary. The policy contains the general conditions governing the insurance, commonly endorsed on the back, and where a policy continues from year to year, variations maybe incorporated by means of endorsement slips which are stuck on the back of the policy.

Valued policy

This is one which specifies the agreed value of the subject matter insured. It can usually be recognized by the use of the term 'so valued' after the details of the subject-matter insured or the term 'valued at' preceding the specified value. The value in the policy is deemed to be conclusive of the insurable value, as between the insurer and the assured, where there is no fraud, whether or not it is the true value.

One must not confuse 'Insured Value' with 'Sum Insured'. The 'Insured Value' is the amount specified in the policy as the value of the insured property, whereas the 'Sum Insured' is the total amount of the subscriptions of the insurers in the policy. Where the property is insured for its full value, both the sum insured and the insured value will be identical. This is usually the case in cargo insurance so that the policy will show for example: '£2,000 on merchandise so valued'.

Unvalued policy

This is a policy which does not specify any 'value' but leaves this to be determined if and when a claim arises. An unvalued policy merely states the maximum amount which the assured would be able to recover. The insurable value of the goods is the prime cost of the goods, plus expenses incidental to shipping and the charges of insurance.

Floating policy

This is a cargo policy with a sum insured sufficient to accommodate a large number of shipments for a single assured. Subject to a limit on any one vessel, each shipment is covered automatically as it goes forward. The sum insured is reduced by each declaration until the amount has been exhausted. A deposit premium paid at inception is adjusted on expiry of the policy to provide the correct premium. A certificate is issued for each shipment. In other words, a floating policy is a contract of insurance the terms of which are described generally, and it leaves for other particulars, such as the name of the ship, to be declared at a later time, that is, when shipment takes place.

Open cover

This has become the most common and most popular form of insurance used in the export trade. It is quite similar to a floating policy. In particular, the assured is likewise bound to declare all individual shipments effected thereunder. However, unlike the floating policy, where the assured receives a formal policy document, under open cover no formal policy is issued. This is because the open cover is not an insurance policy but is a document by which the underwriter undertakes subsequently to issue specific policies within the terms of the cover. The open cover may be limited in time or may be permanent while the floating policy is normally limited to 12 months.

Blanket policies

Such policies usually provide that the assured need not advise the insurer of the individual shipments, as in the case of open cover and floating policies, but a lump sum premium, instead of a premium at several rates, shall cover all shipments.

Aviation Insurance

Air transport operators have a legal liability towards (a) the general public, (b) passengers, and (c) consignors. Insurance cover for liabilities (a) and (b) is beyond the scope of this book. Firstly, it should be noted that so far as legal aviation insurance principles are concerned, these are similar to the ones applicable to marine insurance, for example insurable interest. Lloyd's and the company market use the same basic policy form for aircraft hull and liability business. An indemnity of an insured against the sums he or she may become legally liable to pay, that is, freight liability, is not usually covered in the standard aircraft policy. Such cover may however, be obtained by indorsement, thus covering any or all of the following three types of risks/liabilities; (a) handler's liability; (b) freight forwarder's liability; and (c) freight all risks. War, hi-jacking and similar risks may also be insured, as are strikes, on a separate policy. These risks are normally excluded from the ordinary type of policy. Various factors are considered when effecting aviation insurance such as geographical limits, and general market conditions.

Questions for Discussion

1 Define a contract of insurance. Explain the term insurable interest.
2 What is meant by *uberrimae fidei?*
3 What is (a) a valued policy, and (b) an unvalued policy?
4 What is the difference between 'Insured Value' and 'Sum Insured' under a valued policy? What is a floating policy?

20

General Average

During a sea voyage, the master of the ship has very wide powers of action in time of peril, and at such times he may, if necessary, sacrifice property or incur expense for the general safety. It would be unfair that the owner of the particular property should bear the whole of the loss thus incurred for the general benefit, and the loss is therefore apportioned or adjusted rateably between all the parties interested. Such a loss is termed a general average sacrifice or expenditure.

Where ship and cargo are exposed to a common danger and some part of the cargo or of the ship is intentionally sacrificed, or extra expenditure is incurred, to avert that danger, such loss or expense will be the subject of a general average contribution. It will be apportioned between ship and cargo in proportion to their salved values.

For example, assume a ship which has run aground. If it stays aground then an approaching storm may break the ship up on the rocks and all the ship and the cargo would be lost. To pull the ship back into deep water the engines may have to be used so severely that they are damaged. The shipowner can subsequently ask for a contribution from the cargo owners to make good this damage.

Note, however, that only the loss which was voluntarily incurred for the common safety may be claimed for. In this example the damage incurred by the ship going aground is not a general average situation, only the financial sacrifices subsequently necessary to get her out of danger.

Although the idea is simple in theory, in a real situation the practical application of it can be complicated. Supposing shipper X has a general average loss of £1,000. The shipowner appoints an average adjuster who has to establish the total cost of the ship and cargo which is say £3,000,000. Shipper Y, whose cargo was not damaged but assessed to have a value of £3,000, would be asked to contribute:

$$3,000 \times \frac{1,000}{3,000,000}$$

or £1 as Y's proportion of the general average payment. This does of course take time to calculate – it may well take several years.

The shipowner is responsible for collecting all these contributions, so before he or she loses possessory lien on the cargo the shipowner may therefore ask the agents at the various discharging ports to collect a general average deposit or bond from the consignees before releasing the cargo. Thus, the duty of seeing that the person injured by the sacrifice obtains contribution is on the shipowner. Note that in the absence of agreement, the law of the port where the adventure ends is to be applied.

Very commonly a clause is inserted in the contract incorporating the York-Antwerp Rules, which are a standard set of rules relating to general average. The name 'York-Antwerp' is derived from the places where conferences were held which brought the Rules into existence.

For a sacrifice or expenditure to be the subject of general average contribution the following conditions must obtain:

1 **There must be a danger common to the whole adventure.** The danger must be, in fact, a real one, not merely imagined to exist by the master, however reasonable such fear may be. Furthermore, the fact that a part of the cargo has already been discharged will not preclude the owners of the rest, under all circumstances, from claiming a general average contribution from the shipowner.

Thus in *Whitecross Wire Co.* v. *Savill* (1792), when most of the cargo had been discharged, a fire broke out on the ship, and the remainder of the cargo was damaged by water used in putting out the fire. It was held that the shipowner must contribute in respect of this damage.

2 **The sacrifice or expenditure must be real and intentional.** Where the thing abandoned is already lost, there is no real sacrifice, and consequently no claim for contribution, for example cutting away a mast which is already virtually useless; *Shepherd* v. *Kottgen* (1877).

3 **The sacrifice or expenditure must be necessary.** Generally the duty of deciding whether a sacrifice or expenditure is necessary rests with the master of the ship; *Papayanni and Jeronica* v. *Grampian Steamship Co. Ltd* (1896).

4 **The danger must not have arisen through the fault of the person claiming contribution.** In order to prevent a person recovering general average contribution on the ground that he was at fault, the fault must be something which constitutes an actionable wrong.

Accordingly, a shipowner cannot claim a general average contribution where, for example, he allowed a vessel to sail with smoke in her holds or the cargo had not been properly stowed; *The Ionic Bay* (1975).

5 **The property which was in danger must have been actually benefited by the sacrifice.** If the general average act has been successful but consequently, owing to new causes, ship and cargo are lost, no contribution is due; *Chellew* v. *Royal Commission on Sugar Supply* (1922).

In general, where there is a general average act, the property concerned must in fact come through the adventure, otherwise there will be no benefit to the person who owns such property.

This can be more easily understood if one remembers that the fund from which the contribution to the general average act is made is based on the value of the property saved at the end of the adventure. Therefore, there may be a general average act after which the entire benefit of the adventure may be lost, in which case, there will be no case for a general average contribution, since there will be no fund out of which such contributions may be made.

6 **Only direct losses are recoverable.** Only losses which are the direct consequence of the general average act are allowed as general average. Thus, loss of market, caused by delay due to a general average act, would not be considered to be a direct loss, and therefore, it cannot be recovered.

Figure 20.1: General average

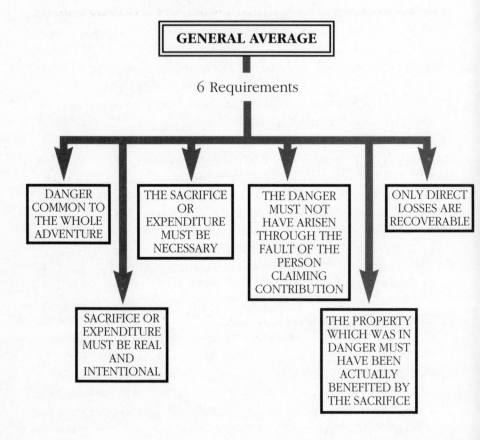

Question for Discussion

Briefly explain the term 'general average'.

21

Institute Cargo Clauses

Introduction

The current insurance policy and clauses were introduced on 1st January, 1982, and they actually came into effect on 31st March, 1983. This form of insurance policy is known as *Lloyd's Marine Policy* and the cargo clauses are described as *Institute Cargo Clauses* A, B and C.

In addition to these three sets of cargo clauses, there are various other clauses such as the Institute War Clauses (Cargo) and the *Institute Strikes Clauses (Cargo).*

Institute Cargo Clauses A, B and C

Risks covered

Institute Cargo Clauses A cover all risks of loss or damage to the subject matter insured, whereas Clauses B and C only cover risks which are specifically referred to. The exporter who, in order to save on the premium, does not wish to insure under Clauses A but prefers to insure under Clauses B or C, should make sure that the specific risks to which the cargo may be exposed are expressly covered, and also are not excluded by the provisions of Clauses B and C.

In particular, the three Institute Cargo Clauses each contain: a risks clause; a general average clause; and a transit clause.

Risks Clause

This is a different Clause in each of the sets, since the cover provided is different between A, B and C. As it will be seen, the widest cover is provided by the Institute Cargo Clauses (A), whereas set (C) restricts cover to the effects of major fortuities, for example fire or collision.

Institute Cargo Clauses (A) define the cover provided by this insurance in Clause 1 as follows:

> This insurance covers **all risks** of loss of or damage to the subject-matter insured except as provided in Clauses 4, 5, 6 and 7 below.

The meaning of the words 'all risks' is wide, and it must be noted that it is sufficient for the assured/insured to show that the loss was caused by a casualty or something accidental without proving the exact nature of the casualty or accident which caused the loss; *British and Foreign Marine Insurance Co.* v. *Gaunt* (1921).

Furthermore, it must be noted that because this type of insurance policy covers 'all risks', as opposed to the type of policies where risks of a specified class or classes, such as a motor policy (for example third party, fire and theft), the insured/ assured discharges his special onus (of proof) when he has proved that the loss was caused by some event covered by the general expression, and he is not bound to go further and prove the exact nature of the accident or casualty which, in fact, occasioned his loss.

Thus, in *Theodorou* v. *Chester* (1951), X had insured a consignment of bleached sponges with Y, on an 'all risks' policy, for a voyage from New York to London. The sponges were tightly packed in wooden cases. X found that they were damaged, and claimed against Y. He (X) alleged that the goods were stained by water, dirt, paint and other substances penetrating the cases.

Y, on the other hand, maintained that the damage was due to normal transit risks of dust and dirt combined with the atmospheric pressure. X's action succeeded since he (X) was able to show (on the balance of proof) that the loss was due to an abnormal peril, and the damage to the sponges was due to an extraneous and accidental cause.

Institute Cargo Clauses (B) state in Clause 1 that the policy covers:

(a) loss of or damage to the cargo reasonably attributable to
   1 fire or explosion;
   2 the vessel or craft being stranded, grounded, sunk or capsized;
   3 the overturning or derailment of a land conveyance;
   4 the collision or contact of the vessel, craft or conveyance with any external object other than water;
   5 the discharge of the cargo at a port of distress; and
   6 **earthquake, volcanic eruption** or **lightning**.
(b) the loss of or damage to the cargo caused by
   1 general average sacrifice;
   2 jettison or **washing overboard**; and
   3 **the entry of sea, lake or river water into the vessel, craft, hold, conveyance, container, liftvan, or place of storage**.
(c) **the total loss of any package lost overboard or dropped whilst loading on to or unloading from the vessel or craft**.

The highlighted risks are not covered by the Institute Cargo Clauses (C).

Institute Cargo Clauses (C) state in Clause 1 that the policy covers:

(a) loss of or damage to the cargo reasonably attributable to
   1 fire or explosion;
   2 the vessel or craft being stranded, grounded, sunk or capsized;

    3 the overturning or derailment of a land conveyance;
    4 the collision or contract of the vessel, craft or
      conveyance with any external object other than
      water; and
    5 the discharge of the cargo at a port of distress.
  (b) the loss of or damage to the cargo caused by
    1 general average sacrifice;
    2 jettison.

General Average Clause

Clause 2 states that the policy covers general average and salvage charges, adjusted or determined according to the contract
of affreightment and/or the governing law and practice, incurred
to avoid or in connection with the avoidance of loss from any
cause except those causes which are excluded.

The Transit Clause

The effect of this clause, which is present in Institute Cargo
Clauses A, B and C, is to extend the sea voyage to include the
risks whilst the goods are transported from the inland warehouse
or place of storage to the time of loading, as well as the risks
from the time of discharge to delivery at the final warehouse or
place of storage at the named destination.

Therefore, an assured can, under this clause, for example, insure a consignment of goods from Manchester to Paris, provided
these places are named in the policy as the commencement and
destination of the transit.

Under the Transit Clause, the goods are covered from the
time they leave the warehouse at the place named in the policy
for the commencement of the transit and continue to be
covered until they are delivered to the final warehouse at the
destination named in the policy or another warehouse, whether
prior to or at the destination named in the policy, but the policy provides an overriding time limit of 60 days after the
completion of discharge overside the overseas vessel at the final

port of discharge. On the expiration of that time limit cover ceases even though the goods may not have reached a warehouse. If before the expiration of the 60 days after discharge the goods are forwarded to a destination other than that named in the insurance, the cover terminates when the transit begins. The 60 days' cover is very valuable for the assured/insured if, for some reason, the goods cannot proceed to the warehouse, for instance, because the buyer has not paid the import duties, and the assured/insured cannot dispose of them quickly.

The principle underlying these provisions is that the assured/insured shall be covered until he or she or a buyer can reasonably be expected to have made further insurance arrangements for the goods. If under the contract of carriage the goods are unloaded at a place other than the contemplated place of destination, due to circumstances beyond the control of the assured/insured, they continue to be insured until they are forwarded to the agreed or another destination and have arrived at the final warehouse, or until they are sold and delivered. The word 'warehouse' has to be given its ordinary and natural meaning.

Risks not covered

Clauses 4, 5, 6 and 7 are exclusion clauses. Clause 4 is the General Exclusion Clause and it is present in Institute Cargo Clauses A, B and C.

Clause 4.1 excludes 'loss damage or expense attributable to wilful misconduct of the Assured'.

'Wilful misconduct' is essentially a question of fact.

Clause 4.2 excludes 'ordinary leakage, ordinary loss in weight or volume, or ordinary wear and tear of the subject-matter insured'.

'Ordinary' refers to the normal transit losses such as the nature of the goods or the loads exerted on them. When the ordinary leakage of one cargo damages a second cargo, the assured in respect of the second cargo can only recover if he or she is insured under Cargo Clauses A, but not if the insurance is based upon Clauses B or C only.

Clause 4.3 excludes 'loss or damage or expense caused by insufficiency or unsuitability of packing or preparation of the subject-matter insured'.

The question of whether packing is suitable or sufficient is often determined according to what is customary and reasonable in a particular trade. Where the packing is such that the cargo cannot withstand the usual conditions appertaining to a particular voyage, the assured cannot recover for any loss or damage caused or for any expenses incurred in replacing inadequate packing. Loss of, or damage to, the contents of a container will not be covered where such is loaded by the insured/assured or his/her servants prior to or after the attachment of the insurance. This exclusion will not apply, however, when the stowing takes place after the attachment of the insurance and without the assured or servants being involved.

Clause 4.4 excludes 'loss damage or expense caused by inherent vice or nature of the subject-matter insured'. This exclusion clause covers situations where the goods insured are damaged or destroyed by an internal development (*inherent vice*). As an example, spontaneous combustion may occur within one cargo damaging a second cargo. The owner of the first cargo cannot recover where the spontaneous combustion is the result of inherent vice, such as may be the case in a cargo of grain, but the owner of the second cargo can recover for his or her own loss under Clauses A, B or C since the risk of loss or damage due to fire explosion is covered.

Clause 4.5 excludes 'loss damage or expense proximately caused by delay even though the delay be caused by a risk insured against'. Therefore, although under the Transit Clause the insurance will remain valid where a delay is beyond the control of the assured/insured, the assured/insured will not be protected in respect of any damage which is proximately caused by that delay. However, in the case of a general average act which causes a delay, the assured/insured is entitled to recover his or her proportion of any expenses incurred during the period of the delay, such as, for example, the contribution to the wages of the crew.

Clause 4.6 excludes 'loss damage or expense arising from insolvency or financial default of the owners managers charterers or operators of the vessel'. If due to financial difficulties, the carrier has to stop short at a port, the insurer will not have to pay the forwarding expenses incurred by the assured/insured. Note that Clause 12 is applicable only to expenses incurred where a voyage is terminated as a result of the peril insured against.

Clause 4.7 of the Institute Cargo Clauses B and C is an additional exclusion not found in A, and provides that the insurance cover will not cover 'deliberate damage to or deliberate destruction of the subject matter insured or any part thereof by the wrongful act of any person or persons'.

Clause 6 is the War Exclusion Clause and is present in Cargo Clauses A, B and C. Deletion of this Clause will mean that war risks are covered in Clauses A, but not in Clauses B or C, since such perils are not present in the risks clause. Where an assured/insured requires war risk cover, the addition of the Institute War Clauses should be requested.

Clause 7 is the Strikes Exclusion Clause and is present in all three Institute Cargo Clauses. Deletion of this Clause will enable an assured/insured to recover for such risks where he or she is insured under Clauses A, since in Clauses B and C the peril is not within the specific risks covered. Where an assured/insured specifically wants cover for strikes and other labour disturbances, the addition of the Institute Strikes Clauses should be requested.

Institute War Clauses (Cargo)

Clause 1 of this set of Clauses states that the insurance covers loss or damage to the cargo caused by:

1.1 war civil war revolution rebellion insurrection, or civil strife arising therefrom, or any hostile act by or against a belligerent power;

1.2 capture seizure arrest restraint or detainment, arising from risks covered under 1.1 above, and the consequences thereof or any attempt thereat;

1.3 derelict mines torpedoes bombs or other derelict weapons of war.

Clause 2 states that the insurance covers general average and salvage charges, adjusted or determined according to the contract of affreightment and/or governing law and practice, incurred to avoid or in connection with the avoidance of a risk mentioned above.

Institute Strikes Clauses (Cargo)

Clause 1 states that the insurance covers with specified exceptions, loss of or damage to the cargo caused by:

1 strikers, locked-out workmen or persons taking part in labour disturbances;
2 any terrorist or any person acting from a political motive.

Clause 2 states that the insurance covers general average and salvage charges, adjusted or determined according to the contract of affreightment and/or governing law and practice, incurred to avoid or in connection with the avoidance of a risk mentioned above.

Question for Discussion

Name the three sets of clauses most commonly used in cargo insurance. Which of these three provides a wider cover and why?

Part 7

Legal Aspects of Carriage by Sea, Air and Road

22

Carriage of Goods by Sea

Before we consider the legal aspects of bills of lading and the Hague-Visby Rules, it is important to understand 1, the distinction between a common and a private carrier, and 2, the way in which a carriage of goods by sea operates.

A common carrier is one who is engaged in the trade of carrying goods as a regular business, and who holds himself out as ready to carry for any who may wish to employ him. Where a person, while inviting all to employ him, reserved to himself the right to accept or reject offers of goods for carriage, it was held not to be a common carrier; *Belfast Ropeword Co.* v. *Bushell* (1918). It is a question of fact whether a man is a common carrier or not; *Webster* v. *Dickson* (1969). The characteristics of a common carrier may be summed up as follows:

(a) Is bound to take any goods brought to him if he has room for them and they are suitable; *Riley* v. *Horne* (1828). The latter means that the goods are properly packed and their destination is the same as the one that the carrier usually travels.

(b) He must charge only at a reasonable rate for carrying the goods, and he must not impose unreasonable conditions; *Garton* v. *Bristol and Exeter* (1861).

Liability of Common Carriers

For any breach of the above characteristics a common carrier could be sued for damages; *Crouch* v. *London and North Western* (1854). Furthermore, a common carrier is absolutely responsible to the owner of the goods carried for any loss or damage to them. Absolutely means irrespectively of negligence; *Siohn & Co. and Academy Garments* v. *Hagland & Son* (1976). However, if such loss or damage is caused by:

(a) an act of God; or
(b) an act to the Queen's enemies; or
(c) an inherent vice in the goods; or
(d) the negligence of the owner of the goods; or
(e) a general average sacrifice,

then the common carrier would not be liable for such loss or damage.

The party responsible for shipping the goods is the **shipper** or **consignor**. This would usually be the seller. The **consignee** is usually the buyer and is the person named as consignee in the bill of lading. The term **'indorsee'/'endorsee'** means a subsequent buyer, that is, a person who buys the goods by an indorsement made by the buyer/consignee on the bill of lading and the delivery of the bill of lading from the consignee to him (indorsee). Either of them may be entitled to delivery of the goods by the **carrier** (shipowner). The shipper (seller) frequently employs a **forwarding agent** and the shipowner (carrier) a **loading broker**. The forwarding agent usually has to ascertain the date and place of sailing, obtain a space and fill in the bills of lading indicating the name of the consignee (buyer), or person to whom the goods are to be delivered (indorsee).

Once the shipper (buyer) or his or her agent (forwarding agent) becomes aware of the sailing schedules of a particular trade, through some form of advertisement, the shipper communicates with the shipowner (carrier) with a view to booking cargo space on the vessel or container. Provided satisfactory arrangements have been concluded, the shipper (or the forwarding agent) forwards the cargo. At this stage, it is important to note that the shipper (buyer) always makes the offer by forwarding the consignment, whilst the shipowner (carrier) either accepts or refuses it. Furthermore, it is the shipper's duty, or that of the agent, to supply details of the consignment; normally this is done by completing the shipping company's form of bill of lading, and the shipping company then signs the number of copies requested.

The goods are signed for by the vessel's chief officer (chief mate), and this receipt (mate's receipt) is exchanged for the bill of lading. If the cargo is in good condition, no indorsement will be made on the document (bill of lading). Conversely, if the goods are damaged or a portion of the consignment is missing, the document will be suitably indorsed by the master or the agent.

Bills of lading are usually drawn in sets of three or four, one copy being retained by the consignor (shipper), one by the master of the ship (shipowner), and one sent on in advance of the goods to the consignee (buyer), and if a fourth exists, then this is sent to the consignee later in case the first is lost or delayed. As a rule the title to the goods passes with this third bill of lading.

Where the shipper had sold the goods under a letter of credit established through a bank, or when he wishes to obtain payment of his invoice before the consignee obtains the goods, he will pass the full set of original bills to his bank, who will in due course arrange presentation to the consignee against payment. The shipowner or his agent at the port of destination will require one original bill of lading to be presented to him before the goods are handed over. Furthermore, he will normally require payment of any freight due, should this not have been paid at the port of shipment. When one of a set of bills of lading has been presented to the shipping company, the other bills in the set lose their value.

In the event of the bill of lading being lost or delayed in transit, the shipping company will allow delivery of the goods to the person claiming to be the consignee, if he gives a letter of indemnity; this is normally countersigned by a bank, and relieves the shipping company of any liability should another person eventually come along with the actual bill of lading.

Bills of Lading

A bill of lading has been defined as a receipt for goods shipped on board a ship, signed by the person (or his agent) who contracts to carry them, and stating the terms on which the goods were delivered to and received by the ship.

The principal purpose of the bill of lading is to enable the owner of the goods to dispose of them rapidly although the goods are not in his or her hands but are in the custody of a carrier. When goods are on the high seas in transit from, say, London to New York, and the bill of lading has been forwarded to the buyer in New York and the buyer thus has become the owner of the goods, the bill of lading representing the goods enables the buyer to pledge the goods with his or her bank in New York or to resell them to a repurchaser in Singapore.

Functions of bills of lading

A bill of lading serves three functions:

1 It is a document of title to the goods, once they are shipped.
2 It is evidence of the contract which has been entered into between the shipper of the goods and the shipowner.
3 It is a receipt for the goods delivered to the shipowner/ carrier.

1 As has been mentioned, the principal purpose of the bill of lading is to enable the person entitled to the goods represented by the bill to dispose of the goods while they are in transit. By mercantile custom, possession of the bill is in many respects equivalent to possession of the goods and the transfer of the bill of lading normally has the same effect as the delivery of the goods themselves. Without a bill of lading, delivery of the goods cannot normally be obtained. Therefore, it enables the consignee to dispose of the goods by indorsement and delivery of the bill of lading.

Thus, in *Horst v. Biddell Brothers* (1912), a contract was made for the sale of hops to be shipped from San Francisco to London, CIF net cash. The buyer refused to pay for the goods until they were actually delivered. It was held that possession of the bill of lading is in law equivalent to possession of the goods, and that, under a CIF contract, the seller is entitled to payment on shipping the goods and tendering to the buyer the documents of title.

Two points should be noted in this connection:

(a) The transfer of the bill of lading is merely deemed to operate as a symbolic transfer of possession of the goods, but not necessarily as a transfer of the property in them. The transfer of the bill passes such rights in the goods as the parties intend to pass. Thus, where the consignee or indorsee of the bill is the agent of the shipper at the port of destination, it is evident that the parties, by transferring the bill of lading, intend only to pass the right to claim delivery of the goods from the carrier upon arrival of the goods, but not the property in them. Where the seller of goods transfers the bill of lading to the buyer, as bound to do in case of a CIF sale, it depends again on the intention of the parties whether the property passes by transfer of the bill of lading or remains in the seller. As far as specific or ascertained goods are concerned, this is in accordance with the fundamental rule laid down in the Sale of Goods Act 1979 (see page 138) which, it should be noted, applies irrespective of whether the goods sold are represented by a bill of lading or not.

(b) Only a person holding a bill of lading is entitled to claim delivery of the goods from the carrier. The carrier is protected if he or she delivers the goods to the holder of the first original bill presented. The bill of lading retains its character of document of title until the contract of carriage by sea is discharged by delivery of the goods against the bill, and the carrier is not responsible for wrongful delivery of the goods against the bill unless he or she knows of the defect in the title of the holder.

If the carrier delivers the goods to a person who is not the holder of the bill of lading, he does so at his peril.

Finally in the event of the bill of lading being lost or delayed, the carrier will allow delivery of the goods to the person claiming to be the consignee, if he or she gives a letter of indemnity, countersigned by a bank.

2 A bill of lading is evidence of the contract of carriage, though not the contract itself, which has been entered into between the shipper of the goods and the shipowner before the bill of lading is signed; *The Ardennes v. The Ardennes* (1951). This is better understood if one realises that bills of lading are issued only when the ship actually sails from the port of loading. Therefore, it could be said that the bill of lading is a memorandum of the contract of carriage, repeating in detail the terms of the contract which was in fact concluded prior to the signing of the bill.

3 The bill of lading, being a receipt of the shipowner for the goods, contains a description of the goods. This description is perhaps the most vital part of the whole bill because the intended indorsee of the bill, who wishes to buy the goods by having the bill indorsed to him, normally has no opportunity of verifying the representation of the buyer as to their quantity and quality by examining them, and parts with the purchase price in reliance upon the shipowner's description of the goods in the bill of lading.

Carriage of Goods by Sea Act 1971

There are two types of contract of carriage by sea: contracts evidenced by bills of lading and contracts contained in charter-parties. Charter-parties are mainly governed by the rules of common law, and thus the shipowner may, by agreement with the charterer, modify his normal liability as a carrier.

Contracts of carriage evidenced by bills of lading, on the other hand, are to a large measure regulated by statute law, in particular by the Carriage of Goods by Sea Act 1971 (giving the Hague-Visby Rules force of law in the UK), which effectively restrains the shipowner from introducing exemptions from his liability beyond those admitted by the standard Rules relating to bills of lading, that is, the Hague-Visby Rules, appended to the 1971 Act.

Charter-parties are of little interest to the 'average' exporter, since the quantity of his shipments is not normally such that the hire of a whole ship would be a viable proposition.

Although the clauses contained in a bill of lading represent the terms of agreement between the shipper and the carrier, the shipper has little discretion in the negotiation of these terms. The terms of the contract which he concludes are fixed in advance, and his position is not unlike that of a railway passenger who buys a ticket. The shipper, like the railway passenger, is protected by Act of Parliament against abuse of the greater bargaining power of the other party. As far as the shipper is concerned, this protection is contained in the Carriage of Goods by Sea Acts of 1971 and 1992.

The Carriage of Goods by Sea Act 1971 came into force in June, 1977. The Act, together with the Carriage of Goods by Sea Act 1992, governs the liabilities and rights relating to carriers under bills of lading as well as to other documents of title. The most important points to remember, in connection with the application of this (1971) Act are:

1 It only applies to outwards bills of lading, that is, from a British port, or Northern Ireland port; the port of destination is immaterial. In particular, Article X provides that the Act will apply to every bill of lading relating to the carriage of goods between ports in two different States if:
   (a) the bill of lading is issued in a Contracting State; or
   (b) the carriage is from a port in a Contracting State; or
   (c) the contract contained in or evidenced by the bill of lading provides that these Rules or legislation of any State giving effect to them are to govern the contract.
2 The Act does not apply to the transportation of live animals, and deck cargo which is carried on deck in pursuance of the contract of carriage. But where cargo is carried on deck without specific agreement between the parties as to the carriage on deck, and no statement appears on the face of the bill of lading that goods carried on deck are in fact so carried, the carriage is subject to the Rules.
3 It applies both to shipments under bills of lading and those under 'any similar documents of title'. Therefore, it applies to

a receipt which is a non-negotiable document, if it expressly states that the contract for the carriage of goods by sea contained in or evidenced by it shall be governed by the Act/Hague-Visby Rules, as if the receipt were a bill of lading. Thus, a forwarder's receipt (or a liner waybill, or data freight receipt) such as a House bill of lading or container receipt would be subject to the Act, if so indorsed. The bill of lading, under the Act, provides *prima facie* evidence of receipt by the carrier of the goods, that is, identification of cargo marks, condition of cargo, number of packages and their weight, and it further provides conclusive evidence when the cargo has been transferred to a party acting in good faith.

4 The responsibilities of the carrier in respect of the safety of the goods entrusted to his care are described in the Act as follows:

The carrier shall be bound, before and at the beginning of the voyage, to exercise due diligence to

(a) make the ship seaworthy;

(b) properly man, equip and supply the ship;

(c) make the holds, refrigerating and cool chambers, and all other parts of the ship in which goods are carried, fit and safe for their reception, carriage and preservation.

Subject to the provision of Article IV, the carrier shall properly and carefully load, handle, stow, carry, keep, care for and discharge the goods carried. (Article III rule 1.)

The principle underlying these provisions is that the shipowner is only liable if acting negligently. Seaworthiness within the meaning of the above Article, includes cargo-worthiness (Art. III rule 1(c)); consequently the vessel is unseaworthy if its condition before loading the cargo constitutes a major and permanent obstacle to the completion of the contract voyage. Thus, a vessel will be unseaworthy if before loading it is infested with insects and for this reason the discharge of the cargo is prohibited by the authorities at the port of destination; *The Good Friend* (1984). Also, the vessel would be unseaworthy if it is provided with navigational charts which are out of date; *The Marion* (1984).

The obligation of the carrier to use due diligence in the cases stated in the above Article is not limited to his personal diligence, but he is also liable if servants and agents in his employment fail to act with due diligence.

5 The Act permits the carrier to be discharged from all liability in respect of goods unless legal proceedings were started within one year of delivery of the cargo or the date when they should have been delivered. Therefore, generally speaking, the Act puts a time-bar to claims made after the expiration of one year. The Act provides that a notice of loss or damage must be given in writing to the carrier or his agent at the port of discharge, and if the damage to the goods is not apparent, then this time is extended to three days.

6 Finally, the Act provides that unless the value of lost or damaged goods has been declared by the shipper before shipment and inserted in the bill of lading, neither the carrier nor the ship will be or become liable for any loss or damage to the goods in an amount exceeding 666.67 (Special Drawing Rights) units of account per package, or 2 (SDRs) units of account per kilogramme of gross weight of the goods (lost or damaged), whichever is the higher. The unit of account is a Special Drawing Right (SDR) as defined by the International Monetary Fund (IMF). The Act also confirms that the maximum liability does not apply if the damage resulted from an act or omission of the carrier done with intent to cause damage, or recklessly and with knowledge that damage would probably result.

Excepted perils

The Act also contains a list of 17 matters in respect of loss or damage arising or resulting from which the carrier is not liable. The burden of proof rests upon the shipowner. He has to prove that the goods were lost without his fault, and if he wants to rely on one or more of these exceptions in order to exempt his liability, that is, that the damage or loss of the cargo is due to one of the exempted perils, he has to establish this fact also. Note that risks which the shipper has to bear under the contract of carriage should be covered by his marine insurance policy.

As has been mentioned earlier in this chapter, a bill of lading is a receipt for the goods shipped and contains certain admissions as to their quantity and condition when put on board; that is, it is a formal receipt by the shipowner acknowledging that goods of the stated species, quantity and condition are shipped to a stated destination in a certain ship, or at least received in the custody of the shipowner for the purposes of shipment.

Description of the goods in the bill of lading

The Carriage of Goods by Sea Act 1971 provides that the shipper is entitled to demand that the bill of lading which the owner is obliged to issue to him should contain the following leading marks and other particulars.

When the shipowner affirms that the goods received are in 'apparent good order and condition', he issues a 'clean' bill. The words 'in apparent good order and condition' denote that 'apparently, and so far as met the eye, and externally [the goods] were placed in good order on board this ship' but the statement does not extend to qualities of the goods 'which were not apparent to reasonable inspection having regard to the circumstances of loading'; *The Athelviscount* (1934). The shipowner who gives a clean bill does not promise to deliver goods 'in apparent good order and condition' to the consignee, and may prove that the goods were damaged subsequent to the issue of the bill by an excepted peril, but he is prevented (estopped) from denying that he received the goods in apparent good order and condition and cannot escape liability by alleging that an excepted peril existed prior to the issue of the clean bill, for example insufficient packing. This estoppel operates only in favour of a consignee/indorsee who relies on the statement in the bill that goods were in apparent good order and condition.

The shipper is deemed to have guaranteed to the carrier the accuracy of the marks, number, quantity and weight as furnished by him, and the shipper has to indemnify the carrier against loss or damage arising from inaccuracies in such particulars. However, note that the right of the carrier to be indemnified by the shipper in these circumstances cannot be pleaded by the carrier in defence against a consignee who tries to hold him responsible.

A bill of lading issued under the Carriage of Goods by Sea Act 1971 is *prima facie* evidence of the receipt of the goods by the carrier as described in accordance with Article III of the Act. This provision applies to 'Shipped' and 'Received' bills alike. Furthermore, the Act provides that the bill shall be **conclusive** evidence regarding those particulars in the hands of a third party acting in good faith. Such a third party, it is thought, would be the consignee, to whom the bill is transferred, and an indorsee.

Finally, a shipper warrants that the goods are fit for carriage in the ordinary way. Furthermore, the shipper warrants not only that the goods will not cause physical injury or damage to the ship or other cargo, but also that the goods can be discharged without delay due to import restrictions or prohibitions. However, the shipper will not be liable under the warranty if he duly informs the shipowner of the nature of the goods or if the shipowner knows, or ought to know, that they are dangerous or that delay in the discharge may be encountered.

Carriage of Goods by Sea: Right to Sue

Section 1 of the Bills of Lading Act 1855 states that:

Every consignee of goods named in a bill of lading, and every endorsee of a bill of lading to whom the property in the goods therein mentioned shall pass, upon or by reason of such consignment or endorsement, shall have transferred to and vested in him all rights of suit, and be subject to the same liabilities in respect of such goods as if the contract contained in the bill of lading had been made with himself.

Therefore, the carrier could have been sued by any consignee or indorsee fitting the description of section 1. Therefore, three 'conditions' were required; (a) the document must have been a bill of lading; (b) the holder of the bill of lading must have been a consignee or indorsee; and (c) property in the goods must have passed to the holder of the bill of lading by way of indorsement or consignment.

Therefore, an indorsee or consignee could sue the carrier for breaches of the contract of carriage even if such breaches occurred before the bill of lading had been transferred to him; *Monarch* v. *Karlshamms* (1949). The problem with the above provisions may be highlighted by the following simple example.

X, the seller/shipper, ships 5,000 tons bulk cargo and sells 1,000 tons of it to Y, the buyer/consignee. As the 1,000 tons out of 5,000 are considered to be unascertained goods, the property in the goods will pass once they become ascertained; section 16, Sale of Goods Act 1979. In such a situation the property in the goods would not pass before the goods are discharged from the vessel. If Y received no goods then it is obvious that one of the three requirements under section 1 of the Bills of Lading Act 1855 would not be fulfilled, and therefore, Y would not be in a position to sue the carrier (see *The Delfini* (1990)).

Other problems also arose as a result of the Bills of Lading Act 1855, which are beyond the scope of this chapter, and as a result the Carriage of Goods by Sea Act 1992 was enacted, repealing the Bills of Lading Act 1855.

The main philosophy behind this new Act is that a bill of lading holder can sue the carrier in contract for loss or damage to the goods covered by the bill of lading, irrespectively of whether property in the goods has passed to the holder. Furthermore, it should be noted that the Carriage of Goods by Sea Act 1992 now covers sea waybills and ship's delivery orders; s.1(3).

The following is a summary of section 2(1) of the Carriage of Goods by Sea Act 1992, on the persons entitled to sue the carrier:

1 The holder of a bill of lading; that is, consignee or indorsee or whoever is in possession of the bill.
2 The person to whom delivery of the goods to which a sea waybill relates is to be made by the carrier in accordance with that contract.
3 The person to whom delivery of the goods is to be made in accordance with the undertaking contained in a ship's delivery order.

Types of Bills of Lading

Shipped bill of lading

The shipper can demand that the shipowner supplies bills of lading proving that the goods have been actually shipped. For this reason most bill of lading forms are already printed as shipped bills and commence with the wording 'Shipped in apparent good order and condition'. It confirms the goods are actually on board the vessel. This is the most satisfactory type of receipt, and the shipper prefers such a bill as there is no doubt the goods being on board and consequent dispute on this point will not arise with the bankers or consignee, thereby facilitating earliest financial settlement of the export sale.

Received for Shipment bill of lading

This type is used more in the USA and in container transport. This arises where the word 'shipped' does not appear on the bill of lading. It merely confirms that the goods have been handed over to the shipowner and are in his custody. The cargo may be in his dock, warehouse, transit shed, or even inland. The bill has therefore not the same meaning as a 'Shipped' bill and the buyer under a CIF contract need not accept such a bill for ultimate financial settlement through the bank unless provision has been made in the contract. Forwarding agents should avoid handling 'Received for Shipment' bills for their clients unless special circumstances require it.

Through bill of lading

These are used for door-to-door container cargo where several different modes of transport may be involved. In such cases it would be very complicated and more expensive if the shipper had to arrange on-carriage himself by employing an agent at the point of transhipment. Shipping companies therefore issue bills of lading which cover the whole transit and the shipper deals only with the first carried. This type of bill enables a through rate to be quoted and is growing in popularity with the development of containerization.

Transhipment bill of lading

This type is issued usually by shipping companies when there is no direct service between two ports, but when the shipowner is prepared to tranship the cargo at an intermediate port at his expense.

Groupage bills of lading

Forwarding agents are permitted to 'group' together particular compatible consignments from individual consignors to various consignees, situated usually in the same destination country/area, and dispatch them as one consignment. The shipowner issues a groupage bill of lading to the forwarding agent who will issue to the individual shippers a Certificate of Shipment sometimes called 'House bill of lading'. At the destination, another agent working in close liaison with the agent forwarding the cargo will break bulk the consignment and distribute the goods to the various consignees. This practice is on the increase, usually involving the use of containers and particularly evident in the deep sea container services. The main reasons for this popularity are: (a) lower insurance premiums; (b) less risk of damage and pilferage; (c) transit times are shorter; and (e) rates are lower for the principals.

Clean/Unclaused bills of lading

Each bill of lading states 'in apparent good order and condition', which of course refers to the cargo. If this statement is not modified by the master (shipowner), the bill of lading is regarded as 'clean' or 'unclaused'. By issuing clean bills of lading the shipowner admits his full liability of the cargo described in the bill under the law and his contract. This type is much favoured by banks for financial settlement purposes.

Claused, 'dirty' or 'unclean' bills of lading

If the master (shipowner) does not agree with any of the statements made in the bill of lading he will add a clause to this effect, thereby causing the bill of lading to be termed as 'unclean', 'foul', or 'claused'. This type of bill of lading is usually unacceptable to a bank.

Although this is an obvious and necessary precaution for the shipowner to take it may create problems for the shipper/ exporter. Very often the foreign importer pays the exporter by a letter of credit which is passed from his bank to the exporter's bank. The exporter can, therefore, expect payment on presenting the bill of lading to his bank. This payment can usually only be made, however, if the bill of lading is clean. If the bill is dirty there may be considerable delay in payment. This, in turn, causes the shipper to ask the shipowner for clean bills of lading even offering him a **letter of indemnity** by which he offers to accept the shipowner's liability for claims made against him for damaged cargo. However, as the bill of lading is a transferable instrument, such letters are illegal as the bill could be sold without the purchaser being aware of the existence of such a letter. Nevertheless because of the financial problems that can arise for the shipper they are still sometimes used.

Negotiable bills of lading

If the words 'or his or their assigns' are contained in the bill of lading, it is negotiable. There are, however, variations in this terminology, for example the word 'bearer' may be inserted in the preamble to the phrase.

'Stale' bills of lading

The expression 'stale bill of lading' is used in banking practice. A bank which is instructed by, or on behalf of, a buyer to make finance available under a letter of credit upon presentation, by the seller, of a bill of lading (and of other documents) might feel obliged, in order to safeguard the interest of its principal, to reject the bill as being 'stale'. By that is meant that the bill, though conforming in all respects with the requirements of the credit, is presented so late that, as the result of the delay in its presentation, the consignee might become involved in legal or practical complications or might have to pay additional costs, for example, for the warehousing of goods. The Uniform Customs and Practice for Documentary Credits (1983 Revision) provide in article 47(a) that transport documents must be presented within a specified time after issuance and that, if no time is specified, banks may refuse documents if presented to them later than 21 days after issuance of the bill of lading or other transport document.

The Date of the Bill of Lading

The correct dating of the bill of lading is a matter of considerable importance. In the case of a 'shipped' bill this is the date when the goods are taken on board and in the case of a 'received for shipment' bill is the date when they are taken into the charge of the carrier. If a 'received for shipment' bill is noted 'shipped', the date of shipment of the goods is that of the notation, that is, when the goods were actually shipped, and not that of the receipt of the goods by the carrier. Where the loading extends over several days, the bill should be dated when the loading is completed, but there may be a trade custom admitting the insertion of the date when the loading commences; *The Almak* (1985). The date of the bill of lading is material in three legal relationships: in the contract of carriage; in the contract of sale; and in relation to the banks if payment is arranged under a letter of credit.

As to the contract of carriage, the shipper is entitled to

demand that the bill of lading should be dated correctly. If the carrier (that is, master or another agent of the carrier) negligently misdates the bill, he would be liable in damages, provided that the shipper can prove that he has suffered a loss as the result of the misdating, but the position may be different if the misdating is due to want of care on the part of the shipper.

The date of the bill of lading may also be relevant in the contract of sale. In one case the contract provided that the bill should be dated December and/or January of a particular year. The bill was dated February but the goods were actually shipped in January. The buyers rejected the bills and the court held that the rejection was justified.

Where payment is arranged under a letter of credit, the credit often states a date for shipment and, apart from this date, every credit states invariably an expiry date. Here the date of the bill of lading is important. An issuer of a bill of lading, who deliberately backdates it in order to bring it within the shipment time, acts fraudulently, and as far as the issue of the bill is concerned, there is no difference between the case where he has forged the bill and where he has deliberately backdated it. However, note that in the hands of an innocent person, the fraudulently backdated bill is valid.

Questions for Discussion

1 What are the characteristics of a 'common carrier'?
2 How can a common carrier be relieved from liability?
3 How would you define a bill of lading? State the functions of a bill of lading.
4 The provisions of the Carriage of Goods by Sea Act 1971 apply to outwards bills of lading. Explain.
5 Under the Carriage of Goods by Sea Act 1992, who are the persons entitled to sue the carrier?
6 What is a 'stale' bill of lading?

23

Carriage of Goods by Air

Introduction

The air law relating to the carriage of goods has reached a considerable measure of international uniformity. The legislation applicable to such carriage consists of the Carriage by Air Act 1932, 1961 and 1962.

The 1932 Act gave effect to a Convention for 'the Unification of certain rules relating to International Carriage by Air' which was signed in Warsaw in 1929. The Warsaw Convention was amended in 1955 by the Hague Protocol, and was enacted in the Carriage by Air Act of 1961. This is referred to as the 'amended' Warsaw Convention.

The basic Convention regulates the legal liabilities and relationships between carriers by air on the one hand, and passengers as well as cargo consignors and consignees on the other. However, as it was found that the Warsaw Convention and its Hague Protocol were vague at some definitional points, it was decided to further supplement the Warsaw Convention by a further Convention which took place in Guadalajara, Mexico, in 1961. This last Convention is embodied in the Carriage by Air Act 1962, which applies to carriage governed by the original and the amended Warsaw Convention.

Other protocols have been concluded since then; The Guatemala Protocol 1971 and The Montreal Additional Protocols 1975. To date, these protocols have not come into force, although legislation exists in the UK in the form of the Carriage by Air and Road Act 1979 to gives effect to them.

Therefore, it would appear that there are three possible legal regimes, in so far as carriage by air is concerned:

1 carriage governed by the original Warsaw Convention;
2 carriage governed by the amended Convention;
3 non-Convention carriage.

Having a knowledge of the basic system of liability and the general application of these regimes is necessary. Therefore, what follows is a brief description of the basic system of liability under carriage by air, followed by an account of the circumstances under which each regime applies.

Basic System of Liability

The carrier of goods by air is automatically liable for destruction or loss of, or damage to or delay of cargo if it occurs during the carriage by air. The carrier has the right to use specified defences if he can, but he cannot contract out of liability or for a lower limit of liability. In return for this liability the carrier can rely on the benefit of maximum limits for his liability. The maximum limits of the air carrier's liability are:

Under the original Warsaw Convention
(i) 250 gold francs per kilogramme; or
(ii) the value declared by the shipper.
Under the amended Warsaw Convention
(i) 17 SDRs (special drawing rights); or
(ii) the value declared by the shipper.

The carrier loses the benefit of the above limits in the event of wilful misconduct; Article 25. The 'gold franc' referred to is a 'diplomatic' unit of currency, not an actual coin in commercial use, weighing 10/31 of a gramme and being of millesimal finess 900.

The only persons who have rights of action are the consignee and the consignor. Note, that the owner has no status and can only raise a claim in his capacity of consignee or consignor.

Like the Hague-Visby Rules, receipt of cargo by the person entitled to delivery without complaint (notice of loss/damage) is *prima facie* evidence of delivery in good condition.

The right to claim for loss, damage or delay to the goods is time-barred if brought after the expiration of two years from the date of actual or expected arrival at destination, or the date on which carriage stopped.

'Carriage by air' comprises of the whole period during which the cargo is in the charge of the carrier, whether in an airport for the purpose of loading, delivery or transhipment of air cargo. Therefore, any damage is presumed to have taken place during the carriage by air, subject to contrary proof.

Carrier's defences

The carrier is not liable if he proves either:

1 that he and his servants or agents have taken all necessary measures to avoid the damage or that it was impossible for him or them to take such measures; or
2 if the carrier proves that the damage was caused by the negligence of the injured person.

Claims in connection to luggage or goods may only be brought by the consignor against the first carrier, or the consignee against the last, whilst each (that is, consignor and consignee) may take action against the actual carrier who performed that part of the carriage during which the loss, damage or delay occurred; Article 30.

Servants and agents of the carrier acting within the scope of their employment can claim the benefit of the limits of liability applicable to the carrier.

Application of the Legal Regimes

The original Warsaw Convention

When, according to the contract between the parties, the places of departure and destination are located either:

1 in the territories of two State parties to the original Convention; or
2 in the territory of a single such State with an agreed stopping place anywhere outside that State

the document of carriage is called the **air consignment note** (ACN). This is not a document of title, but it is *prima facie* evidence of the conclusion of the contract, receipt of the goods, the conditions of carriage, the weight, dimensions, packing and number of goods; Article 11. It comes in three original parts; one is for the carrier (signed by the consignor); the second is for the consignee (signed by the consignor and accompanies the goods); the third is signed by the carrier and handed to the consignor after the goods have been accepted for carriage. In cases of damage complaints must be made in writing to the carrier immediately after receipt of the goods, or not later than seven days after receipt. In cases of delay, the complaint must be put in writing within 14 days from the date on which the goods were delivered.

The amended Convention

When, according to the agreement between the parties, the places of departure and destination are located either:

1 in the territories of two States both of which are parties to the amended Convention; or
2 in the territory of a single State party to the amended Convention with an agreed stopping place anywhere outside that State

if the place of departure is in the territory of a State party to the original Convention whilst the place of destination is in the territory of a State which is not only a party to the original Convention but has also become a party to the amended Convention (for example the UK), then the only obligations which bind both of the States concerned are those contained in the original Convention.

The document of carriage is called an **air waybill** (AWB). Most of the provisions applicable for the air consignment note, mentioned above, apply also to the air waybill. Upon discovery of damage to the goods, complaint must be made in writing to the carrier immediately after delivery, or not later than 14 days after delivery. In the case of delay, the complaint must be put in writing within 21 days.

The non-Convention rules

When the carriage of cargo is governed neither by the original nor by the amended Convention, and there is no agreed stopping place in another State then, whatever the place of departure, no part of the carriage would, as a matter of law, be governed by either of the two Conventions, and in an action before the English courts the carriage would be governed by the non-Convention rules.

Questions for Discussion

1 In what circumstances can a carrier by air be relieved from liability?
2 When does (a) the Warsaw Convention 1929 and (b) the 'amended' Convention 1955 apply?

24

Carriage of Goods by Road

Convention on the Contract for the International Carriage of Goods by Road (CMR)

The provisions of the International Convention concerning the carriage of goods by road (CMR) were notified and enacted by the Carriage of Goods by Road Act 1965 which came into force in 1967. It represents an attempt by the principal European nations to regulate the responsibilities and liabilities of carriers engaged in the international distribution of goods by road.

Scope and Application

The Convention applies to all international carriage of goods by road in vehicles for reward, when the place of taking over the goods and the place for delivery, as specified in the contract, are situated in two different countries of which at least one is a Contracting Party, that is a State which has accepted the Convention. The provision of Article 1 of the convention therefore, can be summed up as follows:

(a) there must be a contract of carriage for reward;
(b) this contract must be one for the carriage of goods;

(c) the carriage must be made by road;

(d) the contract must have international status.

The Act/Convention does not apply to traffic between the UK and the Republic of Ireland. Further, the CMR does not apply:

(a) to carriage performed under an international postal Convention;

(b) to funeral consignments; or

(c) to furniture removal.

It should be observed that the convention continues to apply provided the goods are not unloaded from the vehicle when it continues its journey by sea or some other means of transport; Article 2.

Thus, the CMR applies in the cases in which a container, particularly a groupage container, is taken by road on a trailer or similar vehicle from a Contracting country to another country. But if the loss, damage or delay has occurred during the carriage by the other means of transport and was not caused by an act or omission of the carrier by road, the liability of the carrier by road is determined not by the CMR but by the applicable international Convention; if there is no such Convention, the CMR applies.

Thus, in *Thermo Engineers Ltd* v. *Ferrymasters Ltd* (1981), the question arose as to whether damage suffered by the cargo during its loading on board ship was governed by the CMR or by the Hague Rules, which then applied to the carriage by sea. The cargo was to be transported from the UK to Denmark on a trailer. As the cargo was loaded on board the ship, it struck the bulkhead of the ship and was damaged. The trailer had already passed the outward ramp of the vessel and crossed the line of the stern. It was held that the carriage by road had ceased, although the trailer and its load had not been secured in the ship, and that the damage was governed by the Hague Rules.

If in this case the damage had occurred before the trailer crossed the ship's rail, the CMR would probably have applied.

The consignment note

The contract of carriage is evidenced by a CMR consignment note, containing the following, which is not deemed to be an exhaustive account of all the details required:

1 date and the place where it is made out;
2 the names and addresses of the sender, the carrier and the consignee; the place and date of taking over the goods, and the place designated for delivery;
3 the ordinary description of the nature of the goods and the method of packing and, in the case of dangerous goods, their generally recognized description;
4 the number of packages and their special marks and numbers;
5 the gross weight of the goods or their quantity otherwise expressed;
6 charges relating to the carriage;
7 the requisite instructions for customs and other formalities; and
8 a statement that the carriage is subject to the provisions of the Convention.

Article 6 sets out at length all the particulars necessary.

The consignment note has to be made out in three original copies signed by the sender and the carrier. The first copy is handed to the sender, the second accompanies the goods, and the third is retained by the carrier. When goods are carried in different vehicles or are divided into different lots the seller or the carrier is entitled to require a separate consignment note for each vehicle or each kind or lot of goods. The consignment note is not a negotiable instrument, nor a document of title.

Successive carriers

The CMR (Article 34) provides that if the carriage by road is governed by a single contract but performed by successive road carriers, each shall be responsible for the performance of the whole operation, the second and each successive carrier becoming a party to the contract of carriage, under the terms of the consignment note, but legal proceedings in respect of liability for loss, damage or delay may only be brought against the first carrier, the last carrier or the carrier who was in control of the goods when the event which caused the loss, damage or delay occurred, but several carriers may be sued at the same time. In the case of successive carriers the one responsible for the loss or damage is, as between the carriers, solely liable for compensation but if it cannot be ascertained to which carrier liability is attributable, the compensation has to be borne by them proportionally. If one of the carriers is insolvent, the share of compensation due from him has to be paid by the other carriers in proportion to the share of the payment for the carriage due to them; Article 38.

Finally, note that if a person has contracted to carry the goods to their destination by a single contract but does not take the goods into charge himself and arranges for them to be delivered directly to the actual carrier to whom he has sub-contracted the job, he is nevertheless the first carrier and the actual carrier is the successive carrier.

If, on the other hand, a person undertakes (contracts) to procure carriage, that is, to act as a forwarder, then CMR does not apply to him.

Liability of the carrier

The carrier is liable for the total or partial loss of the goods and for damage occurring between the time when he takes over the goods and the time of delivery, as well as for delay in the delivery. But the carrier is relieved of liability if the loss, damage or delay was caused:

(a) by the wrongful act or neglect of the claimant; or
(b) by the instructions of the claimant given otherwise than as the result of a wrongful act or neglect on the part of the carrier; or
(c) by inherent vice of the goods; or
(d) through circumstances which the carrier could not avoid and the consequences of which he was unable to prevent.

If the carrier wishes to rely on the fourth of these, it is not sufficient for him to show that he did not act negligently; he has to show that the loss could not be avoided.

Thus, in *Michael Galley Footwear Ltd* v. *Laboni* (1982), the carrier, who was driving a consignment of shoes from Milan to England, parked the lorry in an unguarded lorry park in Milan in order for him and his assistant to have a meal. The only guarded lorry park was two hours away and to drive there would have involved breaching the driving period regulations. The alarm on the lorry was left on but thieves managed to by-pass it and to steal the lorry and its load. The carrier was held liable to the owner of the shoes because the loss was avoidable; he and his assistant could have taken turns to guard the lorry.

The carrier cannot rely on any of the relieving events if the loss, damage or delay is caused by the defective condition of the vehicle. In addition, the CMR contains a catalogue of special risks which relieve the carrier from liability. Thus, the carrier discharges the onus of proof if it can be shown that the loss can be attributed to:

1 Permitted use of open unsheeted vehicles.
2 Improper packing, marking and numbering.
3 Handling operations undertaken by the cargo owner.
4 Nature of the goods, that is, ordinary leakage, breakage, etc.
5 Carriage of livestock.

The fact that the goods have not been delivered within 30 days following the expiry of the agreed time limit or, if no time limit has been agreed, within 60 days from the time when the carrier took over the goods, shall be conclusive evidence of the loss of the goods.

The compensation which the carrier is liable to pay in respect of total or partial loss of the goods is subject to a maximum limitation of liability. It is 8.33 SDRs per kilogramme of gross weight short; in addition, the carrier has to refund in full the carriage charges incurred, Customs duties and other charges incurred in respect of the carriage of the goods.

In the case of delay, the measure of damages is limited to the carriage charges if the claimant can prove that he has suffered damage to that amount.

Finally, Article 41 states that any stipulation which would directly or indirectly derogate from the provisions of the convention shall be null and void.

Time limits

If the consignee takes delivery of the goods and does not in the case of apparent loss or damage, at the time of delivery, or in the case of loss or damage which is not apparent, within seven days of delivery, send the carrier a notice of reservations, giving a general indication of the loss or damage, the fact of taking delivery is *prima facie* evidence that he received the goods in the condition described in the consignment note.

In the case where a person intends to claim for compensation in respect of delay in delivery, he should send a reservation in writing to the carrier within 21 days from the time that the goods were placed at the disposal of the consignee.

The period of limitation for bringing an action arising out of the carriage under the CMR is one year.

Road Haulage Association

The normal terms of contracts of carriage by road include those of the Road Haulage Association. The most recent revision of contract terms for the carriage of goods by road, recommended to the members of the Association, are the 'Road Haulage Association Ltd Conditions of Carriage 1991'. The section covering liability for loss and damage under the above is given below:

Subject to these Conditions the Carrier shall be liable for any loss or misdelivery of or damage to goods occasioned during transit unless the same has arisen from, and the Carrier has used reasonable care to minimise the effects of,
(a) act of God;
(b) any consequences of war, invasion, act of foreign enemy, hostilities (whether war or not), civil war,

rebellion, insurrection, military or usurped power or confiscation, requisition, or destruction of or damage to property by or under the order of any government or public or local authority;

(c) seizure or forfeiture under legal process;

(d) error, act, omission, mis-statement or misrepresentation by the customer or other owner of the goods or by servants or agents of either of them;

(e) inherent liability to wastage in bulk or weight, latent defect or inherent defect, vice or natural deterioration of goods;

(f) insufficient or improper packing;

(g) insufficient or improper labelling or addressing;

(h) riots, civil commotion, strike, lockout, general or partial stoppage or restraint of labour from whatever cause;

(i) consignee not taking or accepting delivery within a reasonable time after the Consignment has been tendered.

The Carrier shall not in any circumstances be liable in respect of a Consignment where there has been fraud on the part of the Trader or the owner of the goods or the servants or agents of either in respect of that Consignment, unless the fraud has been contributed by the complicity of the Carrier or of any servant of the Carrier acting in the course of his employment.

Where loss, misdelivery or damage is sustained to the consignment liability is limited to £1,300 per tonne for the whole of the consignment or in proportion to this amount in respect of part of the Consignment. Time limits on claims are designated as follows:

The carrier shall not be liable for:

1 loss from a parcel, package or container or from an unpacked Consignment or for damage to a Consignment; unless he is advised thereof in writing otherwise than upon a consignment note or delivery document within three days, and the claim is made in writing within seven days, after the termination of transit;

2 loss, misdelivery or non-delivery of the whole of a

Consignment or of any separate parcel, package or container forming part of a Consignment unless he is advised of the loss, misdelivery or non-delivery in writing otherwise than upon a consignment note or delivery document within twenty-eight days, and the claim is made in writing within forty-two days, after the commencement of transit.

However, if the Trader (the customer who contracts for the services of the Carrier) proves that: a) it was not reasonably possible for him to advise the Carrier or make a claim in writing within the time limit applicable and b) such advice or claim was given or made within a reasonable time; the Carrier shall not have the benefit of the exclusion of liability afforded by this Condition.

	HAGUE-VISBY RULES	CMR	WARSAW CONVENTION	AMENDED CONVENTION
Relevant Acts	Carriage of Goods by Sea 1971	Carriage of Goods by Road 1965	Carriage of Goods by Air 1932	Carriage of Goods by Air 1962
Application	1 B/L is issued in a contracting State 2 Carriage is from a contracting State 3 B/L provides SO	1 Where the place of departure and destination are in two different States *AND* 2 At least one of those States is a contracting party	1 Where the place of departure and destination are in two States parties to the Convention; *OR* 2 Where the place of departure and destination are in one State party to the Convention, and there is an agreed stopping place anywhere outside that State.	
Relevant Documents	Bill of Lading *OR* "any similar Documents of Title" (Set of 3/4)	Consignment Note (Set of 3)	Air Consignment Note (ACN) (Set of 3)	Air Waybill (AWB) (Set of 3)
Carrier's Liability	Loss/Damage		Loss/Damage/Delay	
Notice of Claim (in writing)	1 Apparent Loss/Damage ... immediately 2 Non-apparent Loss/Damage ... 3 days	1 Apparent Loss/Damage ... immediately 2 Non-apparent Loss/Damage ...7 days 3 Delay ... 21 days	1 Loss/Damage ... immediately 2 Loss/Damage ... within 7 days 3 Delay ... 14 days	1 Loss/Damage ... immediately 2 Loss/Damage ... within 14 days 3 Delay ... 21 days
Limitation of Actions	1 Year		2 Years	
Limitation of Liability	Carrier will not be liable for any loss or damage to the goods in any amount exceeding: 666.67 units of account (SDR)/package; *OR* 2 units of account (SDR) per kilogramme of gross weight of the goods lost/damaged, whichever is the higher.	Carrier will not be liable for any loss, damage or delay in any amount exceeding: 8.33 units of account (SDR) per kilogramme of gross weight short[1]	Carrier will not be liable for any loss, damage or delay in any amount exceeding: 250 gold francs/kilogramme; *OR* the value declared and agreed by the shipper	Carrier will not be liable for any loss, damage or delay in any amount exceeding: 17 SDRs[2] *OR* the value declared and agreed by the shipper

Figure 24.1: Carriage by sea, air and road

[1] Note that in addition the carrier has to refund in full the carriage charges incurred in respect of the carriage of the goods; Article 23.
[2] Section 4: Carriage by Air and Road Act 1979.

289

Questions for Discussion

1 Describe the scope of application of CMR.
2 Under what circumstances can a carrier be relieved from liability under the CMR?

Index